'In Maitland's hands, silence turns out to be another entire, psycho-geographical world laid alongside the one we know and hear and yack about so much. "I learned to tell when it had been snowing in the night by the quality of silence" . . . her book is full of such moments, articulating the common but usually ignored and unexpressed experiences in our lives' *Spectator*

'A healing book about the pleasures to be found alone and how solitude can set you free' *Red*

'Refreshing, insightful, strangely touching and bound to make you want to haul yourself off that sofa in search of a life-affirming journey' *Wanderlust*

'Extraordinary . . . Maitland is blazingly intelligent, and committed to rigorous, interrogative scholarship . . . a justified and valiant response to the widespread frenzy and mindlessness of 21st century life' *Sunday Business Post*

'[Sara Maitland] is right to think that silence is a deep need, ever less honoured in our lives' *Evening Standard*

'Fascinating . . . raises many interesting philosophical questions' *Sunday Times*

'An extraordinary book . . . in our noise-saturated culture' Chosen by the Kew Bookshop in London in the *Independent on Sunday*

'Her artful book, mixing autobiography, travel writing, meditation and essay, describes her route away from urban brouhaha towards increased solitude . . . Her book demands to be taken on its own terms as the vision of a highly educated contemplative who is alert to Western culture's distrust of loners' *Independent*

'Maitland is a bold adventurer and the rest of us, doubtless ill-equipped to deal with the emotional and intellectual challenge of self-sought solitude, are lucky she can give the condition of silence such an articulate voice' *Metro*

'By the end of her brave, honest, fascinating book, one respects her choice of lifestyle, the determination it has taken to bring it about and the sacrifices it has engendered' *Scotsman*

'Offering at once personal anecdotes, cultural diagnoses and soothing antidotes, these memoirs make for a timely and nourishing read' *List*

'The pursuit [of silence] is described with fervour and intelligence that make this book full of insights and explorations, oddities and quirks – about the natural world (some dazzling descriptive passages), about silence in several cultures, about the choice of where to live, about routines, satisfactions, happiness' *Tablet*

'You can't help warming to Sara Maitland ... Maitland is a rottweiler of enthusiasm who pursues her ideas to the end, eloquently and learnedly, and nowhere more than in this, her latest work' *Irish Times*

'Her dedication to the cause is both inspiring and shocking ... There are many beautiful meditative passages in her meditation on silence ... [A] wonderful salutary book' *Sunday Telegraph*

A BOOK OF SILENCE

Sara Maitland

COUNTERPOINT

BERKELEY

Originally published in English by Granta Publications under the
title *A Book of Silence*, copyright © Sara Maitland, 2008.

First published in Great Britain by Granta Books 2008.

Library of Congress Cataloging-in-Publication Data is available.

ISBN: 978-1-58243-517-6

Typeset by M-Rules
Cover design by James Nunn
Printed in the United States of America

COUNTERPOINT
2117 Fourth Street
Suite D
Berkeley, CA 94710

www.counterpointpress.com

Distributed by Publishers Group West

10 9 8 7 6 5 4 3 2

For Janet Batsleer and John Russell
for reasons best buried in silence

CONTENTS

1 Growing up in a Noisy World   1

2 Forty Days and Forty Nights   34

3 The Dark Side   80

4 Silence and the Gods   116

5 Silent Places   154

6 Desert Hermits   189

7 The Bliss of Solitude   223

8 Coming Home   258

Acknowledgements   289

Notes   291

Index   301

1

Growing up in a Noisy World

It is early morning. It is a morning of extraordinary radiance – and unusually up here there is practically no wind. It is almost perfectly silent: some small birds are chirping occasionally and a little while ago a pair of crows flapped past making their raucous cough noises. It is the first day of October so the curlew and the oystercatchers have gone down to the seashore. In a little while one particular noise will happen – the two-carriage Glasgow-to-Stranraer train will bump by on the other side of the valley; and a second one may happen – Neil may rumble past on his quad bike after seeing to his sheep on the hill above the house; if he does he will wave and I will wave back. That is more or less it.

I am sitting on the front doorstep of my little house with a cup of coffee, looking down the valley at my extraordinary view of nothing. It is wonderful. Virginia Woolf famously taught us that every woman writer needs a room of her own. She didn't know the half of it, in my opinion. I need a moor of my own. Or, as an exasperated but obviously sensitive friend commented when she came to see my latest lunacy, 'Only you, Sara – twenty-mile views of absolutely nothing!'

It isn't 'nothing', actually – it is cloud formations, and the different ways reed, rough grass, heather and bracken move in the wind, and the changing colours, not just through the year but through the day as the sun and the clouds alternate and shift – but in another sense she is right, and it is the huge nothing that pulls me into itself. I look at it, and with fewer things to look at I see better. I listen to nothing and its silent tunes and rhythms sound harmonic. The irregular line of the hill, with the telegraph and electricity poles striding over it, holds the silence as though in a bowl and below me I can see occasional, and apparently unrelated, strips of silver, which are in fact the small river meandering down the valley.

I am feeling a bit smug this morning because yesterday I got my completion certificate. When you build a new house you start out with planning permission and building warrant, and at the end of it all an inspector comes to see if you have done what you said you would do and check that your house is compliant with building regulations and standards. Mine is; it is finished, completed, certified. All done and dusted. Last night I paid off my builder, and we had a drink and ended a year-long relationship of bizarre intensity, both painful and delightful. Now I am sitting and regathering my silence, which is what I came here for in the first place.

Three minutes ago – it is pure gift, something you cannot ask for or anticipate – a hen harrier came hunting down the burn, not twenty metres from the door. Not many people have a hen harrier in the garden. Hen harriers are fairly rare in the UK, with slightly over a hundred breeding couples mostly in the Scottish Highlands. They are slightly smaller and much lighter than buzzards, and inhabit desolate terrain. Male hen harriers, seen from below, look like ghosts – pure white except for their grey heads but with very distinct black wing tips. They hunt low and glide with their wings held in a shallow V; powerful hunters, beautiful, free. I do not see them very often, but the first time I came to the ruined shepherd's house, which is now, today, my new home, there was a pair sitting on the drystone dyke. They speak to me of the great silence of the hills; they welcome me into that silence.

The silent bird goes off about his own silent business, just clearing the rise to the west and vanishing as suddenly as he came. Briefly I feel that he has come this morning to welcome me and I experience a moment of fierce joy, but it rumbles gently down into a more solid contentment. There are lots of things that I ought to be getting on with, but I light a cigarette and go on sitting on my doorstep. It is surprisingly warm for October. We had the first frost last week, light-fingered on the car windscreen. I think about how beautiful it is, and how happy I am. Then I think how strange it is – how strange that I should be so happy sitting up here in the silent golden morning with nothing in my diary for the next fortnight, and no one coming and me going nowhere except perhaps into the hills or down the coast to walk, and to Mass on Sundays. I find myself trying to think through the story of how I come to be here and why I want to be here. And it *is* strange.

I have lived a very noisy life.

As a matter of fact we all live very noisy lives. 'Noise pollution' has settled down into the ecological agenda nearly as firmly as all the other forms of pollution that threaten our well-being and safety. But for everyone who complains about RAF low-flying training exercises, ceaseless background music in public places, intolerably loud neighbours and drunken brawling on the streets, there are hundreds who know they *need* a mobile phone, who choose to have incessant sound pumping into their environment, their homes and their ears, and who feel uncomfortable or scared when they have to confront real silence. 'Communication' (which always means talk) is the *sine qua non* of 'good relationships'. 'Alone' and 'lonely' have become almost synonymous; worse, perhaps, 'silent' and 'bored' seem to be moving closer together too. Children disappear behind a wall of noise, their own TVs and computers in their own rooms; smoking carriages on trains have morphed into 'quiet zones' but even the people sitting in them have music plugged directly into their ears.

We all imagine that we want peace and quiet, that we value privacy and that the solitary and silent person is somehow more 'authentic' than the same person in a social crowd, but we seldom seek opportunities to enjoy it. We romanticise silence on the one hand and on the other feel that it is terrifying, dangerous to our mental health, a threat to our liberties and something to be avoided at all costs.

My life has also been noisy in a more specific way.

Because of an odd conjunction of class, history and my parents' personal choices I had an unusually noisy childhood. I was born in 1950, the second child and oldest girl in a family of six; the first five of us were born within six and a half years of each other. If you asked my mother why she had so many children, she would say it was because she loved babies, but if you asked my father he would say something rather different: 'Two sets of tennis, two tables of bridge and a Scottish reel set in your own house.' We grew up in London, and in an enormous early-Victorian mansion house (my father's childhood home) in south-west Scotland. My parents adored each other. I think they adored us, though in a slightly collectivised way. They were deeply sociable and the house was constantly filled not just by all of us, but by their friends and our friends; my mother's father lived with us for a while; there was a nanny and later an au pair girl. What was perhaps unusual for the time was that they were very directly engaged as parents; there was none of that 'seen and not heard' nursery life for us. We were blatantly encouraged to be highly articulate, contentious, witty, and to hold all authority except theirs in a certain degree of contempt. I am appalled now when I think back to the degree of verbal teasing that was not just permitted but participated in: simple rudeness was not encouraged, but sophisticated verbal battering, reducing people to tears, slamming doors, screaming fights and boisterous, indeed rough, play was fine. (You don't grow out of these things – my son's partner has since told me her first encounter with us as a group was one of the most scary experiences of her life – she could not believe that people could talk so loudly, so argumentatively and so rudely without it coming to serious fisticuffs.) We were immensely active and corporate; introspection, solitude, silence, or any withdrawal from the herd was not allowed. Within the magical space they had created for us, however, we were given an enormous amount of physical freedom – to play, to roam, to have fights and adventures.

It worked best when we were all quite small. In 1968, when every newspaper in the country was bemoaning the outrageous behaviour of teenagers, my parents had five of them. I think retrospectively that they lost their nerve a bit. I am not sure what they imagined would happen. If you encourage your children to hold authority lightly, eventually they will work out that you are 'authority' and hold you lightly too. They were better with smaller children – we had fairly traumatic and very noisy teens.

There were good moments. One thing that is hard to insert into this account is just how sophisticated and politically engaged my parents were. I remember the Cuban missile crisis in 1962, for example, with great vividness because one of my parents' closest friends was an admiral in the US navy. He was staying with us, we went on a lovely sunny day trip to Cambridge and as we walked along the Backs, a very young man from the US Embassy appeared. He had been searching for Uncle Harry personally; he had to fly home immediately to Defend His Country against Communism. The following year I knew about the Profumo affair too, though rather lopsidedly. It was the cause of a rare fight between my parents, who usually managed to maintain perfect solidarity against their children's activities. My father taught me a bitter little limerick about it, which he encouraged me to recite at a cocktail party of his Butlerite Conservative friends (several of them eminent) and which rather accurately reflected his own politics.

> There was a young girl called Christine
> Who shattered the Party machine.
> It isn't too rude
> To lie in the nude
> But to lie in the House is obscene.

The fight between my parents was not, interestingly, about the content of these lines, but about my father encouraging me to 'show off'. A bit of me still wonders what on earth they thought would come of it, especially for their girls. You bring them up free and flamboyant, and are then totally surprised and even angry with them when they don't magically turn into 'ladies'. It was, for me at least, a strange mixture of upper-class convention and intellectual aspiration. There was a good, and noisy, example of my father's confused vision a few years later. I was expelled, fairly forcibly, from the House of Commons in 1973 for disrupting a debate on the Equal Opportunities Act, then a Private Members' Bill. I was pregnant at the time. *The Times* (my parents' daily, obviously) made this a front-page item including my name. I was rather anxious about how my parents would react. My mother was appalled that I should do this *while I was pregnant*, but my father was entirely delighted. Not because he favoured such actions or had any particular enthusiasm for Equal Opportunities, but because the person responsible for 'Order in the House' was an old friend of his, whom nonetheless he found both prissy and pompous – he was much amused by the embarrassment that I would have caused this friend, having to deal with 'one of us', with someone he actually knew. He may also, of course, have admired my boldness, without admiring the way I had chosen to exercise it.

We were inevitably sent off to boarding schools, the boys disgracefully at seven or eight and my sisters and I a little later. I am just about prepared to acknowledge that there might conceivably be children whom public school, under the old boarding system, positively suits and that there are homes so dire that boarding is a relief or even a joy, but it remains for me one of the very few institutions that is bad for both the individuals it 'privileges' and our society as a whole. In this context, however, all I want to do is point out that the entire ethos depended on no one ever being allowed any silence or privacy except as a punishment; and where the constant din inevitably created by over two hundred young women was amplified by bare corridors and over-large rooms. I found it a damaging, brutal experience, made worse by the fact that in my parents' world not to enjoy your schooldays was proof that you were an inferior human being – you were supposed to be a 'good mixer', to 'take the rough with the smooth' and enjoy the team spirit. If you are feeling miserable and inferior the last thing you are going to do is *tell* parents who think that the way you feel is proof that you are miserable and inferior.

Perhaps the stakes were too high; perhaps they were too proud of us. At home we were supposed to get into Cambridge, *and* wear long white gloves, a tartan silk sash and our deceased grandmother's pearls, and dance at Highland Balls. I was expected to have my own political opinions, *and* have them turn out the same as my parents'. We were expected to be sociable, active and witty, *and* hard-working, industrious and calm. We were meant to be sociable and popular and bizarrely chaste. At school we were meant to be educated, independent, self-assured, *and* totally innocent. On Saturday mornings we all had to kneel down in the assembly hall so that the mistresses could walk along the rows and make sure everyone's skirt exactly touched the ground. I am still not sure what the terror of the miniskirt was about, really. It all got pretty intolerable and very noisy.

In 1968 I escaped. These were the days before the Gap Year was a well-organised middle-class rite of passage, but if you stayed on at school after A levels to do the then separate Oxbridge entrance exams, you finished school at Christmas and had an inevitable gap until the following October. My father filled this gap by packing us off to any foreign continent of our choice and leaving us to get on with it. It was probably the first time in my life that I had been on my own and responsible for myself; it should have been a time to break out. My skirts were spectacularly shorter than anyone in America had ever seen before – hippies and counterculture and the politics of protest and feminism itself may have been US imports, but the miniskirt was authentically British – and my class accent was less immediately identifiable, but I was not really up to it. It was six months of being the wrong person in the wrong place at the wrong moment, just. I left Washington the day before Martin Luther King was shot and arrived in Los Angeles a week after Bobby Kennedy's assassination. In San Francisco I did go to Haight Ashbury, but I went as a tourist. From that perspective it seemed sordid and scary, and I left at once.

I do remember, though, one bright hot dawn in the Arizona desert when I stared into my first huge nothing: it was the Grand

Canyon. It was red and gold and vast and silent. Perhaps I should have sat down on the rim and stayed for a while, but it was too soon. I gawped for a bit and walked down a little way, then I turned round, got back on the Greyhound bus and went on to somewhere else.

Then, that autumn, I went to Oxford. I became a student at exactly and precisely the right time – for then 'to be young was very heaven'. What more joyful and lucky thing could happen to a privileged public-school girl than to find herself a student at Oxford between 1968 and 1971? It is fashionable now to decry the astonishing, extraordinary period in the late sixties – to dismiss it, or to blame it. I refuse to go there. I am with Angela Carter:

> There is a tendency to underplay, even to devalue completely, the experience of the 1960s, especially for women, but towards the end of that decade there was a brief period of public philosophical awareness that occurs only very occasionally in human history; when, truly, it felt like Year One, when all that was holy was in the process of being profaned, and we were attempting to grapple with the real relations between human beings . . . At a very unpretentious level, we were truly asking ourselves questions about the nature of reality. Most of us may not have come up with very startling answers and some of us scared ourselves good and proper and retreated into cul-de-sacs of infantile mysticism . . . but even so I can date to that time and to that sense of heightened awareness of the society around me in the summer of 1968 my own questioning of the nature of my reality as a woman.[1]

Everything interesting and important that has happened to me since began in Oxford in the three years that I was an undergraduate. There I discovered the things that have shaped my life – the things that shape it still, however unexpectedly, as I sit on my doorstep and listen to the silence: socialism, feminism, friendship and Christianity; myself as writer, as mother and now as silence seeker.

It was not instant. I arrived in Oxford more virginal in more ways than now seems credible. I felt like a cultural tourist, unable to connect directly with the hippies, with their drugs, mysticism and music; or with the politicos and their Parisian excitements, though I went like a tourist to hear Tariq Ali speak at the Student Union; or with the 'sexual revolutionaries' who whizzed off glamorously to London and complained about the repressive college, which expected us to be in bed, alone, by 10.30. I had to cope with the realisation that I was not the cleverest person in the world – a mistaken belief that had sustained me for years. It was culture shock; I had a strange, nagging sense that I was where I wanted to be, but I wasn't quite getting it: an odd mixture of excitement and frustration. I wanted it. I wanted all of it. I did not know how to have it. My life could have gone horribly wrong at this point.

Then, just in time and gloriously lucky, I tumbled, by chance, by grace, in with a new group of people. They were a group of American students, most of them Rhodes Scholars and all of them active against the Vietnam War. They hung out in a shambolic house in north Oxford. I am not entirely sure why they took me under their collective wing, but they did and I was saved. What they gave me was a connection point between politics and personal lives, the abundant energy that comes from self-interested righteousness, a sense that there were causes and things that could be done about them, and large dollops of collective affection. This household has become famous for something other than their sweet kindness to me – because one of the people in it was Bill Clinton, who has always, as far as I am concerned, been a loyal friend and an enormous resource; but it was not just him: it was the whole group of them.

My world was transformed. The sky was bright with colour. I smoked my first joint, lost my virginity and went on my first political demonstration. I stopped attending lectures and my ears unblocked so I started to hear what was going on around me. I realised that a classical education, Whig history and compassionate liberalism were not the only values in the world. I was set suddenly and gloriously free. I made other friends, did other things – and we talked and talked and talked.

A bit later this household gave me, rather unexpectedly, something every bit as important. One evening Bill asked me if I would go with him to hear Germaine Greer speak at Ruskin College, shortly before *The Female Eunuch* was published. He had heard she had terrific legs (she did) but very properly thought it was the sort of event that he wanted a woman to go with. Being Bill he quickly rounded up some more people and that night I met Mandy Merck and thus discovered the brand-new Women's Liberation Movement.

Once I felt secure enough to cope, it transpired that actually one thing my childhood had provided me with were the skills of collectivity. Groups suited me; quick-fire combative talk was something I had practised around the dining-room table from my earliest years. With well-trained energy I engaged in the very noisy, highly verbal student political life of the time – the noisy articulacy of the socialist left and then the emerging verbal culture of early feminism. In an odd way it was like all the good things and none of the bad ones from my own childhood. To speak out, to tell aloud, to break the silence (and, to be honest, to shout down the opposition) was not only permissible – it was virtuous, if not compulsory.

In 1972 I had my first short stories published; I got married and I got pregnant. My husband was an American from upstate New York; he came to Oxford on a scholarship and stayed. By the time we got married he was a trainee Anglican vicar of the extreme Catholic persuasion – high church and high camp went together in those happier days. In the early seventies the best of the adherents of Anglo-Catholicism were all so funny, so witty and so quick, self-mocking, heavily ironic and we all loved talking. While he was training my husband invited a new friend to supper one night; the friend, nervous about dining with a heavily pregnant feminist intellectual, asked someone what we were like. 'Don't worry,' said this mutual friend, 'they all talk at the same time, very loudly; so you don't have to say anything if you don't want to.'

So then I was an Anglo-Catholic socialist feminist. Perhaps the only thing that holds these two together is that they are both very noisy things to be. I quickly extended the din range, though; I became a vicar's wife and a mother. A vicarage is the least quiet place imaginable – a house that is never your own and never empty or silent.

My daughter was born in 1973. Looking back now, I know that my first experiences of positive nourishing silence were her night feeds. My husband's great-grandfather was a carpenter – he had made furniture and when we got married my parents-in-law had sent from America the most exquisite New England four-poster bed made of bird's eye maple with golden candy-twist posts. In the soft darkness of the pre-dawn, propped up in this beautiful bed, with my beautiful daughter contentedly dozing, I encountered a new sort of joy. From where I am now this does not surprise me, because that relationship between mother and child is one of the oldest and most enduring images of silence in Western culture. In about 2000 BCE one of the psalmists wrote:

> I have set my soul in silence and in peace,
> As the weaned child on its mother's breast
>   so even is my soul.[2]

Four thousand years later Donald Winnicott, the child psycho-analyst, wrote, in a totally different context, almost exactly the same thing: that the capacity to be alone, to enjoy solitude in adult life, originates with the child's *experience of being alone in the presence of the mother.* He postulates a state in which the child's immediate needs – for food, warmth, contact etc. – have been satisfied, so there is no need for the baby to be looking to the mother for anything nor any need for her to be concerned with providing anything; they are together, at peace, in silence. Both the ancient poet and the con-temporary analyst focus on the child here – but as a mother I would say there is a full mutuality in the moment.

I remember it with an almost heartbreaking clarity. Some of it is simply physical – a full and contented baby falling asleep at the empty and contented breast. But even so I now think that those sweet dawns, when it turned from dark to pale night, and we drifted back into our own separate selves without wrench or loss, were the starting point of my journey into silence. I am a bit curious that it is the night feed, rather than any of the other times the 'weaned child' lies in the mother's arms, with its wide eyes somehow joyously unfocused. There is something about the dark itself, and the quiet of the world, even in cities, at that strange time before the dawn, but also I suspect that physical tiredness enhances the sensation. More particularly, you are awake to experience it solely and only because you are experiencing it. If the feeding were not happening you would almost certainly be asleep, be absent from consciousness in a very real way. This is not true during daytime feeds, but here, in the fading night, there is nothing else to do save be present. The dark, the 'time out of time' and the quiet of *night* are fixed in my memory along with the density of that particular silent joy.

At the time I did not recognise it for what it was, but I now know that it was an encounter with positive silence, in an unexpected place. For the most part the experience of having small children is not silent.

Meanwhile I was in the process of becoming a writer; more words, more word games. More noise. It is easy to think of writers as living silent lives, but on the whole we don't; when we are writing we usually work alone and usually with great concentration and intensity – but no one writes all the time. Perhaps as a relief from that intensity there is a tendency, at least among younger writers, to seek out people and activities. Anyway it was the seventies; feminist writers were engaged in demystifying our work, opening it up and talking about it. Everyone was in a Writers' Group. I was in a wonderful Writers' Group – with Michelene Wandor, Zoe Fairbairns, Valerie Miner and Michele Roberts. We wrote a collective book and we talked and talked and talked.

I liked my noisy life. All that talking. All my life I have talked and talked. I love talking. I used to say that if I were ever in *Who's Who*

I would put down deipnosophy as my hobby. Deipnosophy means the 'love of, or skill of, dinner-table conversation' (from the Greek *deipnos* – dinner). I have always loved this word and I loved the thing itself. I've been lucky enough to know some of the great deipnosophists of my times.

It is hard to think of a less silent life.

It was – and this is important to me – an extremely happy life. I achieved almost all the personal ambitions I started out with. I am a published writer of the sorts of books I want to write and believe in: I have written five novels, including *Daughter of Jerusalem*, which, with Michèle Robert's first novel, *Piece of the Night*, was credited with being the UK's first 'feminist novel' and which won the Somerset Maugham Award in 1979. I have also written a range of non-fiction books and, perhaps most important to me, I have produced a long steady line of short stories. I made a living doing freelance things I liked to do. I had two extraordinary and beautiful children with whom I get on very well. I felt respected and useful and satisfied. I do not regret any of it. This does matter. When things changed and I started not just to be more silent, but also to love silence and want to understand it and hunt it down, both in practice and in theory, I did not feel I was running away from anything. On the contrary, I wanted *more*. I had it all and it was not enough. Silence is additional to, not a rejection of, sociability and friends and periods of deep emotional and professional satisfaction. I have been lucky, or graced; in a deep sense, as I shall describe, I feel that silence sought me out rather than the other way round.

For nearly twenty years I had a marvellous life. Then, at the very end of the 1980s, for reasons I have not fully worked out yet, that well ran dry.

My marriage disintegrated.

Thatcherism was very ugly. It was not just the defeat of old hopes, but in the impoverished East End of London where my husband had his parish it was visibly creating fragmentation and misery. There was a real retreat from the edge, in personal relationships, in progressive movements of all kinds and in publishing.

Anglo-Catholicism ceased to be *fun*; and became instead increasingly bitter, misogynistic and right-wing; we stopped laughing, and a religion where you cannot laugh at yourself is a joyless, destructive thing.

As a writer I ran out of steam. I lost my simple conviction that *stories*, narrative itself, could provide a direct way forward in what felt like a cultural impasse.

I also went through a curious experience – a phase of extremely vivid and florid 'voice hearing', or auditory hallucinations. Although such experiences are commonly held to be symptoms of psychosis, and often form a central part of a diagnosis of so-called 'schizophrenia', this does not seem to me to describe the experience fully. I continued to carry on with my life. I found the content of these voices more absorbing and engaging than tormenting, and they certainly never urged hideous actions upon me. They were very distinct, however, and belonged to individuals, mainly drawn from fairy stories – a 'lost little girl', a dwarf, a sort of cat-monster. The most threatening were a sort of collective voice which I called the Godfathers and who seemed to represent a kind of internalised patriarchy, offering rewards for 'good' or punishments for 'bad' behaviour. I am still uncertain how much they were connected to the death of my real father in 1982, just a few months after my son was born and named after my father. When they were at their most garrulous there was a genuine conflict between my normal noisy lifestyle and listening to them and attempting to explore and understand what they were saying. There was an additional problem; inasmuch as they gave me any 'instructions' at all, these were about not telling anyone about them. This meant the rather novel experience of having something important going on in my life that I did not talk about.

The worst aspect of all this was the fear, indeed the terror, that I might be going mad. It was the normal cultural response to the voices that was the most disturbing aspect; otherwise and in retrospect they gave me a good deal of fictional material, some interesting things to think about and an awareness that there was something somewhat awry in my life.

In the early years of the 1990s I began to make changes in how I lived.

I became a Roman Catholic, escaping from the increasing strains of high Anglicanism without losing the sacraments, the richness of ritual and the core of faith. I bought a house in Warkton, a tiny village just outside Kettering in Northamptonshire. It was the chocolate-box dream of a cottage in the country – very old with low-beamed ceilings and a thatched roof. At that point I did not seriously think that my marriage was ending. We bought the house jointly. It seemed like a sensible thing to do. My husband's tenure in the Church of England was looking shakier by the day and it seemed reasonable for us to have a house to live in if or when he no longer had a vicarage. Whatever the intention, the reality was very soon that I lived in the house in Kettering and he lived in the vicarage.

Then something unexpected happened. My son decided that he wanted to stay at his school in London. (This did not last long, actually – when he had finished his GCSEs, he came to Kettering to do his A levels and we had an extraordinarily happy two years together there. I don't think he has quite forgiven me yet for selling that sweet house and moving north.) Although he came to Kettering almost every weekend, I was suddenly, and without exactly planning it, living on my own for the first time in my life.

Sometimes one's subconscious plays subtle tricks on one. To be honest I went to Warkton in a bit of a sulk. It was supposed to be a noble way of supporting my husband – he needed more space, but he also needed no 'scandal'. He was part of a group who wanted to become Roman Catholic priests despite being married. A small group of ex-Anglican clergy did in fact pull this off. But while Cardinal Hume was extending the tradition in every way he could manage on their behalf, clearly divorce, or even formal separation, was not going to be taken on board. An agreeable flat in London was not going to pass muster; a charming cottage in the country was much more acceptable. In many ways I felt that this was very thoughtful and kindly of me. I am not sure at that point I would have been up to doing it at all if I had thought how much it would change the trajectory of my life. Too much seemed to be changing too quickly.

The entirely unexpected thing was that I loved it. It is quite hard in retrospect to remember which came first – the freedom of solitude or the energy of silence. If you live alone you have particular freedom: when I first moved into the cottage it needed redecorating and I found myself choosing very deep rich colours. Someone commented on how different this was from all the houses I had lived in before, and I was slightly startled to realise how much of my domestic tastes had been a compromise between my preferences and my household's. (It amuses me still to see how different my house and my husband's house both are from the houses that we shared.) Food was another freedom; to eat what you want, when you want it, is a significant freedom after years of catering for a busy household with all the managing, compromises, effort and responsibility. These are little daily things, but they add up. Suddenly the amount of time in the day expanded, and there was freedom and space and choice. I became less driven, more reflective and a great deal less frenetic. And into that space flowed silence: I would go out into the garden at night or in the early morning and just look and listen; there were stars, weather, seasons, growth and repetition. For the first time in my life I noticed the gradation of colours before sunrise – from indigo through apricot to a lapidary blueness.

One morning very early I was outside and heard a strange noise, a sort of high-pitched series of squeaky protests. It was not a loud noise; I would not have heard it, even if it had occurred, in anything except the silence of a rural dawn. Suddenly something resembling an oversized bumblebee whirred past barely a metre from my face and crashed into the crab apple tree; then after a pause another one, and another. They were five baby blue-tits leaving their nest in the shed wall for the first time, free and flying, however clumsily, into the early sunshine. It was a privilege of solitude and a gift of silence.

For me, from the beginning, silence and solitude have been very closely linked. I know that this is not true for everyone – there are people who love solitude, who spend enormous amounts of time alone, without having any sense of themselves as silent – who have, for example, music or even television on a great deal of the time and who go, in happy solitude, to social or public events – to concerts, plays, films, sporting events and to the pub. Equally there are individuals whose silence is happily communal – you sometimes see this with couples, who need and enjoy to have their partner in the house but whose relationship for long periods of time seems to need no speech to flourish. More deliberately there are the silent religious communities, both Buddhist and Christian, for whom the silence of the people around them enriches their own. But for me personally the two are inextricably entwined. I suspect this is because I am a deeply socialised person; when I am with other people I find it nearly impossible not to be aware of them, and that awareness breaks up the silence. I worry occasionally that this may have something to do with the thinness of my sense of self, which can be so easily overwhelmed by others. But for whatever reasons, I cannot properly separate the two and I have noticed that I tend to use the words almost indiscriminately, so that the phrase 'silence and solitude' can be almost tautological; they both refer to that space in which both the social self and the ego dissolve into a kind of hyper awareness where sound, and particularly language, gets in the way. This was space that I was coming to love.

It took a little while to realise how much I loved it. It was not a sudden plunge into solitude and silence; it was a gradual shifting of gears, a gentle movement towards a new way of living that gave me an increasing deep satisfaction.

I still wonder what created that profound change in me. I honestly do not think I had been suppressing a deep desire for solitude or a need for silence for a long time; I still feel it was something new.

Change. The change. I think perhaps that it really does have something to do with menopause. I am by no means the first woman to shift her life in her mid forties and create a new sort of space for herself. In 1993, quite soon after I moved to Warkton, Joanna Goldsworthy asked me to contribute an essay to her forthcoming Virago collection, *A Certain Age*. At first I said I was too young – indeed, I did not finally stop menstruating for another ten years – but when I thought about it I became aware that there were changes going on – not just the ones I have been describing but more physical basic things. I had always enjoyed a textbook twenty-eight-day menstrual cycle; between 5 and 10 a.m. every fourth Friday I would start to bleed; I would bleed for five days and that would be it. Now that was getting bumpier, I could no longer count on the timing and instead I had backaches, bad-tempered fits and mild cramps. I, who had never shaved my legs or underarms on high feminist principle, was having to think about how I felt about the faint but real moustache that adorned my upper lip. I started to get hangovers and the occasional hot flush.

There are so few clues. No one wants to talk about it. We live in a culture that is terrified of the process of ageing, and in which women are encouraged to take artificial hormones so that they do not enter into this magical condition. But it is not just a modern phenomenon. Middle-aged and menopausal women are conspicuously absent from most myths and traditional stories: first you are the princess and the mother, then you vanish and reappear as aged crone. Even psychoanalysts throw up their hands in despair; at menopause women move beyond their help and good management. Helene Deutsch gives a particularly brutal, but not atypical, analysis of her own helplessness:

> Successful psychotherapy in the climacterium is made difficult because usually there is little one can offer the patient as a substitute for the fantasy gratifications. There is a large element of real fear behind the neurotic anxiety, for reality has actually become poor in prospects and resignation without compensations is often the only solution.[3]

Probably the suggestion that such women might like to go and live alone and experiment with silence would not come comfortably to a proponent of 'talking therapies'.

Unfortunately there is such a taboo around menopause, and such a wide range of ages at which it takes place in individual women, that it is hard to tell whether a turn to silence and solitude might be connected with this life event. There is, however, an interesting group of women saints, who lived highly active lives 'in the world' and then in their forties took a mystical path, joining religious orders often of considerable austerity or becoming recluses. Hilda of Whitby did not become a nun until she was middle-aged; Bridget of Sweden was married, had eight children and was a lady-in-waiting to the queen before she started to experience her visions; she became a nun and founded her new community when she was in her forties. Although Teresa of Avila became a nun at twenty, she had what she called her 'interior conversion', which opened the way for her visionary experiences, in 1555 and in 1562 she began her reform movement, moving her order (the Carmelites) back towards greater silence. So I am tempted to believe that there is something significant in this passage for women at least.

As I became more interested in silence I became intrigued by the negative silence and secrecy that has made menopause almost inaudible culturally – except occasionally, like Sarah or Elizabeth in the Bible, where the restrictions or freedoms of menopause are miraculously overcome by the direct intervention of God. Throughout the 1990s I wrote a series of short stories about menopausal women, refinding them in old tales and inventing new ones.[4] A lot of these, old and new, are about women making unexpected changes in their lives, opening up their imaginations and finding a new self-sufficiency. They are also stories deeply imbued with the countryside, and the rhythms of seasons and growth.

While I was researching for these stories I learned a strange and beautiful thing. Birds have hollow bones – their bones are not solid like mammals' bones, like human bones, but are filled with air pockets, a bit like bubble-wrap only less regular. (This is why when you pick up a dead bird it feels so insubstantial in your hand, unlike, say a mouse.) This is a deft evolutionary development – archaeopteryx, the earliest winged dinosaur, had feathers but solid bones – to make flying easier for them. At menopause women's bones thin out and fill with air pockets – in acute osteoporosis, under a microscope they are almost indistinguishable from birds' bones: at menopause women can learn to fly as free as a bird.[5] Oddly enough, in my own fiction, flying – dragons, witches, birds and angels – has often appeared as an image of women's freedom, so this discovery was especially delightful. When I look back at those stories now I cannot help but sense that something new and happy was going on for me over these years.

Perhaps not surprisingly, parallel with this I discovered the silent joy of gardening. In my childhood gardening, which meant almost entirely kitchen gardening – fruit and vegetables – had been a chore, an unending series of household tasks in which we had all been required to participate; needless to say we did this in a highly organised team spirit and it had never seemed to me like a pleasure or a source of contemplative serenity. My husband had a lovely garden at the East End vicarage, but it was always very definitely *his* garden; I felt no jealousy and was happy for him both to make the decisions and to do the work. The garden behind my cottage in Warkton was *my* garden. Everyone should have her first garden on Northamptonshire loam – it is so encouraging: you stick in a spade and it cuts into this rich, fertile, dark soil, never too dry and never boggy, with few stones and a generous well-balanced nature. Everything grows fast and strong.

And of course it grows silently. In our noise-obsessed culture it is very easy to forget just how many of the major physical forces on which we depend are *silent* – gravity, electricity, light, tides, the unseen and unheard spinning of the whole cosmos. The earth spins, it spins fast. It spins about its own axis at about 1,700 kilometres per hour (at the Equator); it orbits the sun at 107,218 kilometres per hour. And the whole solar system spins through the spinning galaxy at speeds I hardly dare to think about. The earth's atmosphere spins with it, which is why we do not feel it spinning. It all happens silently.

Organic growth is silent too. Cells divide, sap flows, bacteria multiply, energy runs thrilling through the earth, but without a murmur. 'The force that through the green fuse drives the flower'[6] is a silent force. Soil, that very topmost skin coating, is called earth and the planet itself is called earth. It is all alive – pounding, heaving, thrusting. Microscopic fungi spores grow, lift pavements and fell houses. We hear the crack of the pavements and the crash of the buildings – such human artefacts are inevitably noisy – but the fungus itself grows silently. Perhaps we are wise to be terrified of silence – it is the terror that destroyeth in the noontide.

Gardening puts me in contact with all this silent energy; gardeners become active partners in all that silent growth. I do not make it happen, but I share in it happening. The earth works its way under my nails and into my fingerprints, and a gardener has to pay attention to the immediate now of things. In one's own garden one must not be caught unawares – a single sprout of couch grass can grow five miles of roots in a year, while lurking silently behind the delphiniums, which are growing less extravagantly but just as determinedly in the opposite direction: up, up, upwards, and creating a magnificence of blue as though they were pulling the sky down to them. I have to pay attention to that silence.

In Warkton for the first time a garden became precious to me – it became an occupation, a resource and also my first glimpse that there might be art forms that I could practise which were not made out of words. Gardening gave me a way to work with silence; not 'in silence' but *with* silence – it was a silent creativity. The garden itself, through that silent growth, put in more creative energy than I did; it grew silently but not unintelligently. I started to think about gardens; not so much about gardening, which I see as a technical skill like spelling is for writers, but about gardens themselves. This meant looking at other people's gardens and reading about the history of gardens. To my surprise, because he is usually criticised among feminists for his rationalist philosophy and his desire to 'manage' and control nature, I found myself deeply in tune with the Renaissance figure Francis Bacon, who made himself three notable gardens and also wrote *Of Gardens* (1625), a personal and individual essay about beauty and taste, and *Sylva sylvarum* (published after his death in 1626) in which sections 5 and 6 are devoted to his ideas about gardening. Although actually he was a fine experimental horticulturalist, he too saw this as preliminary technique. The skill was necessary to create a garden, but the garden itself was not, in his view, simply a place to display one's gardening skills. He said of his garden in Twickenham that he 'found the situation of the place much convenient for the trial of my philosophical conclusions'.

More important, it got me interested in how gardens might reflect ideas, thoughts and desires, just as literature or painting does. Gardens, I learned, were very central to a great many religious traditions, as places of contemplation and silence of a physical kind: Zen gardens, European monastic gardens, the Persian and Moorish water gardens. 'Professional' silence seekers (hermits for want of a better collective noun) have always gardened. Improbably high in the Himalayas, in northern caves and on rocky islands, in Middle Eastern deserts, there they are, digging, scrabbling, weeding, watering, growing what they can – vegetables, a little grain and flowers, unexpected beauty in the harsh silence of their lives. They are seeking silence as close to the earth, to the silent power of growth as possible, becoming, as they would say, 'grounded'. Traditional Christian monastic life is built around two silent enclosures – the church and the cloister, which is also a garden – the secret, enclosed space, the *hortus conclusus*. The word paradise comes from a Persian word for garden.

I discovered there were modern and secular interpretations of this tradition – gardens that reflect, illustrate and develop personal philosophies and ideas of beauty; gardens that really are a form of art: Little Sparta, the late artist Ian Hamilton's garden in Lanarkshire; Charles Jenks's Garden of Cosmic Speculation; the Veddw, Anne Wareham's garden near Monmouth. These gardens are an open-ended, always changing way of exploring personal meaning and the interior world; they are lovely places that hold together nature and culture; they find meaning in very mundane processes – and these are silent.

With the garden designer Peter Matthews I wrote a book, *Gardens of Illusion*, about such gardens.[7] It was enormous fun to write. The gardens, and their gardeners, were so fabulous, so eccentric and so various. They made me think with a new part of my mind, even as I was beginning to learn how to do it myself.

However, the research for *Gardens of Illusion* had a side effect, which was to prove every bit as important. We had to travel extensively around the country to see these gardens. Up until then my main experience of the British countryside had been of rich green places; Northamptonshire replicated in many ways the rich dairy country of coastal Galloway: a green and pleasant land of pasture and prosperity – deciduous woodland, gentle rivers, prosperous old farms and charming sheltered villages. These are places of peace and contentment. What I encountered in these long drives across the country was another 'mood' of landscape, the wild and desolate places that still, and perhaps surprisingly, occupy a great deal of space in our supposedly overcrowded land. The bony spine of the Pennines and Cheviots running half the length of the country; the high western ranges of the Lake District and Snowdonia; the harsh smooth sweep of the east coast, the fragmented islands strewn west; the naked heave of the Yorkshire dales and the central Southern Uplands, and the vast emptiness of the Highlands. I began to realise that it was not peace and contentment that I craved, but that awed response to certain phenomena of the 'natural' world in which words, and even normal emotional reactions, fail or rather step away from the experience and there is a silence that is powerful, harsh and essentially inhumane. These landscapes have been called 'sublime', a word that also describes an emotion and aesthetic as well as actual scenery. I discovered in myself a longing for the sublime, for an environment that, rather than soothing me, offered some raw, challenging demands in exchange for grandeur and ineffability.

Another of the things I started to do during this time in Warkton was pray. Actually I did not *start* to pray at all – I had been praying for years; I had been a practising Christian since the early 1970s, I had already studied and written some theology and probably thought I was quite religious enough. But as my life became quieter and more solitary I found that my own prayer life was growing in interest and in the time I spent on it. It was not that my faith 'deepened' or indeed altered at all as far as content goes, it was that my living out of this set of convictions and practices shifted inwards. It became more silent, more interior, and I did more of it, in a more systematic and businesslike way. It also became more silent. I started to do what Buddhists normally call 'meditation', or in Christian terms, perhaps, 'contemplative prayer'. This is a discipline of trying to empty one's mind of its egotistical concerns in an attempt to align oneself with reality. For Buddhists it usually means exploring beyond the 'illusion' of matter and individuality; for Christians it means trying, through both the created order and particularly through the life and resurrection of Jesus, to experience and participate in the infinite love and mercy of God. Both traditions offer techniques for attempting this, as well as 'signposts' to discern whether you are on track or not. Thomas Merton, one of the most famous modern contemplatives, summed up the process as 'listening to the silence of God'. Almost all serious writers on contemplative prayer, from all traditions and across history, are clear that this kind of praying can only be developed in a context that includes a great deal of silence.

I find praying difficult, challenging and very hard work, but I also find it necessary, surpassingly lovely and crucially important. It began to supersede deipnosophy as my favourite thing. It became, and remains, one of the central reasons why I went hunting for silence, and why I am now sitting in the sunshine looking down a long silent valley. Of course, at this point in my adventures I did not guess that this was what was going to happen. It was simpler than that: I was on my own, I had a new sort of space and time, and one of the things I turned out to be doing with that space and time was praying.

But the most important thing that happened to me in Warkton was that I got interested in silence itself. At first I was both perplexed and self-critical about this new 'hobby'. We have reached a point in contemporary Western culture where we believe that too much silence is either 'mad' (depressive, escapist, weird) or 'bad' (selfish, antisocial) and I found I had internalised quite a lot of this way of thinking. Nor were the initial responses from many of my friends very encouraging. One of the problems with contemporary ideas about the complexity of our very identities is that if you say you are feeling neither mad nor bad, but on the contrary happy and well, this need make no real impression on one's concerned interrogator – everyone knows that you may be 'in denial' or 'repressing your real emotions', or suffering from 'false consciousness'. I found my efforts to explain what I was doing frustrating and, inevitably, a breach in the dam of the silence I was trying to build.

In these initial efforts I learned quickly that it is extremely difficult to talk about silence. At one level this is so obvious as to be funny – even writing a book about silence has a certain kind of inbuilt irony. But there are some other difficulties that can be swallowed up in this obviousness and I began to encounter a few of them.

The first problem is that the very word 'silence' lacks a clear definition. Everyone thinks they know what it means, but on examination it turns out that there is an enormous range of understanding. Even the dictionary definition is ambiguous. According to the OED, 'silence' means *both* an absence of all noises *and* an absence of speech. To fuzz the issue further, my anecdotal research has led me to believe that most people have a personal use of the word that is somewhere in between these two. 'I was silent all evening' can mean I was at a noisy party but did not myself speak much; it can mean 'I stayed at home on my own and watched TV'; or it can mean that 'it was so calm and peaceful where I was that I did not even hear the wind'. For some people, waves crashing on a seashore are 'silent' but the distant humming of a petrol engine is not. These, usually unexamined, differences matter quite a lot when one is trying to build 'silence' into one's own life. For me personally the exact meaning of silence has grown and shifted as I practise it more, but it remains fairly literal: it is words and speech particularly that break up silence. In addition I find human noises less silent than natural phenomena like wind and water. However, as time passes I increasingly realise there is an interior dimension to silence, a sort of stillness of heart and mind which is not a void but a rich space. What became obvious to me as I thought about this is that for me there is a chasm of difference between qualities like quietness or peace and silence itself. (Although, of course, it is sometimes possible, and lovely when it happens, to have them all at once.) In my personal vocabulary the difference is similar to the one between happiness and joy.

Additionally many people like John Cage, the radical composer, believe there is no such thing as real physical silence:

> There is no such thing as an empty space or an empty time. There is always something to see, something to hear. In fact, try as we may to make a silence, we cannot . . . Until I die there will be sounds. And they will continue following my death. One need not fear about the future of music.[8]

(I do think that Cage has been misunderstood. He was not really interested in silence, because he did not believe it existed. He was interested in forcing situations, removing 'conventional' sounds – like music – so that people would listen properly and become aware that there was no silence.)

A different sort of ambiguity lies in what, using the radio as an analogy, I have come to call the transmitter/receptor problem. The result – silence – is identical whether you turn off the radio in your house or the broadcasting company stops transmitting. Even if both transmitter and receptor are working, static (foul-ups en route between the two) can render the communication meaningless: the speaker has been in effect silenced. If I don't speak, there is nothing for you to hear; but if you are deaf then I can speak (orally) as loud as I want and you still won't hear. We use the same word 'silence' to describe all three of these forms of interference. If I cut your tongue out you are silenced (at the transmission point); if I throw you into a dungeon you may shout and yell, but you are still silenced (no one hears you, the reception is not available); if I make your speaking worthless, 'inaudible', meaningless, if I create static or interference, as it were, around your speech, you are also silenced. (This is very effective and useful for your average oppressor: calling someone 'mad', for example, means they can say what they like but no one will hear – this was the sort of silencing that the Soviet Union went in for.) In terms of shaping a silent life this image raises some interesting questions – is the silence in the hearing or the speaking? If I keep a journal, say, with no intention of 'transmitting' its content to anyone ever, is that a more silent activity than writing this book in the hope that you will read it and hear what I have to say? Is writing, or even reading, which use language but not noise, 'silent' in any case?

But most curious of all, my attempts to describe my experiences of silence, even to people who wanted to hear because they love me, forced me to feel that silence itself resists all attempts to talk about it, to try to theorise, explain or even describe it. This is not, I think, because silence is 'without meaning'. It is 'outwith language'. 'Outwith' is a wonderful Scottish word for which standard English appears to have no exact equivalent – outwith means 'outside of', 'not within the circumference of something else'. 'Without' is necessarily negative and suggests that something is lacking.*

I began to sense that all our contemporary thinking about silence sees it as an absence or a lack of speech or sound – a totally negative condition. But I was not experiencing it like that. In the growth of my garden, in my appreciation of time and the natural world, in the way I was praying, in my new sense of well-being and simple joy – all of which grew clearer the more silent I was – I did not see lack or absence, but a positive presence. Silence may be outside, or beyond the limits of, descriptive or narrative language but that does not necessarily mean that silence is *lacking* anything.

* An attempt to render this concept into standard English has muddled generations of children in the popular hymn 'There is a green hill far away without a city wall'. Like many others, I wondered why any hill should have had a city wall – but what Mrs C. F. Alexander meant was 'outwith a city wall'.

Perhaps it is a real, separate, actual thing, an ontological category of its own: not a *lack* of language but other than, different from, language; not an *absence* of sound but the presence of something which is not sound.

Nonetheless the idea that silence is an absence or lack is the commonly held position in contemporary life and especially – this is why it was painful – among the radical intellectual milieu in which I had for so long lived and flourished.

Towards the end of the 1990s my friend Janet Batsleer, with whom I was discussing all this at great length, sent me a (deliberately) provocative letter:

> Silence is the place of death, of nothingness. In fact there is no silence without speech. There is no silence without the act of silencing, some one having been shut up, put bang to rights, gagged, told to hold their tongue, had their tongue cut out, had the cat get their tongue, lost their voice. Silence is oppression and speech, language, spoken or written, is freedom.
>
> Paolo Freire in his great founding text *Pedagogy of the Oppressed* – founding for so much work in the last forty years – wrote that silence was the great theme of a pedagogy of liberation. That is why literacy preoccupied him and why the paradoxical capacities of the talk of the powerful to silence the 'coming to voice' of the oppressed fascinated him. Call it silence on the one hand; call it false consciousness, too much chatter next. That silence comes before speech and literacy is a trivial point. After all the silence of the oppressed can only be recognised in and through a language of freedom.
>
> That silence is a place of non-being, a place of control, from which all our yearning is to escape. All the social movements of oppressed people in the second part of the twentieth century have claimed 'coming to language' and 'coming to voice' as necessary to their politics . . . In the beginning was the Word. . . . Silence is oppression. It is 'the word' that is the beginning of freedom.
>
> All silence is waiting to be broken.[9]

Janet and I have argued theoretically for years; she has not only a shining intelligence, but also an enormously wide range of reference and an enduring, courageous commitment to justice and truth. On the whole, when we argue, I have the best jokes but she has the last laugh. She is nearly always right. But this time I was sure along my pulses that she was wrong, and I decided that I wanted to prove it.

People do not really change their whole lifestyle because their friends write them provocative letters. Janet's letter clarified and gave a shape to something that had been already growing in me. I was in Warkton for nearly eight years writing my books, pottering about my garden and my prayers, finding in an increasing amount of silence both happiness and fascination. But I was coming to realise that I wanted *more* – not just a greater quantity of silence, but also a more intense and focused experience of it.

The year 2000 was pivotal for me. It was the millennium, of course, but it was also the year I turned fifty, and the year my son finished school and left home. I was free. I could do anything I wanted. What I had learned I wanted was to forge a life with silence at the very centre of it. With this knowledge it also became clear that for me this could not happen in a sweet little West Midlands village. Oddly enough village life, although peaceful and often tranquil, is one of the least silent ways of living. You can be alone in the wild and invisible in a city; in a village or small country town you are known and seen and involved. I never seriously considered the city version of silence, although I deeply admire those who can do it. My ideas about silence had a landscape as well as an interior dimension. This is probably merely an aesthetic choice, but I was free to make that choice, and what called to me was space, wide wild space, neither spectacular mountains nor sheltered woods and fields. For me the terrain of silence is what I have since come to call the Huge Nothing of the high moorlands.

I wanted to live there. I wanted to live there in silence.

People asked me *why*. People still ask me why. Why leave the south where you have been happy for so long, where your friends and your children and your work all are, where your life is established? You are going too far; seemly ladylike retirement for rural peace and quiet, the absence of the din and bustle of the city, makes sense, but why go to such extremes? Sometimes I would just shrug my shoulders and joke, 'It's a tough job, but somebody has to do it,' or, 'Can you go too far in the right direction?' Or say – Like Mallory[10] – 'Because it's there.' But in honesty I was serious. I was not very interested in 'peace and quiet' or in the *absence* of anything. I was interested in silence; in response to Janet Batsleer's letter, which had struck a deep chord in me, I wanted not absence or lack of sound, but to explore the positive power of silence; I wanted the fullness of the experience.

I was much encouraged by other individuals who had sought out extreme solitude. I found myself in profound sympathy, for instance, with Henry Thoreau, the Transcendentalist radical philosopher. He explained his motivation for going to live alone by Walden Pond thus:

> I went to the woods because I wished to live deliberately, to front only the essential facts of life, and see if I could not learn what it had to teach, and not, when I came to die, discover that I had not lived. I did not wish to live what was not life, living is so dear; nor did I wish to practise resignation, unless it was quite necessary. I wanted to live deep and suck out all the marrow of life, to live so sturdily and Spartan-like as to put to rout all that was not life, to cut a broad swath and shave close, to drive life into a corner, and reduce it to its lowest terms, and, if it proved to be mean, why then to get the whole and genuine meanness of it, and publish its meanness to the world; or if it were sublime, to know it by experience, and be able to give a true account of it in my next excursion.[11]

A century later Richard Byrd, a US admiral and polar explorer, said something very similar about his decision to spend a winter alone in the Antarctic:

I wanted to go for experience sake: one man's desire to know that kind of experience to the full, to be by himself for a while and to taste the peace and quiet and solitude long enough to find out how good they really are . . . Must you go off and bury yourself in the middle of polar cold and darkness just to be alone? A stranger walking down 5th Avenue can be just as lonely as a traveller wandering in the desert? All of which I grant, but with the contention that no man can hope to be completely free who lingers within reach of familiar habits and urgencies. I wanted something more than just privacy in the geographical sense. I should be able to live exactly as I chose, obedient to no necessities but those imposed by wind and night and cold, and to no man's laws but my own.[12]

The idea that extreme lifestyles deliver extreme experiences, and that these are desirable, is very ancient. The Greek gods offered the hero Achilles the choice between a long and contented life and a short blaze of glory, and he chose the latter. The desert hermits of the fourth century CE told a number of stories about the gains of going too far:

Abba Lot came to Abba Joseph and said to him, 'Father, according to my strength, I keep a modest rule of prayer and fasting and meditation and quiet, and according to my strength I purge my imagination: what more must I do?' The old man, rising, held up his hands against the sky, and his fingers became like ten torches of fire, and he said, 'If thou wilt, thou shalt be made wholly a flame.'[13]

I did not want peace and quiet; I wanted to be 'wholly a flame'. It is not chance that the words 'whole', 'healthy' and 'holy' are all derived from the same root. I incline to excess.

At a more practical level I had at least four conscious intentions.

First, I wanted to understand silence better. I wanted to demonstrate at least to myself that silence was not just a negative absence or loss, and was not necessarily waiting to be broken. But if it was not simply a lack of noise, then I needed to know what it was, what its positive content might be. I am convinced that as a whole society we are losing something precious in our increasingly silence-avoiding culture and that somehow, whatever this silence might be, it needs holding, nourishing and unpacking.

I wanted to explore my own spirituality and deepen my growing sense of the reality of God, and the possibility of being connected to that reality. Within all the major religious traditions, though to differing degrees, there is a shared recognition that silence is one very effective tool for spiritual development. Of course, there are others, but I had put my hand to this particular plough and wanted to cut a deeper, straighter furrow.

I also wanted to dig deeper into my own writing. I had, as I have said, reached a point where I no longer had the simple confidence in narrative, in storytelling, which had sustained a steady flow of work for over twenty years. I find this difficult to explain, again I think because of our contemporary tendency to see any deviation from the mainstream as a loss or lack. I did not feel that my imagination had 'dried up' or that I was being silenced by a writer's block, but rather that there was something *more*. I wanted to find out what it was. I had been brought up, and indeed had profoundly internalised, the dicta of post-romanticism: 'solitude is the school for genius';[14] creativity is the 'still unravished bride of quietness, [a] foster child of silence and slow time'.[15] I had a sense that I needed a hefty dose of the sublime, of the extreme, to counterbalance the fragmented, psychologically realist babble of so much contemporary fiction. I needed as a writer to escape the pressure to conform, to sing in harmony with what is going on rather than seek out whatever may be beyond that. This journey into silence in extreme terrains has been important for a number of creative thinkers while they prepare themselves for radical new work. Although I did not know it at the time, my motivation feels very close to Wittgenstein's decision to leave Cambridge and its, to him, intellectual triviality, and live in extreme isolation in Skjolden, Norway.

And finally I wanted more silence because I enjoyed the small amount I was getting. I enjoyed it at a great number of levels, intellectually, emotionally, physically. As well as being a silence-avoiding culture, and perhaps linked to this, we are also becoming a profoundly personalist culture, in which only relationships, feelings and psychodynamics are allowed full significance. If I had said to people, 'I am in love with someone and we are going to live on an isolated moor,' I doubt anyone would have said, 'Why?' in quite the same way. We have lost the conviction that Dorothy Sayers, the crime writer and theologian, so vigorous defended: 'It is time to realise that a passionately held intellectual conviction is passionate.' I was falling in love with silence. Like most people with a new love, I became increasingly obsessed by it – wanting to know more, to go further, to understand better.

That was what I wanted and I was in the enviable position of being able to have what I wanted. I don't want this to sound like a midlife crisis, because there was no crisis. It was more a question of, 'Well, what now?' and 'what now' turned out to be silence.

So in the summer of 2000 I moved north to County Durham, to a house on a moor high above Weardale. I was eager and greedy. I wanted both to be silent and to think about silence. I set out to hunt silence and I have been doing so ever since.

2

Forty Days and Forty Nights

The house in Weardale was wonderful. It was also slightly odd: it was perched very high, nearly 450 metres, on the summit of a bizarrely exposed ridge. It was isolated in one sense, but at the same time it was the middle house of a terrace of three cottages. When I first moved there both the other two houses were holiday homes, used only at weekends, so the neighbours created little disruption and, indeed, were immensely helpful as I struggled to learn how to live in such a cold, wind-driven location (drain your pipes before you leave home).

From both the front and the back there were enormously long views. Because of the steep sides of the dale, Stanhope, three kilometres and nearly 250 metres below, was invisible; the view stretched straight over the valley to the moors the other side. At night there were pairs of sharp eyes looking at me – the headlights of cars six miles away, coming over from Teesdale, and shining clean across the valley and in through my bedroom window.

But my house on the hill was not some shepherd's cottage or ancient hermitage. It was part of a major industrial complex. From the earliest times Weardale has been a hive of industrial activity. One of the largest caches of Bronze Age artefacts in the UK was discovered beside the Heathery Burn, between my house and Stanhope. The Romans did not use the A68 (Dere Street), which still runs along the eastern edge of the Durham moors, solely to march troops up to Hadrian's Wall, but also to take the lead and silver from the hill mines down to York. Lead, silver, feldspar, tin and coal were all mined up here, and during the Industrial Revolution of the eighteenth and nineteenth centuries, Weardale became a crucial source of lead and feldspar, which were mined under extraordinarily exploitative and dangerous conditions. In 1834 a railway was opened to bring lead down from the scattered hill mines to the dale itself, then out to the factories on the coastal plain. The sides of the dale were too steep for the trains to climb and a double steam winch was installed to pull them up. The winch engines needed steam twenty-four hours a day, so a line of cottages was built for the winch engineers. Farm labourers' cottages were exquisitely cantilevered in to the landscape to provide them with as much shelter as possible, but the engineers were ruthlessly exposed to the full effect of the elements, 425 metres above sea level, on the very crest of a hill. My house was an ex-winch engineer's cottage.

The ruin of the engine house itself stood derelict a hundred yards from the cottages. There is no winch, no railway and no mining now. The cement factory at Eastgate closed while I was there and the sand quarry beside the old railway line will no doubt follow it. There are no industrial jobs in Weardale, and the machinery and social life of the miners is silenced. But the views of apparently desolate and wild hills have been carved and shaped and constructed and formed by that industrial past. This is 'Famous Five' country[1] because for every fog there is a mysterious mine shaft and for every bog a deserted railway line. The moors are a place of adventure.

At the same time the area is rich in the artefacts of the hermit tradition of northern England – Durham itself, Hexham, Lindisfarne (Holy Island) and a scattering of stones that mark erstwhile chapels and hermitages. In fact, the radical politics of the north-east drew its inspiration from the great hermit Bishop Cuthbert. At the end of the eleventh century, the inhabitants of the north-east resisted William the Conqueror's demands for feudal dues and Norman reorganisation. Their land, they claimed, was the patrimony of St Cuthbert, unalienable, freely given and held. The habit of stubborn resistance has marked most of English history.

There are not many places you can live within such a long history and still have the huge silences and beauty of it all. The dales are full of stories and the vanished silent ghosts of other lives lived very differently in the same place. The emptiness of these moors is not the desolate tragedy of the Western Highlands, where the keening of the dispossessed can still be heard in the silence that followed the Clearances. It is something more dynamic.

I settled in very smoothly, once I had learned how to manage my coal-fired back boiler – my only source not merely of heat but of hot water as well. I started to walk a good deal. Moors are excellent for elementary walkers, especially those who smoke, because once you are above the valleys there are miles and miles of long views, often down on to woods and rivers, but the terrain itself is flat, without steep climbs. There is always something to see but you have to look for it. I felt increasingly pared down, lean, fit and quiet, shacked up, as it were, with the wind and the silence and the cold.

I also found that the landscape worked in a kind of harmony with my prayers. The ruined signs of previous inhabitants reminded me that 'here we have no abiding city'. But the horizon line of the hills abided. It was uncluttered by trees or houses. I could see it out of every window. Wherever I sat to meditate, there was the clear, clean line that divides earth and sky and also unites them. That line was constant. It emerged out of the dark in the first dawn light and was swallowed back into the dark at nightfall. Above the line, infinity; below the line, mortality. But the line itself was both and held them both, and the wind blew along it, fresh and free like the passage of the spirit.

However, I also began to realise that Richard Byrd had been right when he speculated that 'no man can hope to be completely free who lingers within reach of familiar habits and urgencies'.[2] In the contemporary Western world it is very difficult to be silent for very long in the place where you live – people phone, they come to visit, to canvass your vote; the postman needs a signature, Jehovah's Witnesses knock politely, someone has to read the meter; you run out of milk and have to go and buy some more, and the woman in the village shop starts to chat. In fact, it is impossible. Moreover, there are what Byrd calls 'urgencies' – the economic urgency of work, of making a living, and the emotional urgency of love and friendship. I was living more silently than before, but I still was only dabbling on the margins of that deep ocean I sensed was there.

Fascinated by silence, drawn joyfully into the void, I wanted to experience a total version; I wanted to know what it was that I was trying to build into my life before the habits of the quotidian asserted themselves. The nearest analogy I can think of is that of a honeymoon. When this post-wedding holiday started it was in a society in which the newly wed couple had probably not spent more than a couple of hours at a time together, and even less time alone together. Rather than start immediately on the business of building a shared working life, they would spend a period of intense time together away from their normal daily concerns, where they had nothing to do but focus on and learn about each other. Similarly monks and nuns in even the most silent of religious orders take 'retreats', periods of time when they are separate from their community and relieved of all the burdens of work for an intense period of concentration on God. I decided that I would go away and spend some time doing nothing except being silent and thinking about and experiencing it. I decided that forty days would be a suitable amount of time. Obviously this was not a randomly chosen period – but it seemed to be possible but substantial, as well as iconic.

The most straightforward way for someone like me to manage this sort of time and space would have been to spend these six weeks in a religious community where I would have been freed from all the hassles and would have had gatekeepers against any interruptions. But at this point I wanted to separate prayer from silence. My imagination is so 'Christianised' that I felt those sorts of ideas could have overridden other feelings in a monastic context with holy pictures (mostly bad ones!) on every wall. I did not want to go on a 'retreat'. I wanted to explore what this profound pull towards silence might be about. I wanted to examine my conviction that silence was something positive, not just an abstraction or absence. I wanted to know what would happen.

In the end I rented a self-catering holiday cottage on Skye, more because I found a house there that met my slightly off-centre requirements than for any particular engagement with the island. I needed a small house that was genuinely isolated, and had a deep freeze and no TV – and in which I could smoke. My care in checking all these details in advance was rewarded, or else I was lucky – Allt Dearg[3] might have been designed for my purposes.

In all events in late October, my car fully laden with books, notebooks, pens, reading matter, foul-weather gear and six weeks' worth of food and other supplies, I left my sister's lovely and luxurious house near St Andrew's and drove east to west the whole way across Scotland. It was a long, tiring and stunningly beautiful drive, in and out of sunshine and rain, and all the time I had a growing sense of moving away – the roads getting narrower, the houses less frequent, the towns more like villages and the villages tiny. I had forgotten that the ferry crossing from Kyle of Lochalsh over to Skye has been replaced by the muscular sweep of the new bridge and for a moment I missed that sense of being *somewhere else*, in a new and different place, that the ferry provided. But once on the island the bilingual road signs, in both Gaelic and English, provided a strong sense of strangeness. In Gaelic, which about half the population speaks, the island is called An t-Eilean Sgitheanach (The Winged Isle), which refers both to its curious shape and to the wild empty freedom of its terrain.

The Cuillin, the mountains of central Skye, are perhaps the toughest range in Britain, naked jagged rock rising abruptly from the sea, several soaring to some 900 metres. In the shadow and shelter of these mountains, facing west towards the mainland, was Allt Dearg, once a shepherd's croft.

It was lovely. As I drove up the quarter-mile of rough track through yet another smatter of rain, I saw in the wing mirror of my car an extremely vivid rainbow, all seven colours in wide bands. It seemed a good omen.

Allt Dearg sat small, white and welcoming. Although it is nestled under the mountains there is nothing human above it, and below the land drops away to a long narrow bay with steep sides. I could not see the road or any buildings. Close beside the cottage is a burn that leaps and rushes, and makes a good deal of noise. Inside it is compact and tidy. I lived throughout the time I was there entirely on the ground floor, where a tiny bedroom opened off the kitchen-living room, so that I had a strong sense of containment inside despite the wildness outside. Outside, even in the evening light, the colours were extraordinary. Higher above me the mountains were grey; they were like teeth – craggy, broken, fierce. Behind the house is a croft field, still reasonably green, but everything else below those iron heights is gold, gold-bronze, punctuated by very white lichen on stones.

In the fitful sunshine driving across I had thought the colour was sun-on-dead-grass; now I learned it was the grass itself, and dead was not a good word for it. The wind moved fast across it, flapping it like flags. When it reached darker clumps of heather or bog myrtle the rhythm of the movement changed. I kept thinking I'd seen 'something', something alive, moving like an animal running for cover – but no, it was just the wind somehow haunting and energising.

I was exhausted by the time I had explored the house and the immediate surroundings, unpacked the car and settled in, but I also had a powerful sense of excitement and optimism, I was at the beginning of an adventure. I felt oddly foxy – I'd slipped my leash and got away. I felt open to whatever might happen and hungry for the silence.

At one level Allt Dearg was never completely silent. The wind roared down from the mountains more or less incessantly through-out the whole time I was there. There was also the 'voice of many waters'.[4] When it rained, which it did a very great deal, I could hear it lashing on the roof-light windows upstairs; all the old windows of the house, hunching its back against the predominant wind, faced westwards; the modern desire for light has dominated over the older longing for protection. Even when the wind and rain paused the burn did not. Just behind the house it descended sharply in a series of small waterfalls and they sounded like distant aeroplane engines. Nearer to the house the sound of the burn was not dissimilar, in both volume and tone, to the lorries coming up the hill from Stanhope, except that it was continual. Yet my sense was that none of these noises mattered; they did not break up the silence, which I could listen for and hear behind them. I thought a lot about whether it was the constant background nature of these sounds or the fact that they were natural rather than human-made noises that meant they did not disrupt my personal sense of silence.

For the first few days I wallowed in the pure pleasure of freedom: no phone calls, no emails, no neighbours. I snuggled into the private silence of the house and walked out to see the fitful sun on the grass and on the sea, to watch the sharp mountain peaks punctuated by cloud, and to let the wind blow through me. To settle into the silence and somehow lower my own expectations – to plan, scheme, rule, manage the days as little as possible. To experience, sense, live, *be* as much as possible. The experience of most people who voluntarily take themselves off into silence is that it takes a while to settle into it. Of course, it does not grow more silent as time passes, but you do become more attuned to the silence. Unlike sound, which crashes against your ears, silence is subtle. The more and the longer you are silent the more you hear the tiny noises within the silence, so that silence itself is always slipping away like a timid wild animal. You have to be very still and lure it. This is hard; one has only to try to quieten one's mind or body to discover just how turbulent they are. But gradually I discovered a shape for each day and the silence took over.

I was intensely curious to discover what might happen. There are a good number of published accounts of experiences of silence, which could have told me, but I decided not to read any while I was on Skye as I thought it might influence my own experiences excessively; I wanted to discover for myself. However, since then I have read extensively about other people's accounts of it in tandem with my own journal and I have come to believe that there are indeed quite specific things that happen to people who are silent for a prolonged period of time. But it is complicated.

In the first place I had chosen this silence and prepared myself for it; I wanted to do it. Moreover, I enjoyed it. Silence can be terrible and even lethal, most usually when it is enforced or imposed. This is not an absolute rule – Donald Crowhurst chose to enter the Golden Globe race in 1968, and the silence drove him mad and finally killed him. On the other hand Boethius, in the sixth century, and John Bunyan, in the seventeenth, had no choice at all about their isolation and imprisonment, and both found positive and creative resources in the silence. However, in terms of matching my Skye experiences to those of other people I have concentrated on chosen silence.

Another problem I encountered is that most of the accounts that we have of chosen silence are *religious*. Before the mid eighteenth century I can find no detailed reports of voluntary silence whatsoever that are not directed by a religious impulse; even when Daniel Defoe wrote *Robinson Crusoe*, based on the real experience of Alexander Selkirk, he took a totally secular event and turned it into a religious work. All the early accounts share a set of particular expectations, rewards and goals, which are bound to slew both the experience itself and the way it is reported.

There are inevitably biases. For instance, Tibetan Buddhists may not take a permanent vow of silence on the grounds that if they were to achieve enlightenment they would have an obligation to *teach*: finding that silence was a permanent personal need and a primary source of delight would involve admitting (however subconsciously) that one's own silence had 'failed', that it had not brought you to a state of enlightenment.

Specifically religious accounts are most likely to accept ineffability, to feel and say that the experience is outwith language and beyond human expression. Every attempt I have ever seen to diagnose or describe mystical experience uses ineffability as one of the tests. If you can describe what happened and what it felt like, then by definition you have not had an authentic mystical experience. This is not going to encourage mystics to struggle to express themselves. Ineffability goes with the territory. I might even say that the 'best' hermits of both Eastern and Western traditions are those who have least to say about it – or never bother to say it at all. The only thing Tenzin Palmo, a British Buddhist nun who spent three years high in the Himalayas in radical silence, seems ever to have said, at least publicly, about her personal experience is, 'Well, it wasn't boring.'[5]

There is – in my opinion – nothing wrong with this religious bias, but it does distort the evidence; and until recently it underpinned almost all accounts of silence. Luckily for me there are now a growing number of more secular sources to balance out the religious narratives, but they are all modern and cannot offer the cultural spread I would have liked. First there were the Romantic Movement writers like William Wordsworth and Henry Thoreau, who may have been theist in their understanding of nature but were militantly not religious and had quite other fish to fry in their accounts of silence.

Since the mid nineteenth century there has been an invaluable new source of silence stories: the explorers, pioneers, prospectors and lone adventurers. At first too many of these were so stiff-upper-lip that they could not speak of their own emotions at all. 'It was jolly frightening' and 'At the top I felt a certain satisfaction as I sat and admired the magnificent views' do not really meet our contemporary desire for emotional engagement, any more than they enable me to explore the nature of silence.

As late as the 1950s John Hunt, the leader of the first successful Everest expedition, *apologises* for the emotion expressed when Tenzing Norgay and Edmund Hillary returned to the camp after their triumphant summitting of the mountain: 'I am ashamed to confess that there was hugging and even some tears.'[6] In 1958 he wrote the foreword for *Alone*, Richard Byrd's account of his solitary stay in Antarctica, and broods there on whether it is 'healthy' for a man to write about his interior life; or if it isn't a bit indulgent and morbid –

'unmanly'. In addition, a fair number of the solo adventurers have been markedly introverted. In some cases, like Leslie Stephen, Virginia Woolf's father, who was, *inter alia*, an early and dedicated solo mountaineer, this seems to have been why they took to these activities in the first place. As he wrote: 'Life would be more tolerable if it were not for our fellow creatures. They come about us like bees, and as we cannot well destroy them, we are driven to some safe asylum. The Alps as yet remain.'[7]

The last thing someone like this would have wanted was to expose his emotions to any public gaze whatsoever. Although neither seems to have been neurotically misanthropic, Francis Chichester, the first solo circumnavigator of the world, and Augustine Courtauld, who spent six months in a tent alone in the Arctic (one of the most extreme modern silences I have ever come across) were both furious at the attention they received – Chichester from a protective Royal Navy flotilla as he sailed round the Horn and Courtauld by the media 'fuss' that seemed to him to vulgarise the purity of his polar solitude. Women explorers, like Gertrude Bell, have been more willing to give expression to their emotional response, but until recently there have not been a great many of them.

Then, in 1968 the *Sunday Times* sponsored the first 'Golden Globe' race, sailing single-handed, non-stop round the world. Francis Chichester's single-handed circumnavigation, with a stopover in Australia, had caught the public's imagination the year before. Chichester's success established that a non-stop voyage was at least a possibility. More important, though, it demonstrated that the British public would love to hear about such an adventure and what they wanted to hear was not meteorological science, but the gritty little details of courage, endurance and grief; what it *felt* like to be alone at sea.

The *Sunday Times*'s creation of the race itself was somewhat opportunist: there were two experienced single-handed yachtsmen, Robin Knox-Johnston and Bernard Moitessier, already preparing to rise to the challenge for its own sake and who had found other sponsorship. Neither of them took any interest in the idea of a race, Moitessier announcing that the very idea of it made him 'want to vomit'.[8] It was clear that, when either of them was ready, they would set off, waiting for no race and, if successful, leave no role for the *Sunday Times*. In response the newspaper framed the race so that it was impossible *not* to enter it. There would be two prizes – first round the world, and fastest time round the world. These could be different because there was no actual starting date – entrants merely had to set out from any port north of 40°N at any time between the beginning of June and the end of October.

In the end there were nine entries. But there was only one finisher – Robin Knox-Johnston.

One yacht was dismasted in a gale off South Africa and one foundered barely 1,500 kilometres from home. All the other entrants, for one reason or another, 'retired'. In each case it was not the sailing itself that proved the most significant hurdle, but the emotional response to it. No one was killed by wave or wind; their 'will' was warped or altered by isolation and silence. Donald Crowhurst went mad; Nigel Tetley committed suicide some months after his rescue; and Moitessier fell so 'in love' with silence and the sea that in the end he simply could not bring himself to return home.

The reason for elaborating this little piece of history here is simple. Several of the cultural changes of the sixties came together. None of these sailors was independently wealthy, as previous adventurers had predominantly been – they *needed* sponsorship at the very moment when the media had learned that non-specialist readers *wanted* to know about extreme adventures and the interior lives of their heroes. Readers will consume every crumb of emotion, darkness, fear and triumph they can get, so the books of solitary adventure began to include feelings, emotions and inner awareness. All the survivors of this first race wrote books about it.

One effect of the race (not, of course, separated from other cultural developments of the 1960s, which reshaped masculinity as much as they more famously reshaped femininity) was that it led to a new kind of 'adventure writing', a new sort of account of silence and solitude. For sailing, at least, the silence was short-lived the next three decades the public's desire to know what was h. pening emotionally and physically, to 'keep in touch', overwhelmeᴅ the silence. Satellite navigation systems, effective radio communications and the global reach of the rescue services have made it nearly impossible for independent small ships to slip away. The reporting of the silence has destroyed the silence – whatever else her adventure may have been, Ellen McArthur's experience during her record-breaking circumnavigation was hardly one of silence.

Single-handed sailors have produced some of the best accounts of extreme silences. This may have something to do with the psychology of those who put to sea in small ships, but I expect that in reality it is practical: long periods of single-handed journeys are actually quite boring – you are not in the Roaring Forties all the time; nor do you have to shin up masts in high gales seven days a week. You have space and time to brood, think, listen to the silence and moreover a place to write extensive journals. For large parts of Knox-Johnston's journal you would hardly know he was at sea:

> A sedate lunch followed my swim, usually consisting of biscuits and cheese or the like, with a pickled onion on special occasions as a treat. The afternoons would be spent just like the morning, working or reading until 5 p.m. when, if I felt like it, I dropped everything for a beer or a whisky . . . I repaired the Gilbert and Sullivan tape cassette . . . and had a wonderful evening.[9]

The necessary discipline of keeping the ship's log (without which you will not know where you are or how to get to where you are going) means that daily you have to sit down and record your trip. Adding a more personal narrative, which anyway you have already had commissioned and which is enabling you to make the voyage, fits tidily into the pattern of your day. You have the same cabin throughout the journey and can safely store your papers in it. You do not have to lug your notebook or tape recorder around with you day after day. It is patently easier to keep a coherent and consistent account of prolonged silence at sea than under most other adventurous circumstances. For the 1968 Golden Globe yachtsmen we have a solid group of accounts written at the same time, in basically similar external conditions. This race provided me with a touchstone for the experiences of silence.

Of course, there are other accounts too. Almost every extreme habitat has its own silence aficionados. I am not sure what it is that links 'extreme' geography and silence, but I suspect it is something more than the likelihood that such places will be fairly deserted. I know that my own silence is nourished by, even born out of, a particular sort of visual austerity. ('Bleak' is the word more commonly used by my friends.) There are now accounts of prolonged silences in a wide variety of terrain. Deserts, mountains, islands and the Poles are as popular as the oceans; and Jacques Cousteau, the underwater explorer, called his autobiography *The Silent World*.

There are exceptions. For example, I have never come across an account of silence in the jungle, although there are many adventure stories located there. My own limited experience of the jungle suggests that, quite simply, it is not silent. Jungles are noisy – and the noises are sudden, alarming and suggest a density of life, even if not human life, of fertility, movement, surprise. The hot, fetid density of the jungle offers a different kind of physical experience from the sharp, austere atmospheres that seem to be emotionally connected to silence.

Throughout written history at least there have always been individuals who have taken themselves off voluntarily and often alone seeking silence. Some of these expeditions have had important historical consequences. Gautama Buddha's silent meditation under the Bo Tree some time between 566 and 368 BCE, Jesus of Nazareth's forty-day solitary fast in the Sinai Desert *c.* 33 CE and Muhammad ibn Abdullah's annual Ramadan retreat to Mount Hira, near Mecca, culminating in his revelations of 610 CE, are rather obvious cases in point. Most silent adventures, however, have had no particular public consequences – or at least not that we can be aware of. The explicit motivation for these adventures has changed across cultures and across time (religious, artistic, heroic and escapist) but the desire is there constantly. John Hunt, in his foreword to *Alone*, wrote:

> Byrd decided that Advanced Base should be occupied and that he should be the occupant because of an urge that lies very deep in a man's nature – to find out more about himself . . . Imprisoned by darkness and an annihilating cold in a tiny wooden shack, Byrd had [no] distractions. Inaction in the long, silent, bitter, polar night would throw a man upon himself.[10]

On Skye, like Byrd, though less extremely, I was 'thrown upon myself'. People ask me what I did all day. I prayed and meditated a lot more than I was able to do at home; I read a bit, though less than I had anticipated. I walked a good deal when the weather permitted, but I was restricted both by its consistent vileness and by the very early nightfall, that far north in November and December. When I could not walk I drove out in the car and looked at the wild country-side, both the mountains and the rocky coast. I worked on some very intricate sewing. English traditional canvas embroidery, unlike Continental tapestry, does not create pictures but patterns, almost mathematical; it requires endless precise repetitive actions, like knitting but without that irritating click-click sound. And I listened. I listened to all the complex sounds, and I listened to the silence, and I listened to myself and tried to notice what was happening. Every evening I wrote up the day in a journal, usually 2,000 or 3,000 words.

What I saw over those forty days was a group of sensations, most of them oddly physical. Later I was fascinated to find that all of these frequently, even usually, occur to anyone who exposes him- or herself* voluntarily to long periods of silence, for any reason whatsoever. I noted at least eight distinct experiences.

---

* It is usually 'him' – the sort of adventures we learn about have, until very recently, been undertaken most frequently by men. This makes the few accounts by women particularly interesting.

The first effect that I noticed, towards the end of the first week, was an extraordinary intensification of physical sensation. It started with food. One morning I cooked myself my usual bowl of porridge and, eating it, was suddenly overwhelmed by the wonderful, delicious delightfulness of porridge. Eating was an intense pleasure: it tasted *more* like porridge than I could have imagined porridge could taste. The milk was very slightly cooler than the oats; I could distinguish the sugar and the salt tastes independently even though there was no sense that they weren't perfectly blended and balanced. Even cooking it was exquisite – the bubbles rose like lava and created moon craters on the surface in an infinitely pleasing way. It was not a sublimated sexual or religious experience; on the contrary it was an entirely gustatory experience.

Even as I ate it I realised quite suddenly how good all the food was tasting this week, how delicious, how pleasing to cook. It feels slightly foolish at this distance from the moment, but there was something so complete about the making-and-eating. I thank God now that I did not take the alternative option, which I had considered, of buying forty frozen meals and stacking them all prepared into the freezer. The quotidian business, or busyness, of cooking seems extremely important – like weaving the rush baskets was for the desert hermits.[11] Yet it was only and simply porridge – it did not taste of 'nectar and ambrosia' or the Heavenly Banquet: it tasted of porridge! Intensely of porridge.

The sensation that everything sensory was *more so* was the first effect that I noticed in myself and the one that I would say with most confidence was a direct result of silence. I suspect that some of this was simply having the time and opportunity to concentrate. But it was more than this. This is quite hard to describe, but by the middle of the second week I was feeling everything with an extraordinary degree of intensity. Even now when porridge has become just porridge again, I discover in myself a new understanding of little Goldilocks, trespasser and thief, sneaking out of the dark and silent forest and smelling the porridge in the Three Bears House. Even her name can make me salivate, with delight and desire.

All food took on something of this intensity – I cooked well, making more effort, taking more care than I normally do, and enjoyed things for and of themselves. It was not that I cooked very elaborately, and indeed I was confined to the ingredients I had taken with me before I knew that this would be such an important part of my day; it was simply that my sense of taste intensified. But so did my other senses. My hearing, for instance, felt honed and accurate to a remarkable degree.

One evening I noticed that I was suddenly able to separate the different wind noises and follow a bit their relationship to each other – like an orchestra. The wind in the chimney as opposed to 'outside' was quite easy – but there were infinitely more, and subtler, differentiations to be made. The wind (I expect it always does but I am not always so well focused) was changing constantly in volume and strength – so there were almost lyrical moments when it sank down towards silence (brief but intense) and I could rest there. Or there would be just one tone – from the burn or the chimney – then more and more picking up and adding in, including extremely wild moments when all the roof tiles would ripple like a percussion (tympani) line. I could not listen to it in a very sustained way – either all the tones would collapse into one rather formless loud wind noise or my awareness would drift. It was hard work as well as a gift. But the silent falls were exquisite and consoling. It felt, perhaps because of the attention required, entirely NOW and physical – I was not thinking about the wind but listening to it.

My sense of body temperature became more acute – if I was wet, or cold, or warm I experienced this very directly and totally. I have never been so physically tired, so aware of weather, of sound, and of the variety of colour in the wild environment. It seems as though speaking, 'telling' one's feelings, even to the extent of 'look, look how wet I got', acts as a way of discharging them, like lifting the lid of a boiling pot.

Before long my emotions also seemed to swell likewise into monumental waves of feeling – floods of tears, giggles, excitement or anxiety, often entirely disproportionate to the occasion. These roller-coaster rides come up again and again – when I reread the journal I am amazed by them, partly because they often seemed quite normal at the time but also because, even when I did notice them, they did not seem to worry me much. These were not new or inexplicable sensations and feelings; they were the old ones felt more strongly.

Whatever caused this intensification it was not some psychological peculiarity of my own. Almost every account of silence I have ever read contains some version of it. In my journal at the time I commented that this intensification of sensation made me think of St Anthony's sexual torments. Anthony is generally regarded as the founder of Christian monasticism, and especially of eremitical (hermit) spirituality. He was born in 250 CE in Upper Egypt into a prosperous Christian family. His parents died when he was about twenty and (after making suitable arrangements for his sister) he sold all his property and became a hermit, first in his own neighbourhood and later in the Sinai Desert – seeking ever more isolated and extreme situations. The way silence ratchets up the intensity of physical experience makes some sense of his famous struggles with demons. His particular demons frequently disguised themselves as sexy dancing girls. So immediately and powerfully did he become sexually aroused that he felt obliged to rush out of his cell and throw himself into thorn bushes. Actually, I don't share his beliefs about either masturbation or demons, but I can understand how the *intensity* of the physical and mental experience might drive one to seeing such actions as somehow sensible.

In the tradition set by Abba Anthony male Christian hermits do seem to suffer an almost bizarre degree of sexual torment. (Female Christian hermits seem more prone to attacks of masochistic self-harm; Buddhist hermits seem more vulnerable to rage.) Some of this must be related to their earnest pursuit of a rather rigorous kind of chastity since what is most forbidden is most likely to rear up and threaten in any such situation. But I am convinced that a great deal of it is more related to this intensification in silence: feelings about sex, or food, or warmth, or comfort take on a vivid, even hectic, vibrancy. When those are the very things one is hoping to escape from *through* silence, it is not at all surprising that one starts to see one's longings as 'works of the devil' and this sense of the demonic is itself intensified by the silence.

In one form or another a great many individuals report this intensification effect. Richard Byrd, a highly practical man and normally prosaic writer, describes the polar evening:

> The day is not abruptly walled off; the night does not suddenly drop. Rather the effect is a gradual accumulation, like that of an infinitely prolonged tide . . . the on-looker is not conscious of haste. On the contrary he is sensible of something of incalculable importance being accomplished with timeless patience . . . These are the best times; the times when the neglected senses expand to an exquisite sensitivity. You stand on the barrier and simply look and listen and feel . . . the afternoon may be so clear that you dare not make a sound, lest it fall in pieces.[12]

Christiane Ritter, one of the few women to write about extreme terrain, describes the midwinter, twenty-four-hour night in the Arctic Circle in a similar hyperbolic passage:

> There is no longer even a glimmer of day, not even at noon. Around the whole horizon only deep starry night. Day and night, throughout its circular course the moon is in the sky . . . It is as though we were dissolving in moonlight, as though the moonlight were eating us up . . . the light seems to follow me everywhere. One's entire consciousness is penetrated by the brightness; it is as though we were being drawn into the moon itself. We cannot escape the brightness.[13]

Jacques Balmat, who was the first person to climb Mont Blanc, described an earlier long solo climb and the intensity of his hearing. (It is probably worth mentioning, since Balmat's degree of terror may sound a little strained, that he was bivouacking alone at a height which in 1786 was believed to be fatal; he had made the long climb partly in order to disprove this supposition, and made it alone because no one else wanted to risk it.)

> During the short intervals between the crash of avalanches I heard distinctly the barking of a dog at Courmayeur though it was more than a league and a half to that village from the spot where I was lying. The noise served to distract my thoughts, for it was the only earthly sound that reached me. At about mid-night the barking ceased and nothing remained but the deadly silence of the grave.[14]

Jon Krakauer, an American journalist who specialises in stories about 'the wilderness' and who is a climber himself, refers directly to this sort intensification in an account of the first major solo climb he performed, which involved a substantial period of solitary travel to reach his chosen mountain.

> Because I was alone even the mundane seemed charged with meaning. The ice looked colder and more mysterious, the sky a cleaner shade of blue. The unnamed peaks towering over the glacier were bigger and comelier and infinitely more menacing than they would if I were in the company of another person. And my emotions were similarly amplified: the highs were higher; the periods of despair were deeper and darker.[15]

The 'because' that begins this quotation reads to me as if he not only found this 'charged' state normal, but assumed that his readers would too.

A second different experience, which I became aware of in my own silence and find in other people's accounts too, is a sort of disinhibition.

One of the 'harshest' modern silences I know of was the six winter months that Augustine Courtauld spent in a small tent in the Arctic in the 1930s. For over three months of this he was snowed in and unable to leave his tent at all; and for the last six weeks he was in total darkness. His silence was moreover particularly complete – he was confined in a very small space; he had no source of music and no method of communicating even if he had wanted to. I had a telephone, Byrd had a pedal-operated Morse radio, Knox-Johnston had a gramophone.

Although his expedition was given the nominal scientific justification of weather observation, Courtauld had no particular qualifications for this and did not in fact do much of it. Less than halfway through he managed to leave his spade outside his tent and was therefore unable to dig himself out to take the meteorological measurements. He came out of the English gentleman school of adventurers and never said or wrote much about his personal experience. Indeed, his only explanation of his own motives and intentions was expressed as a wish to do something that was not 'mere'. However, Jung commented on a photograph of Courtauld, taken quite soon after the experience, that here was the face of a man 'stripped of his *persona*, his public self stolen, leaving his true self naked before the world'.[16]

This is what I mean by 'disinhibited'. Jung is saying something beyond the simple fact that if you are on your own you can do what you want. This is certainly true: I was quite shocked to find how quickly and easily I abandoned many of the daily activities I'd assumed were 'natural' or necessary, like washing, or brushing my hair, for example: in the journal after barely a fortnight I noted that,

> I managed a hot bath with care, loved the clean underwear. But I realise that all the people who have accused me of being an innate slut are right. I can delight in a hot bath and clean knickers with the simple knowledge that I probably won't bother again this week! I think – without guilt or worry – that I could easily go feral.[17]

Either abandoning customary levels of personal hygiene or creating overriding and strict rules in order to preserve it seems to happen to most people; even among those who are sharing the space of their silence. In some religious disciplines washing, shaving and even dressing are seen as 'worldly' vanities (it is said that Jerome never bathed on the grounds that those who had been baptised needed no further cleaning)* but most silent religious communities adopt rigorous rules to govern personal cleanliness, diet and behaviour, which suggests that regulation is necessary and therefore it is silence, rather than solitude, that disinhibits. Funnily enough for me this has been one of the longer-term changes that Skye made in my life: I still have to put in a great deal of conscious effort to stay vaguely in line with an acceptable level of cleanliness and 'grooming'. There is a freedom in being silent that allows one to challenge a good number of assumptions with less self-consciousness. It was curious to discover on Skye how far I had internalised prohibitions on things like shouting, laughing, singing, farting, taking all your clothes off, picking your nose while eating and so on. These inhibitions fall away at various rates.

But I think Jung was picking up on something more profound. I felt as though the silence *itself* unskinned me, and seems to have done the same thing to Courtauld. As though, to put it crudely, the superego was overwhelmed by the silence. Perhaps this is not surprising. If the contemporary French psycholinguists are right, it is through language, through words, that we enter into the Law of the Fathers – the social controls that allow 'public' life to be endurable for individuals. It is as though language and all its benefits were a 'pay-off' for leaving the pre-lingual, warm, self-absorbed, messy and demanding state of infancy. Language is both the route to freedom and the route to 'good behaviour'. If we abandon language – move back into the silent places we were evacuated from as babies – we might reasonably expect to shed some of the social rules that both govern and empower us. All that self-control I spent so much time learning and mastering; all those infantile joys I gave up – then I stepped outside that social place, back into infancy, out into the wild,

---

* This is a bit more complicated than it looks, because of the social and communal aspects, including nudity, with which bathing was associated in Roman society. It is possible that Jerome just stopped 'going to the baths' rather than that he never washed.

'beyond the pale'.* It seems not at all shocking, really, that I found myself, for example, overwhelmed by seriously bizarre sexual fantasies and vengeful rages of kinds that I had never 'dared' admit.

This sense of disinhibition is almost universal in accounts of silence. There are a very large number of individuals reporting their own loss of concern about social norms, or other people, often critical, taking note of the social peculiarities of 'loners'. At the southern end of Skye Tom Leppard, 'The Leopard Man', an ex-soldier, has been living in a sort of ruin without any modern amenities for twenty years. He is a Catholic who prays for three hours a day and reads extensively. He was also, until recently, in *The Guinness Book of Records* as the world's most tattooed man – his body is covered in leopard spots, even his eyelids tattooed with cat's eyes, and he roams his very isolated peninsula, a two-hour walk or a boat ride away from anyone else, naked and unashamed. In 2002 he explained himself briefly. After he left the army, he said:

> I found it difficult to settle into life as a civilian. And having worked in jobs with terrible conditions and bad pay I needed to do something different. I have everything I need here. I am lonely in the city. I am never lonely here, and I am never bored. This is my Paradise.[18]

There is a timelessness in his response to the rules and restrictions of 'normal' social life – it seems to have been repeated over and over again, at least since John the Baptist went into the wilderness and dressed in camel hair and adopted an unusual diet. (He ate locust fruit – from the carob tree – rather than the insects of the same name.)

This disinhibition may be as good an explanation as any of Bernard Moitessier's superficially strange abandonment of the first Golden Globe race. Moitessier was the most experienced single-handed yachtsman of the entries and *Joshua* was potentially the

* The 'pale' in this well-known phrase was the 'fence' (actual or notional) that marked the limits of English jurisdiction – particularly in Ireland. Within the pale there was law and order; beyond, it was barbaric, lawless, unlicensed.

fastest and best-designed boat in the race. It is clear that single-handed sailing suited Moitessier in a more profound way than some of the other contestants. His mystical bent – and his yoga meditation practice – made the solitary and silent aspects of the race attractive rather than challenging to him.

Peter Nichols, in *Voyage for Madmen*, an account of the race, described Moitessier at sea:

> [His] unceasing close communion with the three constant physical elements of his world – his boat, the sea and the weather around him – filled him with joy . . . a sailing holy man . . . Not since Captain Nemo has a man felt so comfortable and self-sufficient at sea. He had entered into a kind of seagoing stasis . . . deep in the vast middle he was untroubled by anything but the daily concerns of sailing; the rhythm of the sea, the endless passing of waves, the daily surging progress of *Joshua* . . . and his own highly attenuated skills and sensations all blended into a harmonious chord that pealed loud and clear inside and gave him peace.[19]

Moitessier competed fiercely throughout the earlier stages of the race. By the time he was in the eastern Pacific he was very strongly placed to win the 'fastest time' prize and possibly even be first home. (Knox-Johnston, always more concerned with the single-handed record itself than with the speed, had set out two months before Moitessier and was in the lead, but Moitessier was closing up on him in the faster *Joshua*.) Moitessier knew these facts. Nonetheless, somewhere south of Tahiti he simply 'lost interest' in the race. He rounded the Horn and instead of turning north up the Atlantic, he just sailed on, round the Cape of Good Hope at the southern tip of Africa for the second time, back across the Indian Ocean, into the Pacific and finally landed in Tahiti. His 'explanations' of this fairly extraordinary decision do not immediately add up.

> I have set course for the Pacific again . . . I felt really sick at the thought of getting back to Europe, back to the snake pit. Sure there

were good and sensible reasons. But does it make sense to head for a place knowing you will have to leave your peace behind? St Helena yes . . . but I wouldn't have stopped. I would have pushed on in the Trade winds telling myself, 'Don't be a fool, you may as well just put in a little effort, try to pick up the *Sunday Times* prize.' I know how it goes. Trying to reach Tahiti non-stop is risky, I know. But the risk would be much greater to the north . . . I feel a great strength in me. I am free, free as never before. Joined to all nonetheless, yet alone with my destiny.[20]

To me it feels so like the disinhibition that arose in my own silence and in many other accounts. Normal social obligations and commitments to self and others give way, not to selfishness in the normally understood sense of that word, but to buried desires and needs, which have emerged through the silence and overwhelmed the superego, the patriarchal control, so that Moitessier, like Courtauld, was 'stripped of his *persona*, his public self stolen, leaving his true self naked'. (I can hear my own defensiveness here; the number of people – including some who have never met me – who feel free to tell me that my pursuit of silence is 'selfish' still amazes me.)

Third, almost every account of prolonged silence I have ever read or heard about contain mentions of 'hearing voices', whether these come in the form of divine intervention or deeply frightening tongues of madness. As someone who has experienced these voices, I was a bit concerned that prolonged silence might be rather alarming. I know that when I set off to Skye this worried some of my friends as well. Had I known about the loss of inhibition I might have been too cautious to do it at all.

In the event I need not have worried. Although so many people do hear voices in silence, I do not think that this is evidence that freely chosen silence sends people mad. In fact, I now think that precisely because I am a voice hearer it may have been easier for me to distinguish between the various sorts of voices than it might be for others – and therefore infinitely *less* alarming and much easier to think about.

However we choose to interpret 'pathological' or 'visionary' voice hearing (and I am not sure there is much difference except in the eyes of the diagnostician – psychiatrist or priest), there are two forms of voice hearing which seem to me to be slightly different from this and may well be related to silence. The first of these I would call 'stress voices', where a kind of self-splitting occurs under extreme and difficult circumstances. Most of the self is absorbed into the 'difficulty', which may involve great physical pain or vulnerability, but a part of the self continues to act 'sensibly', positively, life protectively. This part of the personality appears to withdraw from the body and instruct it from outside it as an external voice. This voice is often harsh and bullying, but effectively overwhelms the desires to give up, go to sleep, despair or do anything singularly foolish. In his book *Touching the Void* Joe Simpson, the mountaineer whose accident has been made famous by the film of that title, gives a very vivid account of such a voice-hearing episode.

This response to great stress is not uncommon and does not seem to be necessarily related to silence, except in the crude sense that in more social situations someone other than oneself would be around to provide the stimulus and direction that Simpson's *voice* produced. It seems a useful survival mechanism.

But there is a second, more complicated sort of voice hearing, which I think is closely related to silence and can be a positive aspect of the experience.

In my journal I repeatedly recorded my sense that I could hear singing. For example:

> There is a woman, a young woman but not a girl-child, singing outside. I catch myself listening. There are almost words. It sounds as though there were words, but I can't make them out. This does not feel scary or disturbing. Except in the first instance I knew completely that it was the wind, indeed it seems more eerie and beautiful than anything else.[21]

Another evening I heard a male-voice choir singing Latin plainsong in the bedroom. Almost immediately I realised that this was ridiculous; the acoustics were all wrong. The bedroom was tiny, but the sound was like the music at Quorr Abbey, a Benedictine monastery on the Isle of Wight, which concentrates particularly on the very beautiful singing of the daily prayers, or in a large cathedral, heard from a greater distance than between where I was sitting in the kitchen and the bedroom. But I could hear singing, in Latin, and I could pick up occasional words.

I have thought a lot about this phenomenon. It is possible that a great many people who spend a period of time in silence, suddenly and without any particular predisposition, have psychotic episodes, from which they immediately and permanently recover the instant they are back in society. But this does not seem entirely probable. I think there is a better explanation. In *The Language Instinct* Steven Pinker describes an experience which led him to believe, briefly, that he was going mad. He heard human voices emerging from what he knew to be a randomised synthesiser. This phenomenon is called 'sine-wave speech' and can be deliberately manipulated to represent human sentences. Simplifying wildly, some combinations of two or three 'bands' of sound waves create noises that can be heard as human or quasi-human voices. I wondered if the different wind sounds I described earlier could similarly combine and if this was a reason why I was hearing these distant, lovely choirs 'singing'. I have to say that to me, this seems a complex but rather beautiful concept.[22]

To try to make some sense of this I went back to John Cage's idea mentioned in the previous chapter that there is no such thing as 'real' silence. There is always some sound, even if it is only the sounds that the human body makes. Now the human brain is an immensely efficient *interpreter* of sound. Although our hearing is less acute than that of many animals, our capacity to make sense of what we hear, to give meaning to it, is phenomenal. We need this bizarrely sophisticated mental equipment because of language. It is difficult but important to grasp that much of the business of understanding spoken language is a task of interpretation, not of hearing in the physical sense. To take a simple example, in spoken language there are *no aural breaks between words*, no silences that those little blank white spaces on a page purport to represent. This is why it is so hard to understand conversation in a language that one is not entirely fluent in: spoken face-to-face or read it may be possible to have good comprehension, but it is extremely hard for the brain to decide where to put the gaps between the words when they are spoken fast and without full 'lip-sync'. In fact, there is *no* aural difference between 'I scream' and 'ice cream', 'some mothers' and 'some others', 'The good can decay many ways' and 'The good candy came anyways'. Where the word is new to the hearer the ingenuity of the brain is particularly evident: 'They played the Bohemian Rap City,' wrote an American high-school student of a concert, for 'Bohemian Rhapsody'. This is not, as we were too often told as children, 'sloppy mumbling'. These pairings are called 'oronyms' and they seem particularly to delight small children. They are the basis of many playground jokes and rhymes, like:

> Fuzzy Wuzzy was a bear,
> Fuzzy Wuzzy had no hair,
> Fuzzy Wuzzy wasn't Fuzzy was'e?

The brain inserts the gap where it needs to in order to make sense of the continuous stream of sound (vibrations) that the ear sends it via the cochlea nerves.

Particularly in 'adventurous' silences we see people with all their physical and emotional senses intensified, and their normal rational processes disinhibited, who are bombarded with complex sound, where they anticipate and are geared up for silence. The brain is constantly busy at its job of decoding the stream of aural input. There is no actual language to 'test' the sounds against. The brain interprets the sounds as language.

Charles Lindbergh, not someone generally thought of as particularly schizotypic, heard voices while flying the *Spirit of St Louis*. He was alone, 'silent' in one sense but surrounded by the engine noise to which he was obliged for safety's sake to listen continually. He was not under the sort of desperate stress that Simpson was, nor does his description match Simpson's in any useful way. It seems easiest to understand these voices as interpretations of sound.

> First one and then another presses forward to my shoulder to speak above the engine's voice . . . [or they] come out of the air itself, clear yet far away, travelling through distances that can't be measured by the scale of human miles . . . conversing and advising me on my flight, discussing problems of my navigation, reassuring me, giving me messages of importance unattainable in ordinary life.[23]

I spent a good deal of time hovering between two sorts of knowledge. The knowledge that my ears were giving me – that there was, for example, a choir singing in Latin in the bedroom – and the knowledge that my informed intelligence was giving me – that this was a normal effect of high, irregular winds and a long period of solitude.

One of the things that strengthens this theory for me is that these sorts of voices are particularly common among sailors. Sailing ships are exceptionally noisy places and their noises are of precisely the kind that the brain 'likes' to work on – irregular and not immediately easy to identify (unlike, say, a dog barking or a motor car). Peter Nichols describes Knox-Johnston's ship in a storm:

> The singular noise of high wind in a boat's rigging during a gale at sea has no counterpart in the land-bound world, where overhead electrical cable and telephone wires are long and run without great tension. Wind howling through these is low in tone and without multiple a-tonal chords. *Suhaili* was cobwebbed with 30 or more separate lengths of wire and rope, running up its mast, tightened or winched to considerable tension.[24]

It is hardly surprising that Knox-Johnston complained that the 'malevolent eldritch shrieking' of *Suhaili* was 'hard to endure' and it 'ate at his nerves'.

Even without gales, single-handed sailors anticipate that they will 'hear voices', especially those of their yachts. Bill Howell wrote in his log during a single-handed race in 1972: '*Usual* voices in the rigging calling "Bill, Bill" rather high pitched.'[25]

Ann Davison, who was sailing her ship home alone after the death of her husband, noted, '*Reliance* spoke in a multitude of tiny voices from behind bulkheads, under floorboards, everywhere all around, chattering, gossiping, gabbling incessantly and shrieking with gnomish laughter.'[26]

I do not think that understanding the voices that people hear in silence as effects of a specific function of the brain is a reductionist 'explanation', because of course the content, *the meaning*, of what such voices actually say is going to depend entirely on the individual and their moods of the time. What I want to do is clear away some of the negative associations of silence with insanity and make it possible to listen to these interpretations, the meanings of the heart and the 'silent mind'. It seems to me that it ought to be perfectly obvious that the sorts of interpretation the brain will come up with under the pressures of great fear, or loneliness, are rather likely to be more malevolent than an interpretation made in peace, joy or a sense of union with the universe.

A fourth sensation very commonly reported by people who have *enjoyed* the silence they chose (not everyone does) is that they have experiences of great joy, which feel as though they came from 'outside' themselves; a strong sense of 'givenness'.

Several times, especially later on in the six weeks on Skye, my journal recorded moments of intense happiness, followed by a powerful conviction that the moment was somehow a pure gift – that I had done nothing to deserve it and could do nothing to sustain it or repeat it. My only option was to enjoy it.

On one unusually radiant day, with a sort of golden brightness and lovely complex cloud formations, I took a walk up the burn above the house. It was sharply cold but there was less wind than usual. At the top of the valley is the watershed between Glenbrittle and Sligachan. I always found this a strangely haunting place; the water from the hill above collected in two tiny lochs, then flowed out at both ends, north and south. Over the years, walkers have piled up a large cairn here, a sort of mute witness to everyone who has enjoyed this silent space; and far below the river ran down towards the sea in a series of theatrical silver loops. Instead of following the path on down towards Glenbrittle, I climbed on up into the steep-sided corrie. It was sheltered there and magnificent – almost vertical mountains on both sides – a mixture of shining rock and loose scree, and below, tiny stands of water that looked like handfuls of shiny coins tossed casually down. I sat on a rock and ate cheese sandwiches – and thought I was *perfectly* happy. It was so huge. And so wild and so empty and so free.

And there, quite suddenly and unexpectedly, I slipped a gear, or something like that. There was not me and the landscape, but a kind of oneness: a connection as though my skin had been blown off. More than that – as though the molecules and atoms I am made of had reunited themselves with the molecules and atoms that the rest of the world is made of. I felt absolutely connected to everything. It was very brief, but it was a total moment. I cannot remember feeling that extraordinary sense of connectedness since I was a small child.

This feeling of being connected to the universe, and particularly to natural phenomena within it, was central to the sensibility of the Romantic Movement, and appears over and over again in the poetry of the period, nearly always linked to places or experience of silence *in the natural world*. A well-known example is from the famous English romantic poet William Wordsworth's 'A slumber did my spirit seal':

Roll'd round in earth's diurnal course,
With rocks, and stones, and trees.[27]

This 'gift' is experienced both as integrative – the whole self is engaged and *known* to itself, to the subject, in quite a new way – *and* as connecting that self to something larger. This would, of course, be

an expected feeling from anyone who had a strong religious belief –
of almost any kind – and in particular for those for whom silence was
part of a search for precisely that gift. This is a clear example of
where it is useful to look beyond religious descriptions of silence. But
more or less the same set of feelings appears in many accounts of
silence by people who have no particular religious agenda and leads
me to suggest that this is a response to silence as much as to religious
ecstasy, although the latter provides a rich interpretation. Richard
Byrd, contemplating the onset of the polar night (not simply
'evening' in the usual sense) described in almost mystical terms this
experience of everything being connected:

> The day was dying the night was being born – but with great peace.
> Here were the imponderable processes and forces of the cosmos har-
> monious and soundless. That was what came out of the silence,
> harmony, a gentle rhythm, the strain of a perfect chord, the music of
> the spheres perhaps. It was enough to catch that rhythm momen-
> tarily to be myself a part of it. In that instant I could feel no doubt
> of man's oneness with the universe . . . the universe was cosmos not
> chaos; and man was as rightfully a part of that cosmos as were the
> night and day.[28]

Moitessier speaks at length, especially in his film *Song of the Siren*,
about this unitive experience that he often had at sea:

> There was no longer man and boat, but a man-boat, a boat-man . . .
> What you would call isolation, but I call communion. The things
> that mattered at the start didn't matter any more . . . I want to go
> further because there is something more to see.[29]

More specifically, while sailing along the southern coast of
Australia, Moitessier records an extraordinary contact with a large
shoal of over a hundred porpoises. They were not behaving as
porpoises normally do, but were 'nervous' and agitated. In what
seemed to him an almost military way a group of them kept

rushing off, always to the right, always returning and repeating the same manoeuvre. He watched them, entranced and baffled, until he happened to glance at his compass and saw that *Joshua* had changed course on a changing wind and was heading directly towards Stewart Island, a rocky outcrop on which his yacht might well have foundered. As soon as he changed back to his correct course, the porpoises seemed to 'celebrate' and then disappear. He wrote:

This is the first time I feel such peace, a peace that has become a certainty, something that cannot be explained, like faith. I know I will succeed and it strikes me as perfectly normal: that is the marvellous thing, that absolute certainty where there is neither pride nor fear nor surprise. The entire sea is simply singing in a way I had never known before, and it fills me with what is both question and answer . . . I will round the Horn thanks to porpoises and fairy tales, which helped me rediscover the Time of the Very Beginnings, where each thing is simple . . . Free on the right, free on the left, free everywhere.[30]

Christiane Ritter writes of her polar experiences:

I lie down in my little room where the moonlight filters green through the small snowed-up window. Neither the walls of the hut nor the roof can dispel my fancy that I am myself moonlight, gliding along the spires and ridges of the mountains, through the white valleys.[31]

Although a distinctly more prosaic writer, Geoffrey Williams, another single-handed yachtsman, reports an experience extremely similar to these:

I was no longer *Lipton*'s helmsman. I became part of her. I was a limb of *Lipton*, another sail, another tiller; the ship and I were one. But *Lipton* was part of the scene, so I became part of the scene, no longer outside looking in, but inside looking out. I was part of the chorus, neither conductor nor spectator, but singing as part of the environment.[32]

This sense of vast connectedness, of oneness with everything is so central to the core of mystical prayer that it can be distinctly disconcerting to read the matter-of-fact ease with which so many of these adventurers report a parallel experience. Often they sound mildly surprised or even offhand – although it is more usual for them to sense that this is a deeply precious and important moment, born out of an odd mixture of courage and silence.

If you are experiencing a profound level of oneness with the cosmos, you are very likely to experience boundary confusion as well. This was a fifth sensation that I became aware of. If an individual is one with and a part of *everything*, then it is not going to be clear where the self begins and ends.

In *La Nouvelle Héloïse*, Jean-Jacques Rousseau, the influential French philosopher and autobiographer, describes what I mean here very effectively:

There is something magical and supernatural in hill landscape, which entrances the mind and the senses. One forgets everything, one forgets one's own being, *one ceases to know where one stands*.[33]

In a sense this is nothing more than an extension of the connectedness or sense of givenness in silence that I have just looked at, except that is usually less ecstatic and more conscious. As the six weeks went by my sense of difference from everything around me began to dissolve and with it accurate perceptions of all those external factors that shore up our sense of boundaries.

For me the clear, if artificial, demarcations of passing time were among the first to break down under the 'pressure' of silence. As I went further and further into my silent time, I found it harder and harder to maintain a sense of time passing. I ceased to have a 'normal' sense of how long I had been doing something or why I might continue or stop. This did not feel like absent-mindedness and was probably exaggerated because of the amount of the day that was dark, but it did make me realise just how clock-obsessed we have all become, marking our days ritually and shaken by anxiety, like Alice's White Rabbit, if we 'lose' time. It is salutary to recall just how modern a concept this is: until the railway network spread out across Britain, with its need for timetables, there was no 'accurate national time' – the hours were fixed by the daylight and Oxford time, for example, was five minutes behind London time. Once I recognised what was happening, I found it very liberating; it gave me a sense of freedom coupled with a sort of almost childlike naughtiness or irresponsibility. Initially I had removed the clock from the room I spent my days in because its rather loud ticking seemed to break into the silence. For the first couple of weeks I was constantly popping next door to find out what time it was, but gradually it ceased to matter.

Of all the sensations I have been discussing, this loss of time is one from which sailors seem to be more exempt than others – I suspect that this is because navigation, particularly before GPS (the global satellite positioning system that can locate a small boat with pinpoint accuracy, from the boat and from a distance), requires a constant awareness of time and place. Donald Crowhurst, in his final days, more or less abandoned navigation and immediately, judging from his notebooks, became obsessed by the feeling that time was getting away from him. In Rousseau's words, he rather literally ceased to know where he stood.

This sort of confusion is clearly something that a lot of people in silence and solitude find difficult to cope with. Over and over again I found accounts of people going to remarkable efforts to keep time in its place – ordering their days with extreme rigour, appointing precise moments for various activities and finding ways to replace clocks and diaries – marking each day as it passes with a notch on a stick or a stone on a cairn, inventing or at least contriving 'tasks'. However, I particularly enjoyed this sensation. I think there were two reasons why I found it not just interesting but also immensely pleasurable. In the first place I was extremely safe. I knew exactly how long I was going to be there for and had every reason to expect someone to come and let me know if I had completely lost the plot and failed to emerge after the six weeks were over. I had a telephone too if I had needed to use it – and indeed I had a clock, and my car also had a clock. The other reason is more complex: if you believe in a God who is eternal, that is to say outside time, there is a sense of being nearer to, being more permeated by, God as time recedes in both importance and sensation. Almost all the examples of people who have enjoyed this experience of time collapsing have been religious. For us a loss of time is a positive and recognised 'sign' of mystical experience, often described as 'trance'.

Another form that boundary confusions took for me was a very strange inability to distinguish between my own words and other people's. I have a retentive memory, especially for poetry, but in my ordinary life I expect to be able to tell whether something is newly mine or dug up from my memory bank; this is a crucial skill for someone whose own fiction involves so much rewriting of older material as mine does, and confusion here would create serious problems of plagiarism and a radical loss of confidence. Nonetheless, as I moved further into this silent time, my journal increasingly contains phrases, expressions and even quite extended passages that are accurate quotations but with no sign on the page that I was aware of this – not just no quotation marks or other punctuation but with three or four lines of poetry written into my own sentences in continuous (not line-broken) prose. It feels retrospectively as though the boundary between 'creative' writing and memory had weakened.

Later, I had a series of very strange experiences when I stopped being able to distinguish easily between what was happening in my mind and what was happening 'outside'. During the fourth week my journal records a number of such episodes, of which this is one of the clearest:

I heard a car come up the track and a white van crossed the window. Then nothing happened. I was furious at the interruption. But nothing happening was strange – no knock on the door, no sound outside. Then there was a series of piercing whistles. I was hiding from any intrusion in the bed-room and looking out the window I saw a sheep dog – except that it was not really a sheep dog, more some sort of small terrier, but a sheep dog in action – on the far bank of the burn. I pulled on my jacket and went out – the wind was howling and the rain lashing down. I stood at the door. The sheep dog had four sheep huddled on the far side of the burn – and on my side was a shepherd. Not at all a romantic shepherd – neither biblical nor 'gnarled highlander', but a scruffy bloke in a blue woolly hat. When he saw me he called the dog, who let the sheep go and came splashing back across the burn, struggling to make headway. The shepherd smiled at me and said, 'I was looking for a stray.' Then I went back into the house and he – and the dog I imagine – got back into the white van (which had a large dent in the driver-side door) and drove away. I never said anything.

The scary bit is that within a couple of minutes *and still* I am not at all sure whether this actually did happen, or whether I hallucinated or imagined it. His actions were so senseless. Later in the day, I was increasingly perplexed and disturbed by this, so I attempted a little 'reality check': my jacket was bone dry (but then I had not left the shelter of the doorway, and I didn't think of feeling the jacket for several hours). If it was a hallucination it was both bizarrely mundane and ridiculously detailed. But although I remember the dent in the van and the blue woolly hat I cannot remember any other details – local accent/other clothes/attitude or even where he was standing. And if he was 'real' then what the hell was he doing? Why would anyone chase a stray in this weather – or having decided to do so, abandon the project so quickly. I honestly am not sure.

Perhaps more interesting, though, is how little it actually alarmed me. Reading the journal as a whole, I realise with what insouciance, even pleasure, I seem to have regarded episodes like this, which in my pre-silence life would have terrified me as signs of incipient lunacy.

I remain curious, however, about how often this feeling of losing the clear sense of one's own boundaries is experienced *physically*. In almost all extreme situations there is an associated physical phenomenon, where a normal awareness of self-protection ceases to function properly: desert lassitude, the rapture of the deep, mountain madness. In each case there is a sound physiological explanation (dehydration, pressure, oxygen deprivation) but nonetheless they seem somehow to share emotional symptoms. My journal records, several times, things like this:

> Each day it becomes easier to be silent, drowning down into it, but harder to get on the move. As soon as I am walking I feel wonderful – energetic, alive, sane, physically good, 'fresh' – but there is a weighting against it which for the last couple of days I've put down to the weather, but it can't have been that today, as it was, weatherwise, about the best day I've had. I sit and time passes and it does not matter. I feel slightly drunk, elated but uncoordinated; or just dreamy, entranced, and completely uncaring. The Rapture of the Deep. That's the way I feel today.

Jacques Cousteau made the first ever aqualung dive and also invented the term 'rapture of the deep' (*l'ivresse des grandes profondeurs*) to describe Depth Narcosis – the more scientific name for a not dissimilar experience, which attacks deep-water divers.

> The first stage is a mild anaesthesia, after which the diver becomes a god. If a passing fish seems to require air, the crazed diver may tear out his air pipe or mouth grip as a sublime gift . . . I am personally quite receptive to the rapture. I like it and fear it like doom. It destroys the instinct of life.[34]

This 'rapture' is caused by a perfectly explicable biological process, but the emotional content of the experience is so close to what I was feeling that it is hard not to suspect that the silence itself is involved here.

In his book *The World of Silence*, Max Picard, the German existentialist who was to have such an influence on Thomas Merton, quotes a certain Goutran de Procius:

> Here in the land of the Eskimos there is no wind in the trees, for there are no leaves. No birds sing. There is no noise of flowing water. No frightened animals flee away in the dark. There is no stone to become loose under human feet and fall down a riverbank, for all these stones are walled in by the frost and buried under the snow. And yet this world is far from dead: it is only that the beings, which dwell in this solitude, are noiseless and invisible.
>
> This stillness, which has been so solitary, which has calmed me and done good to my worn-out nerves, gradually began to weigh on me like a lead weight. The flame of life within us withdrew further and further into a secret hiding place, and our heartbeats became ever slower. The day would come when we should have to shake ourselves to keep our heartbeats going. We had sunk deep into this silence; we were paralysed by it; we were on the bottom of a well from which we could pull ourselves out only with inconceivable difficulty.[35]

At high altitude climbers lose judgement, cease to take proper care of themselves, act 'as though drunk' or fail to follow even the most rudimentary and ingrained safety codes. In intense cold the mind becomes disorientated; the desire to 'snuggle down and sleep', and to become pleasurably fixated on delusional ideas, is very common – in addition to the more obviously physiological effects of oxygen deprivation.[36]

I am suggesting that alongside these physical responses runs some sort of mental or psychological response to silence. There are so many reports of experiences of confusion about time and/or spatial location – heavy/light and up/down distinctions are commonly lost; falling and flying, for instance, can become synonymous – but even more common and profound is way the self/other (or the I/thou) boundary becomes unclear. It is usually the reassertion of the ego that brings this state to an end and with its closure there is an enormous sense of loss, almost a kind of mourning. This is, of course, a central and classic aspect of mystical experience and can be pursued through the writings of that tradition in both East and West. One of the clearer articulators of what it feels like is the sixteenth-century mystic Teresa of Avila who, over a lifetime of writing about mystical prayer drawing directly on her own personal experience, described a whole series of such confusions including levitation, trancelike loss of chronological time, flying (in the claws of an eagle) and related changes in body weight, limbs dissolving, her body fragmenting, shrinking, enlarging or distorting, and most famously (because of the Bernini statue of the event, *Teresa in Ecstasy*) being pierced by an angel's lance.

We live in a culture that closely associates silence with madness, so the exhilarating sense of peril that is associated with silence may be nothing more than a culturally induced fear of insanity – it is nonetheless a very persistent emotional response and one that I identified as a sixth positive effect of silence. It is not the same as fear or terror. Many people, including me, find it a very positive and exciting experience. Several times my journal describes with delight the knowledge that what I was up to was risky, that I was deliberately exposing myself to peril. The risk felt twofold – one is the danger that disinhibition might allow me to do something *very* stupid; the other is of so losing or confusing one's boundaries that one evaporates into true madness. But despite that reality it remains, for me as for others, a powerfully positive aspect of silence.

Most of us learned in childhood that risk, under particular circumstances, can be very strangely and affirmatively *exciting*. In the late seventeenth century this frisson of thrilling fear became newly fashionable and was seen as part of the aesthetic of the Sublime: 'a delightful Horrour, a terrible Joy'.[37] This in itself can be addictive, and is probably one of the reasons why silence has traditionally been hedged around with disciplines and structures.

In his excellent book about the emotional and imaginative history of mountain climbing, *Mountains of the Mind*,[38] Robert Macfarlane devotes a chapter to what he calls 'the pursuit of fear'. He has little time for sublime peril; his central tenet is that mountains kill people and if we were not still engaged with concepts of heroism and delusions of grandeur we would avoid such sentimentality. Indeed, he is extremely funny at the expense of many of the heroes of romanticism and their wilful production of this emotion. But, because he is focused so specifically on the history of mountain climbing, I think that Macfarlane misses something here. This 'delightful Horrour, a terrible Joy' is far more ancient than he suggests. It was, in fact, the normative reaction to an encounter with the divine. Moses was out in the wilderness (the desert) shepherding his father-in-law's herd when he saw a bush 'burning, but it was not consumed'. Moses, quite naturally, was intrigued by this and 'turns aside' to see what is going on. But when the bush revealed that it is 'the God of Abraham, the God of Isaac and God of Jacob', Moses immediately hid his face, because he was '*afraid* to look on God'.[39] When the angel 'came in' to Mary in the New Testament, she was 'sore afraid'. The physical risks of high mountains and cliff faces are perhaps as much a substitute for the thrill of 'holy fear' as they are a reflex of romanticism. Any extreme situation, particularly one encountered in silence, is capable of putting one's sense of identity, one's self-possession, at risk.

It is the frequency of this thrilling peril itself that suggests to me that silence is the place, the focus, of the radical encounter with the divine, what the theologian Martin Buber described as an (or even the) I/Thou encounter. If this is so, the sense of peril is well founded; there is good reason for it. There is always a risk that our identities may be overwhelmed by something greater, but that need not necessarily mean that there is not equally good reason for the 'terrible Joy'. The desire to break the silence with constant human noise is, I believe, precisely an avoidance of the sacred terror of that divine encounter. On Skye I came to think that silence may be the only 'place' in which the boundaries of the autonomous self can dissolve, can be penetrated without breaking, safely (well, safely-ish). Whether this is a good thing or not is an entirely different and separate question.

Earlier in this chapter I spoke about ineffability and the way that silence itself seems to have a quality of being indescribable, literally unsayable. There is obviously not much I can say about this! The difficulty seems to have caught almost every silence seeker by the neck. 'I can't explain or describe it' is probably the most usual comment – whether the speaker goes on to try to do so or thus evades the effort. Ineffability is the seventh sensation that I noted in my own silence and found again in other people's.

The experience of those intense moments of silence – when the external and the interior silence come together and the subject becomes conscious of that, without thereby breaking it up – is not just difficult to talk about; it is actually very hard to recall, remember, to reconstruct emotionally. It can even be somehow contentless or meaningless – outwith language.

This sense of being 'silenced', rendered mysteriously dumb, both internally and externally, by an intense experience of silence is explicable within many religious traditions, because God is – of God's nature – unknowable and unspeakable. While all things come into being through God's speaking, God is in no way contained or restricted by that speaking. It is harder to understand what might be happening when the silence is not grounded in any willed encounter with whatever there might be 'beyond' language.

And finally almost everyone who describes a positive experience of prolonged silence speaks about a state of bliss – a fierce joy, far beyond 'happiness' or 'pleasure'.

I have come to prefer the French word *jouissance*, with its associations of both playfulness (*jouer* – to play) and joy. There are other terms, like 'glory', and 'beatitude'. In his book *Le Plaisir du Texte* Roland Barthes, the French critic and theorist, contrasts the pleasures of 'closure', of a satisfying resolution, with *jouissance*, which he defines as an infinite opening out to delight and beyond delight. He is speaking of literary texts here, but such inflation or expansion is not confined to literature. For some individuals, indeed, this *jouissance* is the purpose and the goal of silence.

Most small children experience this sensation of profound joy randomly and apparently frequently. Wordsworth mourned its passing in his 'Intimations of Immortality from Recollections of Early Childhood' (1807):

> There was a time when meadow, grove and stream,
> The earth, and every common sight
> To me did seem
> Apparelled in celestial light,
> The glory and the freshness of a dream.
> It is not now as it has been of yore; –
> Turn wheresoe'er I may,
> By night or day,
> The things which I have seen I now can see no more.
>
> The rainbow comes and goes,
> And lovely is the rose,
> The Moon doth with delight
> Look round her when the heavens are bare;
> Waters on a starry night
> Are beautiful and fair;
> The sunshine is a glorious birth;
> But yet I know, where'er I go,
> That there hath passed away a glory from the earth.

This lost glory is not, indeed, particular to silence, but given Wordsworth's frequent association of bliss with storm, wind and wildness, it is intriguing that all the images from nature he uses here are silent ones. Certainly, for me personally, *jouissance* is closely, intimately connected to silence.

Many of the days in Skye were punctuated by these joyful moments. Sometimes they were very gentle and sweet. One magically wind-free day I drove down the Strathaird peninsula beyond Elgol, a tiny coastal village. At one point the road rose along a cliff edge. I got out of the car and it was warm in the sun and at first seemed utterly and completely silent; then, when my ears had absorbed the silence, there was far below me the occasional very quiet boom noise of a wave hitting the cliff, although from above the water looked absolutely still, flat, smooth. There was no wind. All around there were sea and mountains, at every distance: the islands, then Knoydart and Torridons, the Cuillin and the tiny white houses on the Sleat coast.

Then I saw a whale, or porpoise – no, a sea-monster – turning in the water, rolling. A silkie perhaps, a seal woman, lovely and perilous. It was, in fact, a rock with the water rolling over it – but the water seemed to be still while the black shape rolled through it. I leaned against the car and rejoiced. It was not an anguish of loveliness but a complete, huge, calm, silent joy of loveliness. I did not even want to hold or keep it. I did think once, 'If I could look at this view day after day, surely I would grow to be good.' But I immediately knew that was not true and laughed at myself.

I was entirely happy inside the stillness, the beauty. The many islands floated, danced on the sea, and the surface of the water was silky smooth and the snowcaps on the furthest mountains seemed to pour a particular bright light into the air. The soft sound of the sea was a sound of silence.

But on other occasions it was a far wilder joy. The last few days of my stay were quite difficult. Part of me had already moved on from Allt Dearg, and another part of me wanted never to leave. The weather became appalling so that I could not go out for a final walk or round off the time with any satisfying sense of closure. I had to clean the house and then drive a very long way. I had felt quite depressed and lethargic for about forty-eight hours and then, the very final evening, I suddenly was seized with an overwhelming moment of *jouissance*. I wrote:

They say it is not all over till the fat lady sings. Well, she is singing now. She is singing in a wild fierce wind – and I am in here, just. Now I am full of joy and thankfulness and a sort of solemn *and* bubbling hilarity. And gratitude. Exultant – that is what I feel – and excited, and that *now*, here, right at the very edge of the end I have been given back my joy.

For several hours I enjoyed an extraordinary rhythmical sequence of emotions – great waves of delight, gratitude and peace; a realisation of how much I had done in the last six weeks, how far I had travelled; a powerful surge of hope and possibility for myself and my future; and above all a sense of privilege. But also a nakedness or openness that needed to be honoured somehow.

I experienced a fierce *joyful* . . . joyful what? . . . neither pride nor triumph felt like the right word. Near the end of Ursula le Guin's *The Farthest Shore* (the third part of the *Earthsea Trilogy*) Arren, the young prince-hero, who has with an intrepid courage born of love rescued the magician Sparrowhawk, and by implication the whole of society, from destruction, wakes alone on the western shore of the island of Selidor. 'He smiled then, a smile both sombre and joyous, knowing for the first time in his life, and alone, and unpraised and at the end of the world, victory.' That was what I felt like, alone on An t-Eilean Sgitheanach, The Winged Isle. I felt an enormous victorious YES to the world and to myself. For a short while I was absorbed in joy. I was dancing my joy, dancing, and flowing with energy. At one point I grabbed my jacket, plunged out into the wind and the storm. It was physically impossible to stay out for more than about a minute because the wind and rain were so strong and I came back in soaked from even that brief moment; but I came in energised and laughing and exulting as well. I was both excited *and* contented. This is a rare and precious pairing. I knew, and wrote in my journal, that this would not last, but it did not matter. It was NOW. At the moment that now, and the enormous wind, felt like enough. Felt like more than enough.

And once again I am not alone. Repeatedly, in every historical period, from every imaginable terrain, in innumerable different languages and forms, people who go freely into silence come out with slightly garbled messages of intense *jouissance*, of some kind of encounter with nature, their self, their God, or some indescribable source of power.

Now look at the eight particular experiences I have described here: an intensification of both physiological and psychological sensation; disinhibition; a sense of 'givenness' or connection; auditory hallucinations – voice hearing of a rather particular kind; boundary confusions; an exhilarating consciousness of being at risk, in peril; ineffability and bliss.

I would not want to suggest that this was a definitive list. But even as it stands, it does seem to me that to describe these experiences in terms of 'lack' or 'absence' is simply stupid.

Frank Mulville, yet another single-handed sailor, in an article entitled 'The Loneliness of the Long Distance Sailor', wrote about an experience that seems to hold together all the elements of silence that I have been so busy separating out. Mulville got 'blissed out' (his term) sailing single-handed in the Caribbean, in love with his ship and with the long silences. He wanted to see her and himself from the outside, and so one calm day, although the boat was under sail, he attached himself to a long rope, let himself down into the water and floated away.

> It made me feel quite dizzy to look at her. She seemed the most lovely thing dipping in and out of sight as she mounted the long Atlantic swell and then slipped into the hollows. This, it struck me was the supreme moment of my life; I had never achieved anything to equal it and I was never likely to again. This was the ultimate experience . . . it was my dream and I had it. Why not let go of the rope? To melt into the sea at this apex of experience, was the only thing left. Nothing that could happen in the future could better this. Why not trump the ace and walk out?
>
> I stayed at the end of the rope for a while and then I began to get

frightened – not so much at what might happen to me but at what I might do to myself . . . I glanced deeply into the womb of the sea watched the shafts of sunlight as they spent their energy uselessly in its density . . . I slipped the bowline off my shoulders and hung for an instant on the very end of the rope – my fingers grasping the bare end of life itself – then I hauled myself back hand over hand. When I stood on the firm familiar deck I swore I would never do this thing again. I was running with sweat and shaking all over.[40]

This does not feel like loss or absence to me. Driving south from Skye I knew that it was not possible for me to sustain that sort of silence for very much longer than the six weeks I had; but I also knew that it was one of the most significant things I have ever done. It was interesting, demanding, exciting, good fun and deeply joyful. It has informed my choices and my life ever since. I have been engaged trying to build those experiences into a daily and sustainable lifestyle. Skye is both a benchmark and a launch pad for much of my present life.

3

The Dark Side

There appears to be something missing in this account of my sojourn in Skye. It is all very positive and glorious, yet we live in a society that *knows* that silence is dangerous. When I talked about my plans both before I went and since returning, the most common responses have been foreboding concern – 'Are you sure you will be all right? Don't you think that is rather foolhardy? Sara, do be careful.' As a society we will do anything we can to avoid silence at every level. Silence is terrifying, unnatural and drives people mad. Silence is supposed to be very dark, very heavy.

To be honest, after I returned to Weardale I felt I had missed something – that I had not encountered fully the promised 'dark side' of silence. I had indeed had some depressed, angry and destabilised moments and even days, but in a sense they were not different in quality or intensity from the same sorts of days and moments that I experience anyway. In fact, they were probably fewer and milder than normal, because I did not have to deal with other people and their frustrating or inconvenient demands. These sensations, unlike the positive ones, did not feel specific to silence.

I only had one seriously frightening experience that I would interpret as directly related to silence while I was in Skye. One morning I decided that I would take a walk from Luib to Loch Slapin – from sea to sea along a well-marked track between the mountains. From one of the tourist pamphlets in the house I had learned that quite recently some Bronze Age remains had been discovered here, evidence of the oldest inhabitation of the island, and that piqued my curiosity. It was a strange day, very still with no wind. I left the car and walked up the path, and after a couple of hundred yards it turned round a knoll and I walked into *nowhere*. It was a tight, steep-sided glen that I could not see out of. Nowhere. No one. Nothing. 'Desolate' suggests something sad – but at that point I had nothing to be sad about and I wasn't, although the path was really wet and boggy and hard work. It was terribly still and beautiful – but somehow eerie. Soon I came to a little loch with reeds standing in the perfectly clear water, which reflected the hills rising sharply either side – and at first I was enchanted. I could hear, though never see, some small singing birds and I sat beside the water and listened to the silence – and then abruptly, suddenly I was 'spooked'.

It is so hard to describe – the silence, the fact that there was low cloud, or mist, solid on my side of the glen so I could not see how high above me the steep hill actually went. And on the opposite side there were wisps of cloud – at one point apparently emerging from a deep crevasse, like the smoke of dragon's breath from within its lair. I found myself becoming increasingly uneasy, nervous. Gradually I became convinced I was being watched. There were two black shapes on the hill above me. I thought, or rather I felt, that they were alive. They were two dwarf fairy cows, with huge eyes. Before the Highland Clearances brought the sheep to Skye, the crofters farmed the old 'black cattle'. Each year they swam them across the narrow water, from Kylerhea, tied nose-to-tail, to market them on the mainland: perhaps, I thought, these were ghost cattle. They stood perfectly still and watched me. I decided, firmly and rationally, that they were in fact rocks, but I never entirely convinced myself.

The silent staring of the ghost cows or the silence itself overwhelmed me. I felt that the silence was stripping me down, desiccating, denuding me. I could hear the silence itself screaming. Augustine Courtauld in his polar tent recorded strange and inexplicable screaming noises and he said, afterwards, it was the only thing that really frightened him. Commentators have speculated since that it was ice breaking, or grinding, but since that day I have wondered. If I could hear the silence screaming after only three weeks of reasonably active and physically secure and agreeable silence, perhaps it is not surprising that six months immured in a tiny tent might have a similar effect.

What it was for me, and I fully expect for other people in silent situations, was panic. I do not mean those experiences of extreme anxiety which we call 'panic attacks', but something far more primal. Suddenly I understood the full and proper sense of the word, here defined by H. G. Liddell and R. Scott in their *Greek–English Lexicon*: 'Sounds heard by night on mountains or valleys were attributed to Pan and hence he was reputed to be the cause of any sudden or groundless fear.'[1]

Pan is not just the sweet little faun or goat-footed pixie piping away in the springtime, but a powerful and primitive god, representing the whole force of the wild and the inexorable weight of its silence. His name is derived from the Greek word for 'all' or 'everything' – so that, for example, 'pandemonium' means the noise that all the demons together would make. Panic causes senseless and self-destructive responses to imaginary situations, and in groups has an infectious quality, leading to stampedes, irrational aggression and crazed behaviour.

Panic partakes of true horror, physical rather than emotional. It had no meaningful content: I was not 'frightened of' or 'scared by' . . . this was something from much lower down and further in, something really visceral. I fled, literally. I ran and stumbled out of the valley, as though there were something dark in pursuit. Back at the car I found I was soaked to the skin and covered in mud although I had no memory of falling. I felt completely and neatly split in half – a sane me who said 'this is silly' and another bit that was entirely at the mercy of the sensation. This is something I had never felt before – or not since I was a child. It was somehow deeply connected to the silence, but also to the harsh desolation of the landscape.

Nonetheless, although I did genuinely find this scary and troubling, overall I did not find that the silence in Skye reflected in any way my full expectations of sublime horror. The difficult or dark experiences never took on the quality of intensity that the 'highs' did. Where was that madness and desolation that I had been culturally led to expect? Before I went to Skye I know it had worried my friends; some mornings I even woke up glancing over my mental shoulder to see if it was preparing to pounce. No one who goes silence hunting can expect it to be simple or straightforward: it is necessarily complicated and by all accounts can lead to insanity. Even the most positive of the silence seekers whose stories I read were conscious of the threat. The exultant Moitessier wrote, 'Wrapped in total silence, sucked down by a huge inner emptiness I sank into the abyss . . . I felt madness burrowing into my guts like some hideous beast.'[2] And the calmer Byrd recorded: 'Cold and darkness deplete a body gradually; the mind turns sluggish; the nervous system slows up . . . Try as I may I cannot take my loneliness casually. It is too big. But I must not dwell on it. Otherwise I am undone.'[3]

Perhaps I have just been lucky, although, actually, I do not believe it is just 'luck' – I am, I think, reasonably careful about my own self-protection. And there is also an advantage in setting out on this sort of journey when one is older, weighted towards the social and with strong commitments beyond, or outside of, the silence. Most of the things that go horrendously wrong happen to younger adventurers. Naturally one part of me was delighted and reassured – obviously silence suited me and I could enjoy it. At another level, though, I felt somehow slightly 'cheated'. I wanted to experience the whole of silence. I wanted to understand Donald Crowhurst as well as Bernard Moitessier – the dark disintegration, the howling emptiness, the demons of the desert hermits.

Then, that winter I got snowed in.

This was not the usual sort of getting snowed in. Early in 2001 there was a major outbreak of Foot and Mouth Disease. It was horrible. The horror was exacerbated by a feeling that the government was being totally incompetent – the rules and regulations made no sense; the contiguous cull was probably illegal and widely held to be useless; and the disposal of the slaughtered livestock was both unsanitary and insensitive. In many rural areas people felt frightened and powerless, and in isolated places like the Durham moors, social life was completely disrupted. The markets were closed, people did not want to visit other farms or have people on theirs. More immediate to my personal comfort, the moors, like the rest of the countryside, were closed to walkers, so that I could not take my usual exercise and had a sense of being 'cabin'd, cribbed, confined'.

In late March there was a period of severe snow and blizzards. The rural roads of County Durham are normally snowploughed by subcontracted local farmers using their own tractors – but they were confined to their farms by the outbreak, so the road to and from my house was unploughed and soon became unpassable as the snow drifted across it. Without any choice, and without much preparation, I was alone and locked into an involuntary period of silence. Since the telephone lines were down, I had no source of information as to what was going on in the 'real world'. I knew, for example, that my brother's farm was under Special Measures – a legally binding series of restrictions on movement in and out of the farm – and that he was anticipating the slaughter of his stock, but I did not know if this had or had not happened (his sheep were eventually culled but his dairy herd was not, which was in itself rather frustrating and confusing), or how the epidemic was progressing throughout the country, including my own moor, so it was not a comfortable time or place to be confined. Part of me regressed – I built a splendid snowlady in the garden, daily expanding the magnificence of her bosom and the glamour of her costumes, but another part of me became increasingly scared. Some of the anxiety was 'realistic' – would I eventually run out of food (or in my case more seriously, of cigarettes)? What would happen if the weather did not improve? Was my family all right? But more of it was emotional – despite the fact that I was supposedly longing for quiet. I increasingly felt invaded. The silence was hollowing me out and leaving me empty and naked.

The cold intensified that sense of being exposed, and sometimes when the weather was particularly wild just getting the coal in from the coal shed was exhausting and even frightening. When the weather was calmer, however, I realised that snow produces a peculiar acoustic effect: it mutes nearby noises (presumably because the softer ground surface absorbs them) but causes distant sounds to carry further and with a startling clarity. In addition the snow itself flattens everything visually. These effects disorientated me and made me increasingly nervy and jumpy. One day walking to my gate, the collar of my jacket blew up against the back of my head and I screamed aloud, viscerally convinced I had been attacked from behind.

One afternoon I needed to break out and I took a walk up the undriveable road, despite the fact that there were flurries of 'snail' (a mixture of snow and hail) which, driven by a harsh wind, cut into my face. Then, about half a mile from the house, I started to hear the most agonised wailing noises – the wailing, it seemed to me then, of the damned. I was completely terrified. I would be on this hill in this wind forever howling and desolate. I would never see another human being again. I would freeze in hell. It turned out that this strange and deeply disturbing noise was in fact no mani-festation of my inner torment, but caused by a strange and fascinating phenomenon. The unfenced roads in that part of the north-east have snow poles – tall posts, marked in black and white foot-wide stripes that show you both where the road is and how deep the snow is. Older snow poles are made of iron and, to make it harder for them to be blown over, they have holes drilled in them for the wind to pass through. Essentially they were Aeolian harps or organ pipes and they were responding to the wind with these extraordinary sounds. But I know I was lucky that I identified the source of the noise fairly quickly, because otherwise it would have driven me insane. I can only too easily understand how this sort of silence can drive one beyond panic and into true madness.

After the Foot and Mouth epidemic was over I had a letter from the Cumbrian poet Robert Drake in which he noted:

> Time and time again those on culled farms referred to the nature of the silence after the slaughter, either straight away or particularly the next morning. This was something they had never experienced before. The interesting thing is that there must have been sounds – birdsong, distant traffic, wind, trees, etc., but these were ignored, and the silence attained a density and solidity of its own. In a recent poem of mine the final stanza goes:
>
> > At dusk he came back through a silence
> > So hard it ached inside his ear,
> > Abandoned boots and coat in the porch,
> > And found her on all fours, bellowing
> > Over a floor that just would not dry.

Now I can only recall with great effort the extraordinarily powerful feelings of abandonment, desolation, fury and madness that swept over me at times. It did not last very long. My negative experiences have been little ones, but they have been enough to give me some small understanding of how overwhelming and destructive silence can be, and how closely the terrors seem to follow the same paths and patterns as the joys. It has seemed to me important, as I have hunted my own joyful silence, to remember the silencing that other people have endured, suffered and, in some cases, survived.

At first I was baffled about what was going on. Why had six whole weeks far from home and in almost equally unfavourable weather filled me with delight, even ecstasy, and been rich in joyful, expansive thoughts and emotions, while barely ten days in my own home with my own things around me reduced me to semi-hysteria?

Then something superficially minor happened that gave some insight into all this: a friend gave me, as a present, a double session in a 'flotation tank'. This gift was not really meant as a bit of pampering, but as an experiment in a specific sort of silence. A flotation tank is a piece of therapeutic equipment offered by various health spas: it consists of a pod, a large bath with a closing lid. This pod is filled with water heated to body temperature (37 degrees Centigrade – 98.6 Fahrenheit) and highly salinated, so that you float effortlessly with your face above the water level, like the Dead Sea. The pod is completely dark and sound-free (although the one I used did offer customers the option of 'calming music') and you feel neither temperature nor gravity. I was generously given a double session, because my friend felt that I was more used to silence than most people and a single hour would not be enough for me to get the full benefits.

Actually, I did not care too much for the experience. This was partly because the very idea of a health spa, with its odd mixture of 'healthy' and 'luxurious', brought out in me my most dour residue of Presbyterian puritanism. (I have such mistrust of beauty treatments that I have not been to a hairdresser for a quarter of a century.) I was also a bit dubious about provoking so easily the immensely strong emotions I had experienced in silence – it seemed a short cut to a state of being that somehow ought to be the result of a long, delicate and disciplined process, rather like using hallucinogenics to 'find one's soul'. The ambience of the health spa, offering bikini-line waxing, false nails and 'natural' therapies and 'enhanced spirituality and creativity' in a single package, brought all this home to me, a little too strongly for comfort. I was also very tired when I went to the spa; every time I became immersed in the silence I would doze off, then roll or tip over in the supporting water and get my mouth full of vile-tasting liquid. So I may not have been in the right mood for this particular form of silence.

According to advertisers (and, in fairness, users), floating

promotes total calm, peaceful relaxation, eliminates fatigue and jet lag; improves sleep; alleviates stress – mental and physical; energises, rejuvenates and revitalises. Stimulates left/right brain synchronisation; shifts brain waves from Beta to lower frequency Alpha, Theta and even Delta; creates mental clarity, alertness; increases creativity, problem solving; heightens visualisation; deepens meditation; expands awareness, intensifies acuteness of all the senses, accelerates learning. Enhances hypnotherapy and self-hypnosis; increases motivation, diminishes depression, anxiety and fear; facilitates freedom from habits, phobias and addictions. Improves athletic performance. Quickens rehabilitation and recovery; relieves pain – arthritis, migraines, injuries etc.; boosts immune function. Improves circulation and distribution of oxygen and nutrients; reduces blood pressure, pulse, heart rate and oxygen consumption.[4]

(I am only surprised that it does not promise multiple orgasms, world peace and enhanced biodiversity into the bargain.)

As I lay there, trying to stay face up, a hideous thought struck me. 'Flotation' is quite simply 'sensory deprivation'. Indeed, I later learned that when flotation tanks were first introduced as therapy they were even called 'Sensory Deprivation Tanks', until some wily operator realised that this was not likely to go down well with consumers. The connotations are not comfortable. Wikipedia defines 'sensory deprivation' as:

> The deliberate reduction or removal of stimuli from one or more of the senses. Simple devices such as hoods and earmuffs can cut off sight and hearing respectively, while more complex devices can also cut off the sense of smell, touch, taste, thermoception (heat-sense), and 'gravity'.[5]

Sensory deprivation is a technique used for interrogation. Although in 1998 the European Court ruled that it 'did not occasion suffering of the particular intensity and cruelty implied by the word torture' nonetheless it 'amounted to a practice of inhuman and degrading treatment'.

Many experts would go further than the Court:

> Sensory deprivation, as CIA research and other agency interrogation materials demonstrate, is a remarkably simple concept. *It can be*

inflicted by immobilizing individuals in small, soundproof rooms and fitting them
with blacked-out goggles and earmuffs. The first thing that happens is
extraordinary hallucinations akin to mescaline . . . I mean extreme
hallucinations of sight and sound. It is followed, in some cases
within just two days, by a breakdown akin to psychosis. A practice
that may sound innocuous to some [has been] sharpened by the
agency over the years into a horrifying torture technique. . . it is an
obvious choice for interrogators newly constrained by law [my ital-
ics].[6]

Exactly the same technique can produce 'total calm, peaceful
relaxation, mental clarity, creativity, expanded awareness, and pain
relief' *and* 'breakdown akin to psychosis'. Or to put it another way,
the same silence, the same breaking down of his own boundaries in
the enormous solitude of the ocean, that moved Moitessier to
ecstasy, drove Donald Crowhurst to psychosis and suicide. The only
variable in the experience is the individual experiencing it.

We do, sadly, know too much about milder types of sensory deprivation, because solitary confinement as a form of punishment (or
more politely of 'prison management') has been practised far too
extensively, especially within the US and the Soviet Union. It is now
known that keeping people in isolation produces such consistent
responses that Dr Stuart Grassian, a psychiatrist with extensive
experience in evaluating the psychiatric effects of stringent conditions of confinement, defines them as a diagnosable 'syndrome' –
akin to but with noteworthy differences from other psychotic or
stress disorders; it has, he argues, the characteristics of an acute
organic brain syndrome or a delirium. He notes the following
cluster of symptoms: hyperresponsivity; difficulties with thinking,
concentration and memory; intrusive obsessional thoughts; overt
paranoia; panic attacks; problems with impulse control; and perceptual distortions, illusions and hallucinations (his definitions).

Grassian gives examples and details of all these mental states,
often with quotations from the sufferers and concludes that:

Some of [these symptoms] are found in virtually no other psychiatric illness: for example, loss of perceptual constancy (objects
becoming larger and smaller, seeming to 'melt' or change form,
sounds becoming louder and softer, etc.) is very rare with primary
psychiatric illness.* In addition, functional psychiatric illness very
rarely presents with such severe and florid perceptual distortions,
illusions, and hallucinations simultaneously affecting multiple perceptual modalities – auditory, visual, olfactory, tactile, kinaesthetic.
In fact, in the more common psychotic illnesses such as schizophrenia and psychotic depression, auditory hallucinations are by far
the most common type, visual hallucinations come a distant second,
and hallucinations in all other modalities are actually very uncommon; moreover, combined modality hallucinations – other than the
combination of auditory with visual – are exceedingly rare.[7]

Grassian is saying here that these prisoners are not in any normal
sense 'mad', but their reaction to silence and solitude is very closely
akin to psychotic madness. But what really intrigued me about my
own brief experience in the flotation tank and about Grassian's
work with sensory deprivation is that his whole list of symptoms is
extraordinarily close to the list of positive effects of silence that I
drew up in Skye, with the not altogether surprising absence of bliss.
Even though we each give them different names and they clearly
have different emotional meanings, as experiences they are more or
less identical.

What I call 'intensification of both physiological and psychological sensation' he calls 'hyperresponsivity to external stimuli', but
without question both of them describe (one positively and the
other negatively) a very similar condition. So I 'was suddenly overwhelmed by the wonderful, delicious delightfulness of porridge',
and one of Grassian's prisoners reports that he got 'sensitive to
noise – the plumbing system. Someone in the tier above me pushes
the button on the faucet. It's too loud. I can't stand it.'

* Interestingly, though, such phenomena are fairly common in reports of mystical experience – although there they are interpreted positively.

Similarly, what I call a sense of 'givenness' – the feeling that the sensation comes from outside one's own will or power, he calls 'intrusive obsessional thoughts' and his prisoners report a terrifying sense that their individuality is disintegrating; a feeling that they are lost in the universe. What I experience as a thrilling sense of risk or peril he diagnoses as 'overt paranoia'. An experience of 'disinhibition' can be a profound freedom or a 'problem with impulse control'. 'Auditory hallucinations' can just be there in an interesting and thought-provoking way, or they can be experienced as 'perceptual distortions' suggesting an unusual psychotic state. Ineffability can carry all the glories of the divine, but it can also make the experiences inaccessible and overwhelming. Boundary confusions in their darker guises are perhaps the most alarming; one of Grassian's subjects stated, 'You feel like you are losing something that you may not get back.' If the world beyond the limits of yourself is inflicting a series of painful experiences and confusions upon you, and then your ability to know for certain what is 'you' and what is outside yourself (physically or psychically) becomes blurred, that confusion is not going to feel like a joyful freedom but is likely to induce great guilt to be carried along with the burden of these incomprehensible sensations.

Grassian is a psychiatrist and here he is trying, probably for perfectly good reasons like reducing the amount of solitary confinement and sensory deprivation inflicted on his patients, to define a new form of mental illness. He wants to prove that it is silence itself, not some inherent madness in them before their confinement. Naturally he will pathologise these symptoms and argue that the deprivations are the cause of the illness. But I think, when I look at my own experience, and the experience of all the other silence seekers I have been writing about who have experienced similar effects with joy and delight, that it would make as much or more sense to say that these were not symptoms of madness or any other illness, but the effects of silence itself, occurring within a dangerous context.

It was not, I realised, that I had missed out on some aspect or nuance of silence; I had had the same experiences Grassian lists, but I had enjoyed them and they were *therefore* different experiences. The lines between them are almost entirely subjective. Obviously hearing a choir sing in Latin is a very different thing from hearing demons taunting you; and having an intense sensation of delicious porridge is different from having an intense experience of pain. Being disinhibited so that you do not care about singing loudly out of tune is not the same as being so disinhibited so that you cut your own skin without knowing why, as some of his subjects did. There is a parallel in the effects of some drugs – the physiological effects of alcohol have been carefully measured, but I have seen no studies on what sort of person in what sort of circumstances gets happier or more miserable or more violent when drunk. There is no doubt that the effect is caused by alcohol intoxication, but the emotional experience is quite different.

I started to brood on what factors might tip the balance towards positive or negative experiences of extreme silence. I looked at my own silence and again at those of other people who have chosen to write about it. I now believe that the strongest determining factor in whether a silence ends up feeling positive or negative is whether or not it was freely chosen. Quite apart from research like Grassian's on contemporary prisoners placed in solitary confinement, we have a surprising number of accounts of incarceration, isolation, marooning and banishment. It seems such a strange thing to do to another human being – to exile someone not just from his or her own place or family, but also from human society itself. Yet from many cultures and over a long stretch of time there have been tales, legends and myths about exile, exclusion and silencing.

In Greek mythology there are a number of stories of people being immured or exiled in order to prevent them from speaking. One of the most brutal and complex of these tales is the story of Procne:[8] Procne's sister, Philomel, was married to the King of Thrace, who went to fetch Procne for a visit. However, on the way back to Thrace he raped her. He was then so ashamed by his own action that, in order to prevent it becoming known, he cut out

Procne's tongue and imprisoned her in a hut in a forest. He went home and told his wife that her sister had died of a fever. Unable to speak and unable to escape, Procne embroidered a tapestry telling the whole story. After various vicissitudes this message came into Philomel's hands; she rescued her sister and the two of them enacted an extreme revenge on the King: they killed his eight-year-old son – who was also Philomel's son – and served him up to his father as a stew, which he ate with great relish before realising what he had done. Like many Greek myths, one of the issues here is about what might be an appropriate revenge. Here all three characters are equally punished, they are turned into birds, suggesting perhaps that at least in Greek culture the physical silencing of someone, even when it did not serve its intended ends, was seen as a very serious offence indeed, since it is equated with infanticide and cannibalism.

The Hebrew Scriptures told the story of Hagar, Abraham's lover and mother of his (at that point) only child, who was driven out into the desert with her small son. Sarah, Abraham's infertile wife, had used her slave Hagar as a surrogate mother and Hagar had a son, Ishmael, with Abraham. However, after the child was born, Sarah became jealous and persuaded Abraham to expel Hagar from the camp. Abraham gave Hagar bread and water and her child – who was also his child – and forced her to leave, to her certain death. Out in the desert, her child dying in her arms, Hagar clearly encountered the full terror of unchosen silence. She 'cast her child down' under some scrubby bushes and then went and sat a little way away from him, because she could not bear to watch him die. Then the God who had apparently authorised her banishment became present to her; she heard his voice and in an ineffable immediacy not described in any detail she became one of the very few people in the Hebrew Scriptures to 'see God and live'.[9]

Her story has a happy ending; God shows Hagar a well, and she and the child both survive. Inevitably, most such stories have a happy ending, because the likely outcome of driving someone out of the protection of society into the wilderness is death, and then there is no one to tell what happened and therefore no story. In legend and myth, children exiled from their communities, for whatever reason, flourish. Romulus and Remus, raised by wolves, grow up to found the city of Rome. In *Hayy Ibn Yaqdhan*, the first European philosophical novel by Ibn Tufail, a twelfth-century Iberian Arab thinker and writer, which became a major 'bestseller', the eponymous hero is brought up on an uninhabited island by gazelles and achieves religious truth by direct reasoning. Rudyard Kipling's Mowgli, best known in the *Jungle Book* (1894) and its sequels, show Mowgli, who was also raised by wolves, acquiring almost magical powers through his ability to be at home both in human culture and in the wild with animals.

The reality of early abandonment, however, is not so optimistic. There have been approximately a hundred recorded cases of 'feral children', although most of them are hotly contested: how accurate are the records? How long and from how early had the child lived with its adopting animals? Was the child abandoned precisely because it was already brain damaged in the first place? But overall this particular experience of involuntary silence has grim consequences. Children raised outside human society have the greatest difficulty in re-entering; they seldom acquire language or learn to relate to other human beings, and they usually die young. With the subterranean truth of ancient stories this is to some extent acknowledged in the earliest legends. Genesis recounts that although Ishmael survived, he grew up to be 'a wild ass of a man, his hand against every man', to 'dwell over against all his kinsmen. He will live in the wilderness,' while Romulus murdered his brother and organised the mass rape of the Sabine women in order to populate his new city.

Some of the adverse mental effects that Grassian observes in his prisoners may be to do with the physical 'confinement' as much as its 'solitary' nature. But fortunately for me there is also a surprisingly large literature of involuntary silence without close confinement.

For example, a fairly well documented version of involuntary silence is marooning – setting an individual ashore on an isolated island. This course of action was invented by early eighteenth-century pirates. They built the 'terms and conditions' for marooning quite formally into their ship's articles. In 1724 John Phillips, the captain of the *Revenge*, included a clause which read, 'If any Man shall offer to run away, or keep any Secret from the Company, he shall be maroon'd with one Bottle of Powder, one Bottle of Water, one small Arm, and Shot.'[10]

Prior to its adoption by pirates the word 'maroon' had meant an escaped slave, but it was so regularly used on ships that pirates were referred to as 'marooners'. It was a punishment exercised both by captains against insubordinate crew members and by successfully mutinous crews against their captains. The stipulation about the 'small arm and shot', which was conventional in such articles, was so that the marooned could kill themselves if they chose, and they might as well so choose, because the most likely, and to the best of our knowledge the most normal, outcome of marooning was to die alone and slowly. In periods where death was mandated for the most minor crimes this reluctance to execute the traitor directly feels strange. Perhaps it is this awareness of immanent death, endured in silence, that undermines sanity and lets in the dark. It is not an unrealistic fear: silence can kill you, or drive you so insane that you never find a narrative of return. And if you are dead you cannot tell anyone about it – you are finally and completely silenced.

Almost miraculously, though, people do survive and do find a language to tell us about it. And in these accounts, over and over again you see the shadow side of the positive experiences of silence. A different subjectivity, a different day, a tiny piece of good or bad luck, shifts the balance between positive and negative experiences of silence, as it does between life and death.

Marguerite de la Rocque survived. She was marooned on an island in the St Lawrence seaway by her uncle, as a punishment for immorality, in 1542. She survived there for two years and five months before she was rescued. She is probably the first European woman to overwinter in Canada and possibly the first to give birth in the New World. She is one of the earliest modern suvivors of this kind that we know about. She haunts my imagination, as she has haunted the imagination of a number of writers, especially women, from Marguerite of Navarre, who retold the story in the *Heptameron*,[11] onwards. One of my very first attempts to make fiction out of and about silence was based on her marooning.[12]

By any standards it is an extraordinary survival story. Marguerite was a young upper-class woman who had never been out of France before and cannot have had any 'wilderness experience' whatsoever. She was a member of one of the worst-run expeditions in the history of exploration. The leader, her uncle Roberval, patently did not have a clue what he was up to. His 'crew' were a highly unqualified and unstable mixture of convicts and his friends and relations, many of whom seem to have gone along as tourists. He refused to take advice from Jacques Cartier, the most experienced French captain-navigator of his period, who was appointed by the king as Roberval's second-in-command. Cartier finally, and in dereliction of a direct order, left the expedition and returned to France. The basic idea behind this ill-thought-out venture was to sail up the St Lawrence and build a settlement about where Quebec is now as a launch pad for the exploration and colonisation of the Canadian interior. As the expedition was sailing upriver from Newfoundland, very shortly after Cartier had declared the whole mission to be suicidal and had deserted,* Roberval discovered his niece was having an affair with another member of the expedition

---

* Cartier probably should not be too much blamed for this. The expedition was already in chaos. He had sailed the year before Roberval, as an independent captain; Roberval was meant to follow him almost immediately, but owing to his financial crisis he did not in fact leave until the following spring. Cartier meanwhile established a camp and endured the most appalling winter on the St Lawrence, where – without the equipment that Roberval was supposed to be bringing – his crew suffered badly. In the spring, believing that Roberval had got lost, he left the camp and planned to limp back to

and marooned the two of them (plus a maid!) on a small island on the northern shore of the St Lawrence seaway, over 50° N (the Arctic Circle begins at 66° N). The seaway at this point is frozen solid for four months of the year. This was no Caribbean island.

During the first autumn both her lover and the maid died, and later in the first winter so did the baby that Marguerite gave birth to on her own. That spring Roberval abandoned the fort and sailed back past the island; there is no evidence that he even attempted to find out what had happened to her. Marguerite survived alone for more than another year, including a whole winter. We have very few details about how she survived, presumably by hunting and fishing. She killed a bear cub as 'white as an egg'. We know, too, that she was persecuted by demons – they screamed abuse and threats at her in the darkness, and she shot at them through the roof of her hut, and later, when she had no more gunpowder, shouted bits of the Bible at them. But she survived. Eventually she was rescued by some fishermen. (Despite all the talk about exploration and discovery, the fact is that these waters had been fished by both Breton and Basque fleets for years.) She survived; she went home to Picardy and set up a school. At some point thereafter she told her story to a sea captain called Jean Alfonce, who seems to have repeated it to André Thevet, a Franciscan priest, explorer and writer whose written account is accepted as essentially accurate and historical. It is almost certainly through his account that the queen, Marguerite of Navarre, came to know the story.

I sat in the little house in Skye, having chosen it, warm, safe, with a car and a telephone if I wanted to escape, and with electric lighting and plentiful supplies of food. I heard the wind in the roof as

France. By chance he and Roberval met up in Newfoundland, where it transpired that Roberval had got himself appointed as Cartier's admiral. Cartier's insistence that the plan was not viable fell on deaf ears – and he finally sailed east under cover of night. The point here is that the members of the expedition must have known full well that Cartier did not think the plans possible and was prepared to risk criminal charges and death rather than return up the St Lawrence. At the time of Marguerite's marooning there must have been a great deal of tension and unhappiness on board.

a choir singing in Latin – it does not seem to me a huge step to Marguerite in an unimaginably long winter darkness, in a land she knows nothing about, with death all around her and no persuasive hope of rescue; bereaved, post-partum, probably guilt-ridden, certainly without the comforts of home or of religion. I cannot even think about her without tears, but also without a profound admiration at the courage and resourcefulness that enabled her to survive.

Alexander Selkirk survived. There are a number of accounts from the late seventeenth and early eighteenth centuries of marooned sailors who were subsequently rescued but Alexander Selkirk gained immortality by becoming the prototype for Daniel Defoe's novel *The Life and Strange Surprising Adventures of Robinson Crusoe*, or more simply *Robinson Crusoe* (1719), which interestingly is directly influenced by Ibn Tufail's novel. Selkirk, a somewhat truculent Scot who originally went to sea to escape a criminal summons for unruly behaviour in church, spent four and as half years alone on the Island of Juan Fernandez, about 300 miles off the coast of Chile. It would be hard to imagine a better island to be marooned on – as there was fresh water, fertile soil, reasonable weather and populations of feral goats and cats. In addition Selkirk was unusually well equipped because there was a 'voluntary' element in his leaving his ship, which he believed to be ill founded and whose captain was both incompetent and tyrannical (and was later stripped of his captaincy on the accusations of other crew members). This meant that he went ashore with:

> his Sea-Chest, his wearing Cloaths and Bedding, a Fire-lock, a Pound of Gun-powder, a large quantity of Bullets, a Flint and Steel, a few Pounds of Tobacco, an Hatchet, a Knife, a Kettle, a Bible, and other Books of Devotion, together with Pieces that concerned Navigation, and his Mathematical Instruments.[13]

He also had not unreasonable expectations of an early rescue because the island was a favoured watering anchorage for both

British and Spanish privateers. Nonetheless he was said to have run along the beach at the last moment begging to be allowed back on board, which his infuriated captain would not allow. Selkirk himself was, probably unlike de la Rocque, tough, ingenious and skilled in ways that improved his chances of survival.

After his return to Britain Selkirk attracted a good deal of attention. Travel writing was enjoying a vogue and the story had obvious appeal, so we know a good deal about his experiences. In particular, Richard Steele, the Irish writer and politician, interviewed him and published an essay on him a periodical called *The Englishman* in 1713. Unlike most of the accounts, which focused on his physical survival in an exotic location, Steele was explicitly interested in Selkirk's emotional state of mind.

When we consider how painful Absence from Company for the space of but one Evening, is to the generality of Mankind, we may have a sense how painful this necessary and constant Solitude was to a Man bred a Sailor . . . The Necessities of Hunger and Thirst, were his greatest Diversions from the Reflection on his lonely Condition. When those Appetites were satisfied, the Desire of Society was as strong a Call upon him, and he appeared to himself least necessitious when he wanted every thing; for the Supports of his Body were easily attained, but the eager Longings for seeing again the Face of Man during the Interval of craving bodily Appetites, were hardly supportable. He grew dejected, languid, and melancholy, scarce able to refrain from doing himself Violence, till by Degrees, by the Force of Reason, and frequent reading of the Scriptures, and turning his Thoughts upon the Study of Navigation, after the Space of eighteen Months, he grew thoroughly reconciled to his Condition. When he had made this Conquest, the Vigour of his Health, Disengagement from the World, a constant, chearful, serene Sky, and a temperate Air, made his Life one continual Feast, and his Being much more joyful than it had before been irksome . . . I forgot to observe, that during the Time of his Dissatisfaction, Monsters of the Deep, which frequently lay on the Shore, added to the Terrors of his Solitude; the dreadful Howlings and Voices seemed too terrible to be made for human Ears; but upon the Recovery of his Temper, he could with Pleasure not only hear their Voices, but approach the Monsters themselves with great Intrepidity.

When I first saw him, I thought, if I had not been let into his Character and Story, I could have discerned that he had been much separated from Company, from his Aspect and Gesture; there was a strong but chearful Seriousness in his Look, and a certain Disregard to the ordinary things about him.[14]

In fact, though, Selkirk never did return to his previous way of life – after a brief period, apparently enjoying his fame, he became increasingly reclusive, took to living in a cave and died at forty-five. In this account there is a powerful mixture of positive and negative effects of silence.

Joe Simpson survived. For those who have neither seen the film nor read the book, *Touching the Void*,[15] Simpson is a mountaineer. In 1985, climbing with his friend and climbing partner Simon Yates in a very isolated area of the Peruvian Andes, at the end of a successful ascent of the previously unclimbed Siula Grande (6,356 metres), Simpson broke his thigh. At that height and under the circumstances this is usually treated as a death knell and Yates might have acceptably left him there. Nonetheless the two of them began an attempt to get him down the mountain by lowering him on a rope through the night and with the weather worsening. Finally, unable to support Simpson, who after yet another slip was dangling barely conscious over a crevasse, Yates cut the climbing rope – apparently the only chance of either of them surviving – and allowed Simpson to fall to his presumed death. The next morning Yates got himself back to their base camp only with the greatest difficulty.

However, Simpson was not dead; seriously injured and in great pain, without food or fresh water, with a badly broken leg, additional injuries from the fall and alone with the knowledge (from the rope end) that this had not been 'accidental', he spent four days struggling out of the crevasse and down the intensely inhospitable terrain, arriving back only hours before Yates and the third member of their party, the non-mountaineering Richard Hawking, were planning to strike camp. *Touching the Void* is a barely endurable account of extreme human isolation, and both physical and mental suffering, yet for Simpson there is an element of negative ineffability: 'For me this book still falls short of articulating just how dreadful were some of those lonely days. I simply could not find words to express the utter desolation.'[16]

One of the things that kept him alive was a *voice* (which, in his book, he always refers to in italics). It drove him relentlessly, not towards destruction and disintegration, but towards the opposite:

> There was silence, and snow, and a clear sky empty of life and me sitting there. It was as if there were two minds within me arguing the toss. The *voice* was clean and sharp and commanding. It was always right, and I listened to it when it spoke and acted on its decisions. The other mind rambled out a disconnected series of images and memories and hopes which I attended to in a day dream state as I set about obeying the orders of the *voice* . . . The *voice* had banished the mad thoughts from my mind. An urgency was creeping over me, and the *voice* said, 'Go on, keep going . . . faster.'[17]

As soon as he found the camp and his companions the *voice* disappeared, leaving him a sobbing, collapsed wreck.

> The minute I knew help was at hand something inside me had collapsed. Whatever had been holding me together had gone. Now I could not think for myself, let alone crawl. There was nothing to fight for, no patterns to follow, no *voice* and it frightened me to think that, without these, I might run out of life.[18]

In one sense this was a short 'involuntary silence' but the intensity of the experience – the altitude, the bizarre circumstances, the extreme emotional trauma, the absolute uncertainty and above all the physical pain seem to have forced a high-speed version of the psychological effects of enforced silence on Simpson – and his book is by far the most distressing account of such an experience I know. It contains, in an intensified form, many of the effects of negative silence: as well as the voice hearing, he fell into confused ritualistic patterns of behaviour; he lost a normal sense of time; he experienced wild mood swings and an increasing loss of mind control.

Anthony Grey survived. He was a Reuters journalist in Peking at the height of the Cultural Revolution. In 1967 a 'frenzied' group of politicised Red Guards invaded his house at midnight, tortured and hanged his cat in front of him, daubed him with black paint and then kept him in isolation in his own basement, which the Chinese government described as a 'restriction of movement', for over two years. Essentially he was a political hostage – and at one level a well-chosen one because he was not a diplomat. His 'solitary confinement' was a peculiar sort of silence because at one level it was not silent at all. Grey set himself in the later stages of his ordeal to learn Chinese, but until then he had to listen endlessly to his guards talking together, singing and chanting the aphorisms from Mao's *Little Red Book*, but no one spoke to him, he could not understand what they were saying and apart from two half-hour consular visits he spoke to no one during this time. In his account of the episode he speaks very movingly of the additional pressure that the constant noise, supervision and uncertainty imposed on him, while he himself was silenced. But, despite the differences, his account of his own emotions is surprisingly similar to Steele's account of Selkirk's. He describes a practical phase where you deal with the physical realities of your situation and test their boundaries, followed by an escalating inertia, overwhelming depression and a mounting sense of claustrophobia, paranoia, terror and fantasy, and an increasing dependence on ritual – in his case daily prayers and yoga (interestingly, much the same routine as Moitessier seems to have adopted in his joyful and free isolation) as well as a strange, almost Gnostic ritual numbering and naming of days.

In these particular cases not only did the individuals survive, but so did their stories. Simpson and Grey are both writers; Selkirk and Marguerite de la Rocque encountered writers who had an interest in their stories and the ability to tell them. There are other examples, too, that we know about, and innumerable ones that we cannot know or tell.

Obviously there are far fewer stories from those who went into a silent place or a silent period and did not survive.

Chris McCandless did not survive. A young American from a prosperous east-coast American family, McCandless 'dropped out' after graduating from college in 1990 and two years later was found dead in the Alaskan outback – the autopsy gave starvation as the most probable cause of death. He had been living 'in retreat', alone and in silence in a derelict bus, endeavouring to live 'off the land' in an extreme terrain, for four months before his death. In *Into the Wild*[19] Jon Krakauer has made a bold attempt to explore those final months. *Into the Wild* is an extraordinary meditation on solitude, the call of the wild and particularly the seductive thrill of peril, adversity, and what he calls 'Tolstoyan' asceticism and renunciation. Krakauer, a journalist of extreme adventure, incorporates into his book detail of his own experiences and those of other modern 'wandering hermits', and despite the different context and intention that he and his characters had from mine, I find this book both moving and helpful.

One reason for my sympathy is perhaps that I feel my own trajectory into silence is quite close to McCandless's in some particular ways. He, too, clearly started by simply enjoying the sense of being alone and free of family and other responsibilities. He was intensely idealistic; he gave his life savings, nearly £12,000, to Oxfam before setting off, and was strongly motivated by contempt for contemporary Western culture (something I strongly shared at his age and have not entirely grown out of yet) and also by authors like Tolstoy and Thoreau, who offer a free-ranging and ecstatic view of both 'nature' and personal renunciation. Like me he decided to go off somewhere desolate, isolated and extreme, and explore his own identity in silence. He kept it up a good deal longer than I did – 113 days of similar highs and lows to mine – but it was clear that he did not mean to stay for ever and also that, given his lack of equipment and experience, he managed surprisingly well for quite a long time. As Krakauer tracks down the last two years of McCandless's life I can see an individual pushed by a particular and contemporary constellation of ideals further and further towards the challenge of absolute silence.

There are differences, though, and I expect the most important one was quite simply age; and the experience and sense (or fear) that go with it. I have learned to respect, rather than despise, my own limitations. With an almost staggering stupidity or arrogance or both, McCandless went into the Alaskan outback without a map. (Had he had one, he could very easily have seen that there were other ways out from where he was than the track he came in by, which was closed by a flooding river, and that he was a mere six miles from safety.) I not only had a large-scale Ordnance Survey map – I also, perhaps more crucially, had interior maps and compass. I had a solid, deeply enjoyable life to want to come back to. Another difference is that I am neither male nor American – and so not acculturated within that extraordinary wilderness mythology about courage, masculinity and the frontier. I also believe that my religious conviction – a steady, reasoned, critical faith – may help to make someone safer in silence.

No one will ever know what happened to Chris McCandless or what he thought he was doing. But there is one detailed personal account of a fatal silence, which we can follow to the sorry end. This brings me back again to the Golden Globe race in 1968.

Donald Crowhurst did not survive, but he kept up his 'ship's log' until some very last moment and we know in great detail what was happening to him, even if it is hard to make sense of. It is a strange story. Donald Crowhurst, an electrical engineer and 'inventor', entered the Golden Globe race with a newly built, radically designed multihull, *Teignmouth Electron*, which it transpired was not fit for purpose and which Crowhurst could not in fact sail. Because of delays in building her, *Teignmouth Electron* had no sea trials. Crowhurst left Devon on the last day permissible under the race rules – 31 October 1968. Within a fortnight he was recording in his log that the situation was desperate, nothing on the boat worked properly and that he ought to retire. At this point he seemed entirely rational. He recognised that although retiring would almost certainly mean bankruptcy, he 'would have Clare [his wife] and the children still', and he comforted and encouraged himself with snippets from Kipling's poem 'If'.

Some time in the first week of December, however, he cooked up a bizarre plan. On 6 December he started keeping two different logs – a true one of his increasingly passive drift around the western Atlantic and a fake one that showed him whizzing at ever more exciting speeds (breaking the world record at times) south and east and round the Cape of Good Hope. As this got more untenable he cut off radio contact altogether and disappeared for eleven weeks. It seems clear that he was planning to pretend to have sailed round the world. He would work his way to the south Atlantic, then reopen radio contact and sail home as though he had completed the circumnavigation. When he reopened radio contact he learned that Robin Knox-Johnston had arrived back in Falmouth on 23 April – the first non-stop solo circumnavigation of the world had been achieved. He also learned that Nigel Tetley was pushing up the Atlantic well placed to win the 'fastest time' prize. Crowhurst must have felt that he had a good chance of getting away with his deception. He could come in behind Tetley, with his reputation intact and his obligations towards his sponsors met, although he must have been aware that there might be some awkward questions asked.

At this point an ironic tragedy occurred. Tetley, in the now badly damaged *Victresse*, learned in his turn that Crowhurst was still in the race. Had he not believed that Crowhurst was close behind him and making apparently extraordinary speed, he could probably have nursed *Victresse* home for the fastest-time prize; as it was he felt obliged to push on harder than his damaged little boat could bear and on 23 May *Victresse* literally broke up in the water a scant 1,000 miles from Britain. Tetley was rescued, but when Crowhurst heard the news on his newly established radio connection, the full implications of what he was doing crashed home on him: he was going to *win* the race, and this would lead to a highly undesirable level of attention and examination, and his deception would almost certainly be exposed. After 23 May he stopped sailing anywhere; *Teignmouth Electron* was allowed to drift. In early June his radio genuinely failed. Although he repaired it and made connection again on 22 June, it was too late: all the communications coming to him from his publicist were exultant plans for his 'victory'. After that Crowhurst stopped communicating with anyone and sank into his own silence. His logbooks changed: in eight days he wrote 25,000 words of incomprehensible delirious rambling, in which he debated with Einstein, prophesied the end of the world and offered magical insights into the universe. Like most psychotic discourse there was a coherent central image – the coming superman (himself) could, by will alone, free himself from the limitations of the physical world.

When he came to himself on 30 June all his clocks had stopped and he knew neither where he was nor what time or even what day it was. For any deep-water sailor this is the ultimate disaster. He attempted to calculate both time and position from the sun, and came up with an answer that was palpably absurd. Increasingly desperate and aware that time itself was dissolving for him, he went back to writing his bizarre ship's log. Between 10.03 (if that is what the time really was) and 11.17 he continued writing – now marking the minutes, and towards the end even the seconds in a final attempt to control them. At 10.29 he wrote:

I will only resign this game
if you will agree that this
game is played it will be played
according to the
rules that are devised by my great god who has

revealed at last to his son
not only the exact nature
of the reason for games but
has also revealed the truth of
the way of the ending of the next game that
   It is finished –
   It is finished
IT IS THE MERCY[20]

At 11.20 he stopped writing mid sentence (but at the bottom of a page).

It is unclear, of course, what happened immediately after that. On 10 July *Teignmouth Electron* was found unmanned and drifting. The weather had been so calm that on the cabin table a soldering iron was still balanced neatly on a milk tin. Crowhurst was not there – nor, oddly enough, was the brass chronometer from the bulkhead, which had been unscrewed and was not on board. Crowhurst had tried to take time with him when he travelled into the final silence.

It could be argued that both Chris McCandless and Donald Crowhurst *chose* their danger and isolation; it was not involuntary or compulsory. Nonetheless it seems to me significant that it was precisely at the point when they felt they could not escape that things started to go wrong for them. McCandless survived very well and his journals seem reasonably sane up until the point he discovered that the track back to civilisation was flooded and inaccessible. Given that he did not know (even though he should have) that there were other ways out, he must have felt imprisoned. Likewise with Crowhurst – it was only when he realised that *Teignmouth Electron* was completely unmanageable, that his own skills were inadequate to the task in hand, and that his own fantasies and deceptions had in effect imprisoned him, that his grip on sanity began to slip.

What bound me into all these stories is how closely many of them matched my own experience of the dark side of silence when I was briefly snowed in, just as I had found that sets of responses to 'good silence' seemed remarkably consistent when I was in Skye. Indeed I have, as I have suggested, come to believe they are the shadow side of the positive responses.

So, once the road was finally cleared and the late spring lengthened the days and greened the trees, I was glad to have gone through this brief imprisonment. I knew retrospectively that it had given me some real understanding and also a deep sense of security – there was nothing in my own freely chosen silence that I needed to be frightened of. I turned my attention joyfully to the task of discovering how much of the intense joy and excitement I had found in Skye could be built into my daily life.

Or so I thought. Later that summer I encountered a rather different negative effect of silence. I had an attack of accidie.

Accidie is a state of mind that is so deeply associated with silence that the OED defines it 'the mental prostration of recluses induced by fasting and other physical causes', although none of the desert hermits or their commentators made any connection between accidie and asceticism. It occurs in so many accounts of silence that are not associated with other ascetic practices like fasting that this definition smacks to me of nineteenth-century rationalist scientism. The 'recluses' themselves saw it as a sin and later it became the theological term for the fourth deadly sin – sloth or laziness – but originally it had a very specific meaning related to silence. Accidie is a form of torpor or, to translate the original Greek word more literally, a 'not-caring-state' (a = 'not' + $kedos$ = 'care'). Rather pleasingly, the medieval spiritual writers, whose Greek was less sound than after the Renaissance, mis-derived it from the Latin *acidum* – sour or bitter (the same source, obviously, as 'acid' and with a similar corroding power). It certainly turned the joys of silence sour for me.

It is very difficult to describe the effects of accidie, because its predominant feature is a lack of affect, an overwhelming sense of blankness and an odd restless and dissatisfied boredom. I would get up in the morning, make earnest resolutions about work or prayer or exercise, all things that I knew would make me feel better if I did them, but I would in fact find, in the evening, that I had spent the whole day rereading detective novels or playing patience, despite the fact that these activities felt boring even while I was doing them. For me, and for others, one very marked 'symptom' was an enormous difficulty in moving from one activity to another – just one more chapter, one more game of sudoku, one more embroidery thread and *then* I will go for a walk.

In the early fifth century CE John Cassian wrote an account of accidie, which seems close to the mark still. He had been an ascetic in the Egyptian desert as a young man, but left as a missionary for southern Gaul, where he founded monasteries and spread the desert tradition. Although he sensibly advised his French monks to moderate the rule of the desert because of the colder climate, he nonetheless harked back to his youth and described the lives of the earlier saints with affectionate detail. His voice is an unexpectedly modern one because, as Helen Waddell puts it,

> His ironic human perception makes intelligible the more alien experience of the desert, its concentration within the four walls of one's cell. To read Cassian on accidie is to recognize the 'white melancholy' of Gray in Pembroke and the sullen lethargy that is the sterile curse of the scholar and the artist.[21]

Cassian wrote a specific passage on accidie and how to 'contend' with it:

> Accidie, which we may describe as tedium or perturbation of heart. It is akin to dejection, and especially felt by solitaries, a persistent and obnoxious enemy to such as dwell in the desert, disturbing the monk especially about midday . . . When this besieges the unhappy mind it begets aversion from the place, boredom with one's cell and scorn and contempt for one's brethren. Also toward any work that may be done within the enclosure of our own lair, we become listless and inert. It will not suffer us to stay in our cell, or to attend

to our reading . . . It produces such lassitude of body and craving for food as one might feel after the exhaustion of a long journey and hard toil; one is for ever in and out of one's cell, gazing at the sun as though it were tarrying to its setting; one's mind is in an irrational confusion, like the earth befogged in a mist, one is slothful and vacant in every spiritual activity.[22]

The early hermits were very much aware of this affliction, but it does not seem to be a consequence of the ascetic life per se, but rather a result of silence. The same thing is reported over and over again from people whose silence, for one reason or another, did not involve any 'mortifications of the flesh' or harsh physical discipline in the sense that Cassian understood that. On the other hand it does not seem to be a problem for elite athletes, whose physical disciplines and renunciations are every bit as rigorous as those of the hermits. There is a very similar and powerful description of this torpor in *Hostage in Peking*, Anthony Grey's account of his two-year imprisonment in 1968:

> I want to record my complete feeling of emptiness at the moment. Often in my prayers I ask to be delivered from this 'vacuum of hell'. I have somehow developed a dead feeling, which makes it hard for me to make up my mind to do anything active. In some moments I am seized with despair but most of the time I can contemplate long weeks ahead as empty as this without any feeling. . . . It is becoming increasingly difficult to remain enthusiastic about Yoga or anything else for that matter. My life seems becalmed on a flat sea never to become mobile again.[23]

Christiane Ritter, in more poetic language, seems to be wrestling with a similar condition when she writes:

> For humans this stillness is horrible. It is days since I have been outside the hut. Gradually I have become fearful of seeing the deadness of the land. I sit in the hut and tire myself out with

sewing. It makes no difference whether the work is finished today or tomorrow, but I know what I am up to. I do not want to have my mind free for a moment to think, a moment in which to become aware of the nothingness outside . . . I know with certainty that it was this nothingness, which over the past centuries has been responsible for the death of some hundreds of men here in Spitzbergen . . . There is no longer even a glimmer of day, not even at noon. I take it particularly badly and the hunters maintain that I am moonstruck. What I would like best of all is to stand all day on the shore where in the water the rocking ice-floes catch and break the light and throw it back at the moon. But the men are very strict with me and often keep me under house arrest.[24]

Accidie feels rather different from the other negative effects of silence because it is not the shadow side, or the subjectively warped expression of any positive feeling at all that I have been able to locate. I have tried to see it as the reverse side of the sense of 'givenness' that I have described: if everything is a gift from outside one's own ego, then one may well experience an unnerving sense of passivity – that no action or decision is worth taking for oneself, that no act of the will can have any results, so why bother? However, that is not what it felt like. It felt like a thing in itself, quite separate from any of the other states I have described.

It is particularly hard to work out what is going on in attacks of accidie because of our modern understanding of depression, and especially the contemporary notion that depression is a physical illness which, like a broken leg, exists completely outside our will. It is now more or less normative to reduce every negative experience we have to some neural malfunction or imbalance. Early theologians and the medieval Church, however, ascribed accidie to sin. The very gentle and sane writer of the *Ancren Riwle*, the early thirteenth-century handbook for anchoresses (solitaries whose cells were attached to parish churches, like Julian of Norwich) is very blunt and writes sternly of accidie, urging his anchoresses to cast it aside with prayer and determination.

There is a lovely and relevant demonstration of this confusion between depression and accidie: the Desert Fathers, as Cassian reiterates, associated accidie with the 'demon' in Psalm 91:

> You will not fear the terror of the night,
> Nor the arrow that flies by day,
> Nor the pestilence that stalks in the darkness
> Nor the demon that lays waste at noonday.[25]

In 2002 Andrew Solomon published an excellent comprehensive account of depression and he called the book *The Noonday Demon*.

I think it is possible that depression and accidie are just different words for the same condition, but as someone who has suffered from both I think there are real differences; at the simplest level accidie was perceived as connected with silence (not simply with ascetic hermits, but with the excessive confinement of scholars, and with prolonged isolation in convalescence for the ill) and there is no suggestion that depression is. In fact, if depression were directly affected by silence we would be seeing less and less of it in a society where there is an ever-decreasing amount of silence. All the evidence – for example, the number of people using anti-depressants or the number of working days lost to depression – suggests that this illness is reaching epidemic proportions.

The writers who wrote about accidie also recognised depression, which they usually called melancholy. For them there was a clear distinction. They had very much more experience of the effects of silence, solitude, ascetic practice and the life of prayer than we do today and it seems to me wise to learn from their experience: accidie is not depression. They are two very different things, even when the 'symptoms' look very alike, and it is important to distinguish between the two.

The reason it is important to distinguish is very simple – the 'cures' for these two conditions are precisely opposite, as Richard Burton, standing as it were on the cusp between the medieval and

the modern understanding of human emotion, acknowledged in
The Anatomy of Melancholy (1621).[26] The generally accepted treatment for depression, with or without pharmaceutical intervention,
is gentleness. Eat well, avoid stress, do not feel guilty; be kind to
yourself, seek quiet but real amusement, rest a lot. But such a regime
would find little sympathy with the spiritual directors of those
afflicted with accidie. The classic cure for accidie is penance, a strict
'rule' of life, self-discipline and hard work. Cassian addresses this
energetically:

> And so the wise Fathers in Egypt would in no way suffer the monks,
> especially the younger ones, to be idle, measuring the state of their
> heart and their progress in patience and humility by their steadiness
> at work. Not only might they accept nothing from anyone towards
> their support, but out of their own toil they supplied such brethren
> as came by or were from foreign parts and did send huge stores of
> victuals and provisions to those that pined in the squalor of the pris-
> ons. There was a saying approved by the Fathers in Egypt; a busy
> monk is besieged by a single devil but an idle one is destroyed by
> spirits innumerable.[27]

This ancient prescription is endorsed in the practice of those who
have best survived long and difficult contemporary silences.
Drawing up 'rules of life', schedules or timetables and exercising
one's will to *keep to them* seems to be a necessary defence against the
sluggish torpor of accidie and its attendant dangers. Cassian goes
on to tell a commendatory story about Abba Paul, a hermit 'in that
vast desert of Porphyrio' whose physical needs were met by a
fortunate date palm and his small garden, and who lived in such isolation that there was no way of marketing any surplus or handicraft.

> Nevertheless did he gather palm leaves, and every day exacted from
> himself just such a measure of work as though he lived by it. And
> when the cave was filled with the work of a whole year, he would set
> fire to it . . . Thereby he proved that without working with his hands

a monk cannot endure to abide in his place, nor can he climb any nearer the summit of holiness. So though necessity of making a livelihood in no way demand it, let it be done for the sole purging of the heart, the steadying of thought, perseverance in the cell and the conquest and final overthrow of accidie itself.[28]

Ritter's sewing, Grey's decision to create crossword puzzles, to learn Chinese and to practise yoga, Tenzin Palmo's gruelling meditation hours, the carefully timetabled threefold discipline of study, physical work and prayer that Benedict recommended to his monks; the regular washing routines and daily weather observations that Byrd struggled to maintain even when he became ill, these are all proven and effective tactics against the noonday demon of accidie.

But it is not easy; not only do silence dwellers have to diagnose their condition accurately and treat it wisely, they also have to keep an eye on the opposite danger. Rigorous busyness, as Adam Nicolson points out very perceptively in *Sea Room*, his account of life on the tiny isolated islands he owns in the Outer Hebrides, can also easily be an evasion of or a defence against the silence and one's own fragility in the face of it.

I have spent weeks on the Shiants . . . making enough noise in working on, mending and setting creels, repairing fences, digging a vegetable patch in one of the old lazybeds, setting up winches on the beach, putting wire netting on the chimneypots to keep the rats from scampering down them, painting the house inside and out – all this, in the end, to keep the silence away.

Always at the back of that hurry is the knowledge that it is a screen against honesty. More than on anything else, Crusoe expended his energy on fences. He built huge palisades around both his island houses, the stakes driven into the ground, sharpened at the top, reinforced, stabilized, all designed to keep the world out. It was not the world he was fencing out but his own profoundly subversive and alarming sense of isolation.[29]

It was in many ways a long winter: a journey through the glories and *jouissance* on Skye, the fears that being snowed in had thrown up for me, and the 'slough of despond' thereafter. I found the necessary monitoring of myself tiring and at times irritating; I was often amazed at the gap between my desires and my actions. But underneath all that I knew I was learning and growing in silence, and I was excited.

4

Silence and the Gods

The summer comes late and slowly on the high moors; it comes from two directions at once, out of the sky in the longer days and the shining brightness, and simultaneously creeping up from the valley, green and gold. In the spring there would be daffodils in full flower at the bottom of the dale while the same plants up at my house on the moor had hardly poked their first hard green spikes above the ground. Going up and down the road between my house and the village I could see the bright yellow clumps laboriously struggling up the hill, pulling the new green of the trees behind them. This gentle but inexorable movement of the seasons is yet another of the silent elemental forces that shape our lives and of which we remain mainly oblivious.

As slowly as the seasons, that summer after I had come back physically from Skye and mentally from the various difficulties of that winter, I began to settle down. I felt both determined and eager. What I had learned, for good and bad, about both silence and myself reassured me powerfully. This was what I wanted.

However, the first thing I had to absorb was that sadly but inevitably the intensity of that winter could not continue indefinitely. Over the next three years I joyfully explored how I might create a sustainable lifestyle that would contain as much silence as possible. One part of this was simply doing it – building up internally and externally a practice of silence, persuading my friends and family that this was really what I wanted, developing and maintaining a disciplined pattern of meditation and prayer, unplugging the phone, taking life gently, walking, looking, listening to the silence.

Another part of it, though, was about learning more about silence; looking at the ways silence had been understood in the past and how it was used in the present. I was investigating silence – its history, its landscape and its culture. I wanted to understand *why*, in the face of my experiences in Skye, Western society increasingly sees silence as an absence, and a dangerous absence at that. This drew me back to Janet Batsleer's letter, which I described in chapter 1.

> In the beginning God *said*, God spoke.
>
> Silence is a place of non-being, from which all our yearning is to escape. All the social movements of oppressed people in the second part of the twentieth century have claimed 'coming to language' and 'coming to voice' as necessary to their politics . . . In the beginning was the Word. . . . Silence is oppression. It is 'the word' that is the beginning of freedom.
>
> All silence is waiting to be broken.[1]

My writerly imagination has always been deeply grounded in myths and ancient stories of various kinds. This retelling has been both a way of finding strong and enduring stories, and a way of looking at ideas that puzzle me. So high on the moor and revelling in that silent beauty, and especially the silent coming of the light, I started to look at and think about creation stories.

> In the beginning . . . God *said* 'let there be light' and there was light.[2]

> In the beginning was the word and the word was with God and the word was God.[3]

In the beginning . . . In the beginning of the creation story that Christianity and Islam both learned from Judaism, there was nothing. There was chaos, emptiness, fall without direction, vacuum, void, notness. There are no words for this nothing, because there were no words. And as there were no words, there was no silence either, because silence in this story is the absence of words. Language creates the possibility of silence through absence. In the beginning there was nothing, not even absence or silence. There was nothing, no thing. 'The world was without form and void.' God creates *ex nihilo*, from nothing, out of nothing, by speaking.

'In the beginning God created the heavens and the earth . . . God *said*, "let there be light" and there was light.' God speaking broke the void. The silence was broken and because there was light, there was dark. Because there was word, there was silence. Time began 'and there was evening and morning, one day'.[4]

After that it was pretty straightforward, although each phase of the creation took longer and longer sentences, more and more words, to accomplish. The final act – the making of human beings – was the most complicated; God had to communicate directly, establish an I and a You. Not just speaking but speaking to, being heard.

> In the beginning God spoke.
> In the beginning was the Word . . . all things were made through the Word, and without the Word was not anything made that was made.[5]

This story has proved itself a *very* powerful creation myth.

Now, here is another creation myth. It is rather shorter:

> At the beginning* there was the Big Bang.

I am not using the word 'myth' here to suggest that the theory that the universe was created by the extraordinary explosion of a singularity – the energy of which triggered the whole process of the universe including time itself – is fictional; or that I don't believe it.

* I think the change of preposition is fairer to the modern story: it is not a rerun, whatever some Christian apologists would like to think – it is a brand-new story. It just has some remarkably similar features . . .

I am using the word more technically. The Big Bang is an attempt to express the inexpressible, in terms of images and story. To break the silence, indeed. It is not 'literally' so; it is an image, a chosen not an inevitable image – a representation, a set of words. The Big Bang was not 'big', it was sub-nuclear; and it was not a bang, because there was nothing to make or hear any noise. It is not exactly sophisticated language either – BANG. In fact, I could argue that the Genesis writers did a better job, but under the circumstances it will do. It will have to do.

It is not by chance that the discoverers – or reporters perhaps – of this initial singularity event used this set of images rather than another. Silence is absence, is nothingness. For the world to come into being silence has to be broken, ended, replaced. Even in this most modern of myths, this creation by random accident, without intention or purpose, without a Grand Narrative or a divine directive, we still apparently need an articulation of sound; a noise, a very specific and precise moment in which the silence is broken.

But, I began to think, there is something missing from these stories, with some version of which we were all brought up. Who is this 'we'? It is a very Western 'we'. This 'we', and I am part of it, lives within a primal myth about creative activity. Creation happens when silence is broken; when someone speaks, when the formless and meaningless void is pushed back by sound or word. This particular mythological *structure* in all its diverse forms has proved so successful in terms of colonisation, scientific description and prediction, political stability and military power that it is difficult to notice what a very unusual and odd myth it actually is. The Children of the Book, as Islam describes us – that is the heirs of the three world religions whose roots lie in the cultural drama of the Middle East – are unique. The invasive military and cultural success of both Christianity and Islam should not feel surprising. According to the foundation story of both religions, you have rights and powers over everything you name. By naming it you make it and what you make is yours. It is not by chance that the words 'author' and 'authority' are connected.

Indeed, the biblical version of this story, which I started above, immediately moves on to God giving Adam the right to name the beasts, 'and whatever the man called them, that was their name'. Thus, we are told quite precisely, Adam established his 'dominion' over them, by speaking, by naming, by breaking the silence of the wild. Having created Adam in his own image, God immediately gives him some of God's own particular creative power.

The idea of gift is important here. This is not a Prometheus story, a Loki story or a Babel story.

Prometheus, in Greek mythology, stole fire from Olympus to give to human beings. It is for this presumption that he is pinned for ever to a rock while birds of prey pluck out his liver, unless you believe with Shelley[6] that he was finally released from the gods' bondage by scientific rationalism.

Loki, in Norse mythology, is a strange figure, a god who is both childlike and wicked. He frequently stole treasures, material and spiritual, from other gods and let humans get hold of them. It is his constant mischief that puts the gods, and the virtuous heroes who will fight with them, at real risk of defeat at the final battle of Ragnarok.

In Genesis 11, the collapse of the Tower of Babel, and consequent 'confusion of tongues' (the division of human speech into mutually incomprehensible languages) was a punishment for overweening pride.

In this Genesis story, however, people do not steal the power of naming and making from God. God gives it to them freely, without cost. Language, and with it the power to name and dominate, exists before the Fall, not evil but good. Part of the initial Grand Plan. All the three religions concerned – Judaism, Christianity and Islam – are highly verbal narrative faiths, their adherents *speak* directly with their God, and their God speaks to them through texts as well as face to face. All three religions see the creative capacity of language as 'innocent' rather than arrogant; as divine rather than demonic.

Naturally a culture that sees power in speaking is likely to develop a creation-by-fiat story. And such a culture will obviously see silence as lack, silence as absence, not merely as negative, but as blank. Paul Davis, the cosmological physicist and writer, has argued that the question 'what happened before the Big Bang' is a non-question; it is the equivalent of asking, 'What is north of the North Pole?' There is nothing north of the North Pole; the whole point about the North Pole is that there is nothing north of it. The whole point about the biblical story and the Big Bang story is that there is no 'before'. There is nothing. In such a poetic-religious context it is not at all 'unreasonable' to argue that all silence *is* waiting to be broken. Once it is broken, the myth suggests, the human situation improves radically. Matter, order, intricacy, socialisation, language, representation, identity, the individual, ME can emerge and evolve. From here it follows, all too easily, that silence – since 'I' am the purpose, centre and goal of the whole project – was waiting to be broken, longs and desires to be broken and should, ought to, be broken. The word desires to break the silence; that is the word's job.

However, there is a problem. Although this myth has proved extremely effective, especially for those who wish to conquer the world and banish the darkness, or at least bring it firmly under control, it is not actually necessary or inevitable. The global power that this myth has given its owners obscures the fact that it is a very unusual, indeed very peculiar, story. There are lots of other creation myths, all of which get the show up and running without this primal fracture. The world is littered with them. Gods, Prime Movers and their newer scientific substitutes, create the origin of matter by ingesting, by brooding, by birthing, by killing, by withdrawing, by defecating, vomiting and masturbating, by fucking, by desiring, by self-mutilation and even quite simply by mistake.

Here is a Maori creation story:

In the beginning was Te Kore – the Nothing, the silence. The beginning was made from the nothing and the nothing existed for a long, long time. Then there was Te Po – the Great Night and it was dark and silent and it went on for a long, long time. In the silence and the dark there was nothing, and there were no eyes to see that there was nothing and no ears to hear that it was silent, not even the gods'.

Then Papa Tu Anuku, the earth, the mother, and Rangi Nui, the sky, the father, embraced and lay with each other and loved each other. Locked together, they lay so close in their love that there was no light between them; and they did not speak because there was no space between them. And though their love was rich and fruitful their offspring were trapped between them, sealed in the darkness so they could not grow and take shape and live. It was like this for a long, long time: *from the first division of time unto the tenth, and unto the hundredth, and unto the thousandth, all was darkness and silence.*

But at last the children of Papa and Rangi agreed that their parents must be separated so that they could live. Tane, who would be the father of the forests and whose strength was the strength of growth, lay down on his mother and he placed his feet against his father and, as slowly as a tree grows, he pushed and pushed until, with cries of pain and loss Papa and Rangi were separated. Light flowed into the space between them and their many offspring were uncovered and took shape and lived.

Later, Tane took some earth, red with the blood of his parents' severed love, and made a woman Hine Ahu One, the Earth-formed maiden. And she gave birth to a lovely daughter, Hine Titama, the Dawn Maiden – and the children of Hine Titama and her father Tane became men and women in the world, and for a long, long time death had no power over them.

Here is a Norse myth:

In the beginning was Ginnungagap – the void, the chasm. Because there was nothing there it was cold and dark in Ginnungagap. It was so cold and dark there that layers of everlasting salt ice formed in that dark void. Then Authumla, the Great Cow, came to lick at the ice and with her rough warm tongue she licked out the giant

Ymir. When he came out of the ice she fed him with her rich warm milk until he was grown up. Then alone, using the material from his feet and his armpits, he created the giants. From the giants, the Aesir and the Vanir, the gods of the north, were all descended.

After many generations Odin, Lord of the Aesir, and his brothers killed Ymir and used the pieces of his dismembered body to construct the worlds, with Yggdrasil, the world tree, at the centre. After the three worlds were built Odin went for a walk on the beach of Middle Earth with two of his colleagues – Lodur and Hoenir, the silent god. They found two trees on the shore – Askr and Embla – and they breathed humanity into them. Odin gave them life, Lodur gave them form and Hoenir the silent gave them understanding. That was the beginning of people and time and speech and song.

I love this story and find it hard not to push for some connection between Authumla and the idea of a 'mother tongue' – the first language we all learn. In honesty the connection is not there. Authumla is silent, animal, licking not speaking – she is before language. That is the point.

And here's an Egyptian version:

In the beginning was a limitless expanse of dark water – inert and sullen. The *benben*, the primal mound rose out of the water, as the islands and sandbars and banks rise out of the water when the Nile floods recede. And Atum, lord to the limits of the sky, created himself out of nothing and stood on the *benben*. Atum was the sun, the totality, containing within himself all potential, all being, the life force of every deity and every animate and inanimate thing yet to come. Atum stood alone on the *benben* while light flooded into the world; then he masturbated every thing into existence.

'No sky existed, no earth existed . . . I created on my own every being . . . my fist became my spouse . . . I copulated with my hand . . . I sneezed out Shu, I spat out Tefnut . . . and later Shu and

Tefnut gave birth to Geb and Nut . . . and Geb and Nut gave birth
to Osiris, Seth, Isis and Nephthys . . . and ultimately they produced
the population of this land.'

Well, this is how they told it in Heliopolis. But Egyptian mythology
is extremely complex – mainly because Upper and Lower Egypt
were originally two different countries and cultures, each with its
own mythological hierarchy, divinities and stories. It was essential
to pharaonic authority to synthesise these into a single narrative.
The seams still show. In Hermopolis in the distant south they
thought Atum a Johnny-come-lately. In the beginning, they said,
there was the dark water, the primeval matter. Within it there was
power: there were eight gods who appeared to be like frogs and
snakes, and who contained in themselves the four deep energies of
water, flood, darkness and dynamism. After a long time these forces
broke through the inertia of the water, and the energy of their col-
lision threw up the *benben*, not in the Delta but at Khemnu in the
south. Thoth, the ibis god, flew down bearing the cosmic egg,
which was laid on the *benben*. Atum was born from that egg and the
rest is history.

I have picked these stories more or less at random from an enormous selection: I could just as easily have told the story of Vishnu's
lotus, or Pangu and the Yellow Emperor, or Crow's flight, or
Uranus's castration. I have told them in my own words and to my
own ends as the old stories are always and necessarily told, though
I hope I have told them with respect. However, I am going to tell
one more here, because it comes from a mindset so utterly unlike
my own.

There are numerous examples of myths that express the sense
that there *was no beginning*. For the Cherokee, for example, the land
was always there. However, it was flat until the Great Eagle flew
over it, and each downbeat of his wings pushed in the valleys, and
each upbeat pulled up the mountains. But in the following Australian aboriginal myth, humans are themselves active in the creation,
which is continuous, ongoing and is a creation not by word, but by

acts. The *songlines*, the ancient sung poems of the Australian people, record the creation of meaning for the land, but they do not create it. It is the ancestors travelling, and the people replicating those journeys, that are the creative moments.

> In the beginning is the land and the land has no beginning – it is before the beginning and it is for ever, everlasting. But in the beginning the land was flat, dark and featureless. It had neither shape nor meaning. It had no places in it or on it, until the ancestors went travelling the paths of it. The ancestors did not create the land, but they created its meaning and shape. As they travelled they were creating the mountains and the hills and the rocks and the animals, people, places. They did not do it once and for all, they do it still – they do it in the walking and the dancing and the singing and the dreaming. The paths must be walked. The creation work must be done. The ancestors start the process, but the land is for ever and the creating of it is for ever. The ancestors are not gods – they die and go to be stars, or to be animals or to be mountains, but they are still walking the paths and creating the land. In the beginning, still, always, without beginning. The dreaming, singing, dancing, walking goes on and on, for ever.

It is hard to see what most of these stories have in common, except for the things they do not have in common with the verbally creative, highly intellectual, monotheist God of the Children of the Book. They represent a different way of seeing, a different way of telling about what can only be imagined. For example, the current story, the one we call the Big Bang, could equally well have been named the Tiny Egg, but it was not. And that is not accidental.

In all these stories, instead of having an abrupt singularity, a sharp-edged instant marking the beginning, a sound breaking the silence, the whole process is much more gradual. Time and silence come together in a slow, even piecemeal, creative drama. In one of the classical Greek versions the first god is actually called Kronos – Time.[7] Language here really is the 'foster-child of Silence and slow

Time'.[8] It comes into play late in the story, usually after emotions, divisions and growth. Silence is not broken by the word, not outwith the beginning, but an integral, if separate, part of the creation.

There are good reasons for taking note of these stories. The first is obvious – they give a positive and active role to silence itself, not a negation or lack or castration or something to be 'broken', but a creative, generative power. The Gnostics – who tended to think that the creation of matter was a shocking error, unimaginable to the true God who is pure spirit – narrated long genealogical creation myths. These start with a Primal Being as the beginning of all things, who gave rise to other beings (often called aeons or demiurges) by a process of emanation. These in their turn emanate further beings, and so on, each generation slightly further removed from pure spirit, until one of them, usually by mistake but sometimes through wilful error, creates matter and thence the world as we experience it. Valentinus, one of the most important of the Christian Gnostics of the second century, names silence as one of the active demi-urges who (tragically from the point of view of Gnostic philosophy) made the material world. Silence is a god, or at least a divine force, herself (and not the feckless one who finally created the world – that was Nous – intelligence). It is rare for silence to be personified in this way; even the medieval Christian Church, which loved to make physical representations of most abstract qualities, virtues and vices (Justice with her blindfold and scales, for example), does not seem to have given silence a human face.[9]

In a real sense, these sorts of creation stories better correspond to our contemporary knowledge of evolution and the scientific account of the 'creation' of the universe, and particularly of our species, than the God (or other force) who creates *ex nihilo* by suddenly breaking the silence. We know, now, of evolution's slow, inexorable, chancy, silent movement through vast fields of time. We see both intricacy and accident in our own making and in the making of the world around us. If, in our imaginations, we could really accept the information from evolution and from astrophysics, we might find that the most complex genealogies of the gods and their creative methods were actually less alien than the notion of humanity popping up, on a single verbal command, sophisticated in all matters except fashion sense.

Perhaps even more important, since it is myth – the poetry of the soul – that I was looking at here, these complex, convoluted stories of division and change and mixed motives and chance feel closer to our experience of our own 'creation' as individuals. Despite our potent ideas about our unalienable human rights, inherent from birth, we tend to *experience* ourselves as individuals in the process of becoming, rather than as finished and fixed, all complete when our parents picked out our names. The moment of our emerging, becoming, the moment of our creation as fully rounded autonomous selves remains blurred and gradual: a journey from infancy towards self-hood.

Moreover, at least since the romantic revival of the eighteenth century, we have accepted that *human* creative activity requires time and effort, and a withdrawing from the social bustle. Creative individuals – in both arts and sciences – are supposed to be detached, to withdraw into a silent introspection and self-examination, which is not simply about practice and experiment, but somehow a brooding process, which gives birth to new ideas or creative works. All myths are complex and cannot be interpreted too literally, but it seems curious to me that the three monotheistic religions want to claim *both* that we are 'made in the image of God' and that God creates in a radically different way from the way we create. George Steiner has suggested that all artists set themselves up as 'rival gods' – they are in creative competition with God.[10] Certainly we assign a rival *method* to them. God creates by breaking the silence in a single abrupt instant – God *speaks*. But when we mythologise ourselves as creators we seem to accept that silence plays an indispensable part in the process.

So when we think of silence as a lack, something that needs to be broken in order to let in life and meaning, we must not forget that this is a singular, though powerful, viewpoint. It is not 'natural', obvious or inevitable. There are indeed many creation stories that do not see a violent breaking of silence by the voice of God or any other force as either necessary or desirable. And there are some that see silence itself as a creative agent, an active power, a vital ingredient.

There is, of course, a huge, probably unanswerable question about *why* different cultures come up with different sorts of creation stories. But the God who creates everything from nothing by speaking is a desert God. The silence of the desert has a horror to it, as well as, born of the horror, a deep and joyful beauty. The desert is vast, cruel and very silent. Perhaps there is an inevitable attraction to a God who speaks – to creation through sound.

But there has to be a story to explain why we came up with this sort of mythology and particularly why we hold to it so tightly that even the most rational scientific minds of the secular twentieth century reverted to it apparently subconsciously and very illogically when they wanted a name for a radically new narrative of creation – the Big Bang. This looks like fear to me and I sense that the fear of silence is very deeply embedded in the Western psyche. I began to get extremely curious about why we are frightened, where the fear comes from. I think there is a plausible story that goes something like this:

Once upon a time, almost at the very beginning, there was the Great Chthonic Terror.* No one, back in these earliest human societies, has time to worry about abstractions; at this point there is a far more pressing question. Actually, there are *two* pressing questions that are quite closely linked. One of them (the other of them) is 'Are we sure? How can we be sure that we aren't animals?' And

---

* Chthonic is a word that deserves wider use. It is derived from the Greek *khthōn* (earth; pertaining to the Earth; earthy). It is one of several Greek words for 'earth'; it typically refers to the interior of the soil, rather than the living surface of the land (Gaia) or the land as territory (*khora*). It is usually restricted to discussions of Greek religion, although Jung uses it in the sense that I am here. Essentially it carries a very similar meaning to 'primitive' but without any pejorative associations.

one of the mythological ways we can answer this is by speaking – language is what humans have, and what by definition animals do not have. But the first pressing question is simple, 'How do we stay alive?'

The Great Chthonic Terror is that the dark may swallow the light, may gobble it up, terminate or destroy it. That the night will conquer the day; that the sun will not rise, that the fires will go out, that the cold will triumph; and we will all be dead. Light is life; dark is death. This is not symbolic at all; this is actual and biological.

Everything we can do to allay the Terror, to assist, persuade, seduce, propitiate, cajole, reward or bully the sun, which, for all its power, seems oddly fragile and recalcitrant, we must do and we will do. Anthropologically 'sun encouragement' rituals are as nearly universal as anything is, from the Aztecs to Beltane. They are gruesome, expensive and ruthless. They are creative, beautiful and symbol-rich.

What is more, they *work*. Every morning the sun rises; and further north, where it matters more, every spring the sun returns.

Though, interestingly, the doubt remains and the colder the terrain the deeper the doubt. The Vikings were never entirely confident: Norse mythology is the only theistic theology I know of where the issue remains in serious peril. The gods will go out to fight at Ragnarok. They will do their best, for themselves, for humans and for the light; but Baldur the Beautiful is dead and we do not know if they or the forces of the dark will triumph. Even if the gods do win, it will be at great loss and with a tragic diminishment (like the Hobbits at the end of *The Lord of the Rings*). The Terror is fobbed off but never defeated; the issue remains in the balance. I think this may be why Viking culture is the only one I have so far encountered that has never valorised, desired, or found any positive cultural space for silence. Valhalla is also the *noisiest* heaven I have ever come across, no everlasting rest and sweet music for the heroic Norsemen; their dream is of drunken rioting and a great deal of crashing and banging.

For most cultures, though, the magic works – and since we worked the magic we feel pretty clever (with, it must be said, some considerable justification). We have won. The sun rises; the spring comes, the ice melts, the rivers flood the fertile plains. And eventually we feel smart enough and secure enough to invent 'science', in the sense of non-theological, non-magical rules, to explain why the sun has not been swallowed up and – equally important – why it is *not going to be* swallowed up tomorrow. This is not only comforting; it is also an immense saving of energy, time and expense. It is a massive victory – it really is. *Our* rules – our *own* laws, not the gods', not the light's, ours – enshrined in *language*. Our language – not the animals' – keeps the sun (the light, life, food, future, the species, the world) alive.

Now what happens? What always happens when we try to suppress real fears without acknowledging them. The Terror appears somewhere different; it shifts, in language, as language always does, from the material to the abstract; from the present actual to the symbolic. Now the Terror turns up elsewhere.

(Of course, it is possible that the psychoanalytic story is true, and all this is repressed Oedipal stuff really – will daddy's laws swallow up mummy's love? Will mummy's chaos gobble down daddy's order? But, frankly, I doubt it.)

Now the abstract terror is that silence will gobble up (down) the words – will overwhelm the meaning, reinsert the void and the light will go out and we will all be dead; and the dead are very silent. By now we've given up magic so we can't use ritual to force language into better health, as we once did with the sun. We need some new strategy. Needless to say we think of rather a crafty one: we deny the reality of silence, we reduce it to a lack or absence and make it powerless. We say that silence 'needs' – and therefore is waiting – to be broken: like a horse that must be 'broken in'. But we are still frightened. And the impending ecological disaster deepens our fear that one day the science will not work, the language will break down and the light will go out. We are terrified of silence, so we encounter it as seldom as possible, even if this means losing experiences we know to be good ones, like children wandering alone or unsupervised in the countryside. We say that silence is a lack of something, a negative state. We deny the power and meaning of silence. We are terrified of silence and so we banish it from our lives.

Before I went to Weardale I did not notice the noise in public places, but as soon as I was experiencing periods of silence I also became increasingly overstimulated by noise. Before I had fully realised this I went one day to the Metro Centre in Gateshead to buy a waste-paper basket; something I needed, though not urgently, something that was not very important and which I could comfortably afford to buy – so it was not the shopping itself that led to the subsequent distress. Shopping malls are more or less designed to be noise boxes – they tend to have a great number of smooth hard surfaces, off which sound waves bounce energetically; they have roofs through which the sound waves cannot pass and are projected back like echoes; many of the shops play background music, which spills out into the passageways; electronic announcements blare out over the continual hubbub and there are a great number of people often in small groups. I very quickly found it extremely stressful – it caused me actual physical discomfort, an escalating feeling of panic and exhaustion. I was entirely unable to purchase anything at all and after less than an hour had to leave in tears.

It took me a little while to work out what was happening. I have never suffered from either agoraphobia or claustrophobia, to which on investigation the symptoms seemed quite close, and subsequently do not seem to have developed either. I am convinced that it was aural overstimulation – and it has not got better. Now I know what it is I can manage it well enough, but going to cities, to large parties, or to any place where there are a significant number of loud, overlapping but different sounds remains stressful and tiring at best. I had lived in London for years and had never noticed let alone been distressed by the noise, but now I do find it nearly intolerable; when I go to towns I sleep badly, I drink too much alcohol and I feel physically depleted very quickly. Literally millions of people live in a constantly noisy environment the whole time: it must be unhealthy, and to me at least provides part of an explanation of the tension and violence and the grim, closed-down faces that you see on the streets. The extensive use of personal stereos to deliver more freely chosen sounds directly into ears while cutting off the noise of the environment makes sense in this context, although of course what it actually delivers is more sound – noisy earplugs.

This is not merely subjective. There is good evidence now that exposure to excessive noise has damaging physiological and psychological effects, including hypertension, aggression, insomnia, high stress levels, tinnitus and hearing loss; and these in themselves can lead to other health problems, like cardiovascular diseases. The origins of the word 'noise' are uncertain but two of the suggested derivations are from *nausea* (the Latin for sickness) and *noxious* (the Latin for harmful).[11] I have come to believe that we are at risk of underestimating the danger: lower levels of sound, particularly when it is sustained and out of our control, seem to have unnoticed but nasty effects. Noise may be damaging even when we are not experiencing it as excessive.

Like other forms of environmental pollution, this is a relatively recent problem. The more densely inhabited any given area is the more noisy it inevitably is; it is impossible for a human being to move without making some sound. The more human beings there are in any one place the more noise there will be. Over the last 200 years the population of Europe has increased enormously, but the rural population has declined radically and continues to do so: more people occupy less space and are therefore subject to more noise than would have been imaginable in the eighteenth century. This shift is continuing still: the population of the Scottish islands, for example, has fallen a further 3 per cent in the last decade.[12] Moreover, the more hard flat surfaces and the less horizontal space there is the more any noise will increase. One of the points that Henry Mayhew, the nineteenth-century journalist and sociologist, made in his most famous book, *London Labour and the London Poor*, is how damaging intellectually and morally the dense population, and the constant hubbub that it inevitably generated, was to the urban poor; the effect was compounded because people who had worked alone or in small units outside in agricultural labour were now transferred to the immensely loud, steam-powered factories of the Industrial Revolution. For extremely long periods of the day more and more people worked in the enclosed spaces and hellish din of industrial units and mines.

If the volume of ambient sound increased in the nineteenth century because of urbanisation and industrialisation, in the twentieth century yet more noise arose as a side effect of technology, and indeed of increasing prosperity. Horses make more noise than feet; cars and trains make more noise than horses; and aeroplanes make more noise than any of these. Almost every labour-saving device – vacuum cleaners, refrigerators, liquidisers, central heating and air conditioning, computers, even hair dryers – makes more noise than the manual version of the task that it replaced. Radios, stereo sound systems and television – along with other recreational devices – also add volume. Our homes may be more private than they were but they are not quieter. Above all, communication technology has, in increasing human contact, decreased the amount of silence around us. The ubiquitous mobile phone (117 per cent of the population of the UK own one) is the latest form of instant communication.

In the Middle Ages Christian scholastics argued that the devil's basic strategy was to bring human beings to a point where they are never alone with their God, nor ever attentively face to face with another human being. In the Christian tradition Satan has always been hampered by her inability to create anything new – she lacks both imagination and artistry. The mobile phone, then, seems to me to represent a major breakthrough for the powers of hell – it is a new thing, which allows the devil to take a significant step forward in her grand design. With a mobile, a person is never alone and is never entirely attentive to someone else. What is entirely brilliant about it from the demonic perspective is that so many people have been persuaded that this is not something pleasurable (a free choice) but something necessary. Of course, I am fully aware that mobile phones have radically improved working conditions for some people – but oddly enough this is used in peculiar ways. Doctors, for example, have told me how much easier a mobile makes their house calls, without apparently noticing that at the very moment this ease was granted them they gave up making house calls at all.

In *The Screwtape Letters* C. S. Lewis, the Christian apologist now best known for his children's books about Narnia, has his devil write:

> Music and silence – how I detest them both! How thankful we should be that ever since Our Father entered Hell . . . no square inch of infernal space and no moment of infernal time has been surrendered to either of those abominable forces, but all has been occupied with Noise – Noise, the grand dynamism, the audible expression of all that is exultant, ruthless and virile – Noise which alone defends us from silly qualms, despairing scruples and impossible desires. We will make the whole universe a noise in the end. We have already made great strides in this direction as regards the Earth. The melodies and silences of Heaven will be shouted down in the end.[13]

This ambition seems very nearly to have been achieved. I believe it has psychological consequences. In 1985 Ernest Gellner, the philosopher and sociologist, commented, 'Our environment is now made up basically of our relationships with others.'[14] And in *The School for Genius* Anthony Storr developed this notion:

> The burden of value with which we are at present loading interpersonal relationships is too heavy for those fragile craft to carry . . . love and friendship are, of course, an important part of what makes life worthwhile. But they are not the only source of happiness.[15]

This idea, that we feel ourselves to be happy and fulfilled only when we are interacting with other people, creates a dissonance with the equally popular mythology that stresses individual autonomy and personal 'rights'. If I need interpersonal relationships and I have a right to what I need, it is obviously very difficult to have relationships of genuine self-giving or even of equality. However, this problem is not addressed, is indeed concealed, within popular culture. The consequence of this, almost inevitably, is the creation of an increasing number of lightweight relationships – relationships that appear to connect people, but are not vulnerable to the requirements of love, and therefore tend to lack endurance and discipline. The overstimulation, of which noise is a major factor, of modern society has an addictive quality – the more stimulation and novelty you get, the more you feel you need.

Incessant noise covers up the thinness of relationships as well as making silence appear dangerous and threatening. The nervous chatter that is produced to cover over even brief periods of silence within a group is one manifestation of this. A more alarming one is the move away from honouring disaster by silence to celebrating the event with applause. What on earth is going on when groups of people gather to cheer and clap as a response to sudden or shocking deaths, as a crowd of strangers did outside Liverpool Cathedral at Rhys Jones's funeral? It is a serious tragedy that an eleven-year-old should be shot dead on the street. What are we celebrating; why are we not silenced?

Noisy applause replacing silence as a way of marking these sorts of events is, moreover, a break with a very ancient tradition and one that seems to occur in a wide range of cultures. The traditional response to awe, positive or negative, has been silence. In the Apocalypse the whole of heaven falls silent 'for one little hour' before the mystical Lamb can 'break the seal' which will bring on the judgement day.[16] This idea seems to have been derived from the poetry of the psalms – 'The Lord is in his holy temple; let all the earth keep silent before him,' or, 'Be silent all flesh before the Lord; for he has roused himself from his holy

dwelling' – and from classical Greek custom. Philip Howard out-
lined the history:

> Silence has been the ultimate human response to enormity. A
> Munch *Scream* may be the initial response to tragedy, but silence is
> the awe for something too deep for words. The Romans called the
> inspiration for such otherworldly feeling *numen* [hence 'numinous'].
> The priests of ancient Greece called on their citizens to keep silence
> in the presence of tragedy or disaster . . . the awesome ceremony
> has survived ever since.[17]

Awestruck and dumbstruck (struck dumb, and dumbfounded are
similar terms) are almost synonymous.

Oddly, in the face of the increasing noise, the two-minute silence
on Remembrance Sunday is one of the very few remaining acts of
social ritual that commands wide support in Britain, and this annual
ceremony seems to be increasingly observed, with about 75 per
cent of the population participating.

The organised minutes of public silence in honour of the war
dead and more recently of other groups has a complicated history,
with various different countries and individuals claiming to have
invented it. France was probably the first country to have a national
annual period of silence after the First World War, although in
1912 large parts of the USA kept a ceremonial silence to mourn
the sinking of the *Titanic* and the *Maine*, while the Portuguese
Senate kept a ten-minute silence on the death of Rio Branco – the
Minister for Foreign Affairs of Brazil. The British silence, originally
on Armistice Day and subsequently on the Sunday nearest to 11
November, began in 1919 after a formal appeal by George V,
through the pages of *The Times*. The foreign ministers of the EU
asked for a three-minute silence following the destruction of the
Twin Towers, a curious example of a war memorial occurring
before a war. I cannot help but feel that such a silence is both more
appropriate and more meaningful than inevitably artificial
cheering.

Silence, even as an expression of awe, is becoming uncomfortable. We are asked to be silent less and less; churches and public libraries are no longer regarded as places where silence is appropriate, or even more simply polite. Even the acceptable length of silence in radio programmes is being reduced. Silence is not experienced as refreshing or as assisting concentration, but as threatening and disturbing.

Perhaps it is not surprising, then, that in 1994 the Criminal Justice and Public Order Act undermined a very specific silence: the right of a person accused of a crime not to answer questions, nor to have prejudicial inference drawn from such a silence. Although this right was only codified in statute law in 1912, it is a very ancient Common Law provision – probably emerging from the seventeenth-century protests against the Star Chamber and High Commissions, which could compel (by torture) the accused to answer questions without telling them what they had been charged with. This right to silence is based on a number of legal principles. People were held to have a 'natural duty' of self-preservation and therefore could not be 'bound to accuse themselves'. In law people must be treated as innocent until proven guilty; it is not their job, as it were, to demonstrate their innocence – it is the prosecution's duty to prove their guilt. Such ideas must have been connected to, or at least have drawn force from, the fact that at his trial Jesus declined to answer questions: 'he was silent and gave no answer'.[18] The contemporary erosion of this right suggests to me that, consciously or unconsciously, silence is perceived as sinister, dishonest and contemptuous. It must not be permitted or encouraged.

Yet we know historically and emotionally that silence as resistance can have a bone-shaking power – as anyone who has had to deal with a sulking teenager does not need telling. Silent protest, the freedom not to speak, to challenge the supposedly rational speakers, to give no ground, to refuse to enter the arena, is not simply negative; it is an occupation of space with a symbolic and powerful meaning. The right to freedom of expression – the right to speak out and be heard – loses meaning if it separates itself too far from the parallel right to be silent.

Nonetheless, despite the rising tide of noise, there are some real pools of silence embedded even in the noisiest places and I began to search them out and test them, starting with what was in easy reach of Weardale. One of the most obvious places to begin was with religiously inspired silences.

It was by lucky chance that there was a Zen monastery less than twenty miles from Weatherhill and by an even luckier chance that I discovered this. I will always think of Throstlehole with gratitude as well as affection; the monks were extraordinarily generous and hospitable, open to explaining their own faith tradition, while never probing into mine, just offering the resources of their evening meditation whenever I wanted to come and sit with them.

Zen is a form of Buddhism which emerged during the trans-mission of Buddhist teaching from India to China, although its principal development was in Japan and Korea. Part of Zen philosophy is that it is impossible to describe Zen; but individuals have tried. In the early twelfth century a seminal work, *Ts'u-t'ing shih-yuan*, attributed this description of Zen to the fifth-century master, Bodhidharma:

> A special transmission outside the scriptures,
> Not founded on words and letters;
> By pointing directly to mind
> It allows one to penetrate the nature of things
> To attain the Buddha-nature.[19]

In *Gödel, Escher, Bach: An Eternal Golden Braid* Douglas Hofstadter attempts a more modern description:

> Zen is intellectual quicksand – anarchy, darkness, meaninglessness, chaos. It is tantalizing and infuriating. And yet it is humorous, refreshing, enticing . . . one of the basic tenets of Zen Buddhism is that there is no way to characterize what Zen is. No matter what

verbal space you try to enclose Zen in it resists and spills over . . . In general, the Zen attitude is that words and truth are incompatible, or at least that no words can capture truth.[20]

If words and truth are incompatible then you are better off not even trying to articulate your understanding of truth in language, but to explore other less logical* routes to realisation. The concept that everything is absolutely one allowed Zen to seek out many paths to enlightenment and this may account for its enormous cultural impact, since architecture, and especially landscape gardening, together with calligraphy and painting and even 'flower arranging', *ikebana*, are seen as valid ways of seeking an end to all dualities. But at the heart of Zen practice is a rigorously disciplined method of meditation, *zazen* (derived from the Japanese words for 'sitting' and 'absorption').

It was into this daily practice that the monks at Throstlehole made me so welcome: I would go to their evening *zazen*, which was entirely silent, and their silence was extraordinarily potent, rich. Whenever I was there, there were at least forty people present. Everyone sits facing the wall (or as it happens rows of lockers, because the *dojo*, or meditation hall, is also the communal dormitory for the novices who sleep on the floor. So other people are there, but because you do not see or hear them, they are present in a rather strange way. Each person brings their own *zafu* (cushion) into *zazen* with them, so there is nothing redundant or cluttered. The *dojo* is vast and airy, high-roofed, so it feels spacious even when there are a lot of people in it. The monastery is rural, isolated, surrounded first by its own garden and beyond that by the Cumbrian hill country – there is a silent ambience. Everything external is set up for good silence. Within the monastery itself there was always a strong flow of energy, silent energy; people seemed purposeful and engaged without ever seeming *busy*. The long hours of

---

* 'Logical' derives from the Greek *logos*, which means 'word'. Logical thinking means thinking amenable to the conscious processes of language.

silent meditation flowed out into a gentle orderliness. As a neophyte silence practitioner I cannot say how supportive and enriching and moving I found this embracing, generous silence, and how much it has informed and shaped my own, profoundly Christian practice: at the most superficial level I now meditate sitting on the round black Buddhist *zafu*.*

Zen silence is an *oppositional* silence. You are silent in order to escape from the self, and the dualisms of the world, to 'protest' against the veils of illusion and transcend them. Zen philosophy, and *zazen* as the practical working out of that philosophy, sees all the differentiations of the world as delusion. As Hofstadter explains it:

> At the core of dualism are words – just plain words. The use of words is inherently dualistic, since each word represents, quite obviously, a conceptual category. Therefore a major part of Zen is the fight against reliance on words.[21]

The famously confusing Zen Koans are *meant* to confuse. Being bewildered allows the mind to operate non-logically and getting outside logical systems allows you to make the leap to enlightenment. Zen is profoundly anti-dualist, far more so than any Western philosophy. It urges people to stop categorising – there is no I/thou; no here/there; no differentiation, no categorisation; no autonomous self – there is only Buddha-nature and all the rest is illusion. Words create categories.

> What is the way? asked a curious monk.
> It is right before your eyes, said the master.
> Why do I not see it for myself?
> Because you are thinking of yourself.
> What about you? Do you see it?
> So long as you see double, saying 'I don't' and 'you do', and so on,

---

* There is an amusing irony here. When I first started meditating seriously I used to sit not on a *zafu* but on one volume of the Compact Edition of the *Oxford English Dictionary*. Same colour, same height, but full of words!

your eyes are clouded, said the master.

When there is neither 'I' nor 'You', can one see it?

When there is neither 'I' nor 'You', who is the one that wants to see it?[22]

During that summer for similar motives I also started to attend Quaker meetings. At first sight the externals could not have been more different from Throstlehole. The Meeting I attended in Durham took place in a slightly grotty 'community hall' that lacked both the beauty and the glamour of the *dojo* – and we sat in a dowdy circle on stacking chairs. But in another sense Quaker Meeting is not unlike *zazen*, although Quakers come into silence for the silent meeting while the Zen monks bring their existing silence into meditation. The Quakers – or the Religious Society of Friends, as they are more properly called – are probably most famous in Britain for their commitment to pacifism and for the radical lead they have given since the seventeenth century in various forms of social work – the abolition of slavery, women's suffrage, prison reform and mental health care. But at the heart of Quaker life is the Meeting for Worship and this is primarily silent – or, rather, a meeting in which any words emerge from silence. The modern Quaker, Pierre Lacout, describes the silence of the Meeting thus:

> In silence which is active, the Inner Light begins to glow – a tiny spark. For the flame to be kindled and to grow, subtle argument and the clamour of our emotions must be stilled. It is by an attention full of love that we enable the Inner Light to blaze and illuminate our dwelling and to make of our whole being a source from which this Light may shine out.
>
> Words must be purified in a redemptive silence if they are to bear the message of peace. The right to speak is a call to the duty of listening. Speech has no meaning unless there are attentive minds and silent hearts. Silence is the welcoming acceptance of the other. The word born of silence must be received in silence.[23]

Theologically what Zen Buddhism and the Friends share in common is a belief that we contain 'enlightenment' (Zen) or the 'Inner Light', the 'divine spark' (Quakerism), within ourselves and that all external definitions and codes – dogma, rituals, conventions, language itself – will only get in the way of dissolving the barriers between us and the infinite. But the differences are in fact profound.

Quakerism has its roots in the turbulent religious politics and political religion of the English seventeenth century. Initially Quakers found themselves in trouble not only because they would not serve in the armed forces, take oaths or pay tithes (a form of taxation to support the established Church), but because they would not show respect for outer forms – for example, they refused to 'doff their hats' in the presence of a social superior or legally constituted authority; worse still, they upheld the equality of women, who were able to speak, travel and bear witness equally with men. Within the Society itself there was no leadership, no paid or trained ministers, no credal formularies and no set rituals. Quakers gather together and sit in *collective* silence seeking to become 'gathered' – it is a gathered meeting, where hearts and minds are united beyond words, that can discern the fullness of truth. A Quaker friend described his experience of Meeting for Worship:

Not sure what I think of 'a gathered meeting' – it changes as I continue to attend – it started off as a quite private experience with me meditating and then praying, but amongst people. And when people ministered [spoke out in the meeting] it felt like an interruption that I couldn't assimilate and had to make some effort not to be annoyed by before I returned to my private experience. But recently it's begun to feel more seamless and I'm able to listen to people without feeling disrupted in what I was doing even if they don't 'speak to my condition'. I can see how it's all reflective of my default settings with regard to other people and I expect other people's experience must be quite different. There are similarities to

the appeal of scuba diving – another private experience in the essential vicinity of other people . . . Is one person's gathered meeting
another person's fragmented one? And how do you know?
Sometimes I've felt the room is 'gathered' and then someone ministers with obvious out-on-a-limb anxiety, which I can sometimes
incorporate and continue in being gathered, but other times kicks
me out of that collective feeling into a sense of us being a bunch of
unconnected strangers sitting in a room. A lot of times people minister in rather obvious preaching-to-the-converted kinds of ways
(especially about the Iraq war). But is being gathered about sameness
of opinion? Isn't true gatheredness about being able to articulate and
bridge difference? Perhaps both gatheredness and fragmentation are
true at once and the meeting is an attempt to cultivate the former.[24]

I enjoyed going to Meeting, especially once I discovered the
older Quaker places of worship, often small, where 300 years of
silence are gathered in buildings marked by simplicity and a lack of
decoration. There was an earnestness and simplicity in Quakers
that touched me, and I liked the sense of being linked back into a
long radical history; in an odd way Meeting reminded me of early
women's liberation consciousness-raising groups – but without any
of the din. I wonder retrospectively if we would have done better
to 'gather' ourselves in silence rather than 'speaking out'. It led me
to question what Evelyn Underhill, the twentieth-century English
writer on mysticism, *meant* when she said that the Quaker 'sacrament
of silence' or 'communal mysticism' has offered us 'nothing, no
new understanding of the human soul'.[25] Underhill can only see
mystical experience as essentially and absolutely individual and
'private'. I would have agreed with her, I suspect, before I had
experienced Quaker Meetings and seen that you *can* run an international organisation for 300 years without a hierarchy; that out of
shared silence a shared voice can emerge; that shared listening to
the spirit leads to social action, especially for peace. The Quakers
offer me at least a profoundly optimistic 'new understanding of the
human soul' – a positive value for silence.

However, this sort of silence is quite different in its intention from Zen silence. Quakers are profoundly egalitarian: the Spirit may speak through anyone and therefore the silence of the Meeting for Worship is a *listening* silence. This is indeed 'a silence that is waiting to be broken'. Because of the Friends' understanding of the Inner Light there is no difference between an authentic breaking of silence from within an individual and the direct voice of God, but the silence is there to enable hearing, and hearing is meant to enable Quakers to 'speak the truth in love'.

At both Throstlehole and at Quaker Meetings I found a silence that felt deeply liberating and spacious, but I know had a certain detachment because intellectually I do not believe in the underlying principles of either. However, when I went on Christian retreats I began to find the silence rather thin. Perhaps this was simply the name – retreat. I did not want to retreat from anything, but to move forward. Perhaps life already had enough silence in it for me not to need the rather oddly constructed silence of the monastic guest house. I found, even on private retreats, that however silent the monks or nuns may be, the retreatants were outsiders. The silence here was being given to us as a gift that we could somehow *use* when we returned to the noisy world, rather than being an invitation to help create the silence. Christian retreats really do seem to treat silence as an absence of sound – albeit a more positive rather than a purely negative one.

I did try various forms of formal retreat over those three years but I came to feel that I got a better understanding of Christian silence by reading about it than by going on retreat. Thomas Merton's *The Seven Storey Mountain* describes in some detail the Trappist vision of silence in community. Trappists are a Roman Catholic religious order, growing out of a reform of the Benedictine rule, who live in extreme silence and austerity. Trappists are different from other silent orders like the Carmelites, or Carthusians: these orders emphasise their eremitic (hermit, solitary) nature; their communities are formed *functionally* to make being hermits easier and safer. Trappists, on the other hand, see community as an essential part of their lifestyle. Carthusian novices, when they enter, are installed in their cells; Benedictine monks are installed literally – they are given a stall, a seat in the choir. This difference, like most of the practices of the older religious orders, is saturated with symbolic meaning.

Unlike Zen or Quaker silence, Trappist silence is about discipline. Its intention is to enable an individual to live 'as perfectly as possible the Rule and Spirit of St Benedict – obedience, humility, work, prayer, simplicity, the love of Christ'. The community and the silence are two slightly different disciplines of *love*. The community is moreover a sign of mutual dependence, and as such is a corporate responsibility. This is not a silence that is waiting to be broken, like Quaker silence, but waiting to be completed.

Strangely enough Christian churches have never been seen as primarily silent places: the Victorian hush from which we are still emerging seems to have been a brief and short-lived exception. As late as the 1770s boys were still playing skittles unreproved in the aisles of Westminster Abbey.[26] Very occasionally I would find deep pools of silence, usually in small country churches. When I found myself exhausted and overstimulated in a city I could seldom take silent refuge in churches – they were either locked up or, if more famous, filled with tourists, restless and noisy. One day, though, I discovered a new and for me unexpected sanctuary. I went to the Tate Modern and by chance found myself in the dim light of Room 3, where Rothko's Seagram paintings hang: nine huge pulsating dense pools of silent energy.

Rothko himself said the paintings were designed for 'contemplation' and Simon Schama has described them as 'A space that might be where we came from or where we will end up. They're not meant to keep us out, but to embrace us.' For me, that hot nervy afternoon, they were silence made visible; I was shaken by their power and their fierce dark beauty. This was something new for me, and I have become increasingly interested in painting and sculpture. The visual arts are obviously silent in a way that literature and music can never be, although there is a great deal of 'noisy art' around – from the energetic business of medieval Christian narrative painting through to contemporary installation art. Nonetheless I began to look for and find silence in both traditional and contemporary art: the serene tender gaze of Raphael's *Madonna del Granduca*; the startling moment of metamorphosis of Bernini's *Daphne and Apollo* – where the still rigour of marble holds transformation steady for a silent moment; Turner's sunsets; Andy Goldsworthy's *Springing Arches*, leaping with silent joy across the Border hills of Scotland. These were all images that used silence itself as part of the work and generated silence in me. In all these, and many others, the silence seems to pour out of the work into the space around it. I came to believe that my silence was making my seeing more sensitive.

But more than any of these silences I found myself thinking about and experimenting with reading. Reading is a rare activity in that it is normally regarded as both silent and entirely positive. When I tried to describe my life to people they would often say, 'I expect you read a lot' and obviously feel reassured. But when I started to think about reading, I found myself in the presence of something very mysterious. Is reading silent in any sensible understanding of that word? Does it deepen the silence around us or break it up? When we read are we listening to the author, conversing with the author, or are we looking more directly into the author's mind, seeing the author's thoughts, rather than hearing her voice? How might one define silence in relation to the written, as opposed to the spoken, word?

I realised that the ambiguity I pointed out in the meaning of the word 'silence' itself became crucial, though tricky, here. If you take the first OED definition and understand silence as an absence of *language* then simply there is and can be no silence on a printed page, because it is made up entirely of language. If, on the other hand, you take the second definition, that silence is an absence of *sound*, then written language is silent, because whatever else it does, a printed page of text does not make any sound.

What does it mean to say that a blank piece of paper is 'more silent' than one with writing on it? Or with writing in a script that the person looking at it cannot decode at all; for me that would include cuneiform, hieroglyphics, Chinese ideograms or Cyrillic.

I began to speculate that it might be easier to understand written-and-read English as a different language from spoken-and-heard English. Reading, like British Sign Language, is a hand–eye language not a mouth–ear language, even though they start from the same place, both in the large historical perspective and in individual readers. Beginners tend to read 'aloud' or at least moving their lips, full 'reading competence' is usually judged by the ability to read silently. As a person learns to read fluently the connection between the arbitrary black marks on the page and aural language evaporates and practised readers absorb meaning from texts entirely visually, as can now be neurologically proven. Spoken English and written English (for example) have a different vocabulary and a different grammar as well as a different function. They generate different genres of literature – the distinction between storytelling and fiction writing is now fully recognised; 'performance poetry' is understood as a different form from written poetry. These differences are extensive, though usually invisible.

If the page 'speaks', it is not silent, but everyone who can do it knows that reading silently feels *different* from reading aloud or being read to. This is treated as so normal now that it comes as a surprise to discover that it was not always like this. Until the fourth century everyone who read, read aloud.

Andthescripttheyreadinthewestwaswrittenwithoutthewordbreaksinasinglestreamofphonemesorlettersperfectlyreplicatingspeechitiscalledscriptacontinuaithadnopunctuation.

(And the script they read in the West was written without the word breaks – in a single stream of phonemes, or letters, perfectly replicating speech. It is called *scripta continua*. It had no punctuation.)

Around 385 Ambrose, Bishop of Milan, learned to read silently. The young Augustine saw him do it, recorded this and was immensely influenced by it.

Before his conversion Augustine was a teacher of philosophy and rhetoric. Along with his contemporaries, he followed Aristotle and saw writing as 'signs of sounds'. He was explicit about this: 'When a word is written it makes a sign to the eyes whereby that which pertains to the ears enters the mind.' It is in this context that we have to see Augustine's account of Ambrose reading.

In 385 Augustine was thirty-one. He was very brilliant, very troubled and highly sensitive. He ran away from home in North Africa and went to Rome, where he was laughed at for his provincial accent – for his speaking voice – and was unable to make a living as an independent teacher, so he accepted a government post in Milan. Once there, he went to call on Ambrose who, as well as being the bishop, was a friend of his mother.

> I could not ask him what I would when I would, being shut out both from his ear and speech by multitudes of busy people whose weaknesses he served. When – which wasn't often – he was not taken up with them . . . he was refreshing his mind by reading. But when he was reading his eye glided over the pages, and his heart searched out the sense, but his voice and tongue were at rest. He never read aloud.[27]

Clearly this way of reading was a novelty and a bit of a puzzle to Augustine. It is the first explicit description of someone reading silently (without moving his lips). There has of course been considerable debate about whether Ambrose was the very first person ever to do this[28] but I am persuaded, partly by Augustine's *Confessions* themselves and partly because in 349, less than half a century before Augustine watched Ambrose reading, Cyril of Jerusalem exhorted the women in his congregation to read during gaps in the ceremonies, 'but quietly, so although the lips speak no other ears may hear what they say'. Following Paul's exhortation

that women should not speak during worship[29] there was considerable anxiety in early Christianity about keeping women *silent* in
church. I cannot help but feel that if silent reading had been known
to him, Cyril would have urged it upon them.

We know that Augustine himself quickly learned to read this way,
because his famous conversion scene in the garden in *The Confessions*
pivots around reading. After a long day talking about faith and reading aloud with his friend Alypius, Augustine had worked himself
up into something of a state. Finally he went off alone, burst into
floods of tears and heard the famous child's voice saying, '*Tolle, Lego*'
(Take, read). There was a codex of the Epistles lying near by, so
he 'seized, opened and *in silence* read the section that my eyes first
fell on' and immediately, 'No further would I read, nor needed I: for
instantly at the end of this sentence, by a serene light infused directly
into my heart, all the darkness of doubt vanished away.' What works,
what dispels his doubts, is silent reading, which infuses the light of
knowledge 'directly into the heart'.

Ten years after his conversion Augustine wrote *The Confessions*.
Their publication marked a distinct turning point in the history of
self-understanding. The role that silent reading played in this shift
felt to me like yet more evidence that we cannot treat silence simply
as a lack or absence – here we see it as a passionately strong positive source in the making of the modern self. One way to
understand this is by looking at some aspects of modern reading
and seeing how things have changed since Augustine watched
Ambrose read without moving his lips.

First, there has been an enormous social change in reading.
Literacy is now seen as a necessary life skill. In the sitcom *Friends*,
Joey always moves his lips as he reads – this is a stock joke to show
that he is thick and uneducated and viewers understand this.
Before Augustine's time it was seen much more as an aristocratic
accomplishment. There is a nice little story in Petronius's *Satyrica*,
where a character excuses himself by saying that he did not kiss a
particular youth because he was beautiful but because he 'could
read a book on sight': there is no modern version of this excuse.

The level of interpretation required to read sensibly meant that fluent reading was subsequent to an extensive education, rather than prior to it. For instance we have records of an argument about whether the phrase from Virgil *collectamexiliopubem* (in scripta continua) should be read, '*collectam exilio pubem* – a people gathered for exile' or '*collectam ex Ilio pubem* – a people gathered from Troy'. Obviously you need some considerable knowledge of the plot of the *Aenead* before you can hope to decide; reading could not be about unravelling plots and discovering secrets. This limitation was not as extensive as it would be now because one of the effects of easier reading is that it has radically reduced the depth of textual memory in even the well educated, just as calculators have reduced people's capacity to do mental arithmetic.

The ability to read is now also far more closely linked to the ability to write (the single term 'literacy' covers both). Because reading was so much more of an aural skill in the late classical world, most writing was dictated to scribes. The modern literate person has access not only to silent reading, but also to silent writing. Reading and writing were social events, whereas now they are deeply private activities.

Adam Phillips explores some of this new privacy in *Promises, Promises* where he links it specifically to dreams and silence:

> Whenever I read a book someone is communicating with me in their absence. Modern technology masks how truly incredible it is that people can communicate with us in their absence and after their deaths. So what difference does a person in the room make? We might think of children as experimenting with what is possible in the absence of the object, of finding out what they can do, what experiences they can have without the palpable presence of another person . . . a time comes, ideally, when the child discovers the pleasures of her own solitude. One of the things that a child might do with this solitude is read . . . Like the dreaming experience, the reading experience is conducted in silence, unless of course one reads out loud in which case, oddly enough, one hears only one's

own voice. What kind of exchange goes on between a book and its reader? What can a book give us that a person can't? One possible answer might be 'the experience of a relationship in silence' – the unusual experience of a relationship in which no one speaks. Our present interest in biography, in knowing about writers is, I think, a wish to break this silence.[30]

Along with this social change in reading since Augustine's time there have been enormous physical changes in the written text. For example, silent reading strips away certain aspects of language like pace, volume and inflection, which we primarily use in speech to insert emotional rather than intellectual content. To replace this loss, punctuation was invented. Punctuation marks both assist sense (especially because the natural rhythm of breath has also disappeared; you cannot speak on an in breath but you can carry on reading perfectly well) and emphasise mood or emotion.

Silent reading also changed our relationship to both books and readers. A person reading is 'private' even in public places. It would be considered rude to lean over the shoulder of a person reading a book on a train and share the text; but we will shamelessly listen to and engage with other people's conversations. Within that privacy readers 'own' the text in a new way; they can read subversively, secretly. Augustine himself was aware of this. He became very anxious about independent 'interpretations': private (silent) reading could – and he was right it *did*, as Luther was happy to confess – lead to heresy. The practice of silent reading led to individual, or independent thinking. This sense of independent ownership of a text established itself quite quickly. From this new relationship between reader and text stems the long struggle about Authority in the interpretation and translation of sacred writings – still a rather crucial issue for all text-based faiths like Judaism, Islam and Christianity.

If reading is a separate language by which authors communicate with readers, in what sense can we properly describe it as 'silent' at all, particularly if we think of silence as predominantly an absence of language? Should a person seeking true silence be reading?

Here there have been a variety of traditions. In mainstream Western Christianity reading – scholarship – has been seen as central to the contemplative, or silent, life. Protestantism maintained this part of Catholic practice even when they abandoned the monasticism, which had originally promoted it. Benedict, the founder of Western monasticism, laying down his rule in the sixth century, was very clear that reading was a part of the harmonious rhythm of monastic life. He argued that 'a cloister without books is a fort without armoury'.

In classical Buddhism, on the other hand, reading has generally been seen as antipathetic to meditation and enlightenment. The Eastern Orthodox Churches have, broadly, taken up an intermediate position; while scholarship and books were preserved through intensely difficult periods within the monasteries of Greece and the Middle East, there is also a strong ascetic revulsion from too much reading. In *From the Holy Mountain* William Dalrymple relates a contemporary encounter with this approach. He is visiting the monastery of Mar Saba in the West Bank – a notoriously austere community – where Fr Theophanes, the guest master, is shocked to discover that Dalrymple is a writer. He announces that,

> 'I've stopped reading books myself . . . The Divine Liturgy contains all the writing I need. Once you've read the Word of God everything else becomes very dull.'
>
> 'They say books are like food,' pointed out Fr Evodimos. 'They feed your brain.'
>
> 'But Father,' said Theophanes quietly, 'monks should try to eat as little as possible.'[31]

I read; of course I read. I cannot really imagine not reading. But I gradually became aware that, through silence, I was beginning to read in a new way. I still, too often, use reading as a way to escape from silence, either into a noisy mental dogfight with authors I disagree with, or simply by being sucked into fictional worlds. This often happens in certain sorts of genre novels, particularly (for me) romance. Such writing can leave me entranced rather literally – feeling empty at the end and even slightly nauseated, as lost to myself as those characters who were stolen by the fairies and could not calculate how long they had been away but were left semi-enchanted, deranged and febrile when they returned. Lost to the real. These are not 'silent' reading experiences – they are overwhelming, even oppressive. Such novels are too easy, too successful; they don't 'nourish', they drain; they are escapist in the technical sense of the word, and even addictive.

But during my time in Weardale I discovered a new way of reading. I read more slowly and therefore in a sense I read less, but I read more carefully and attentively. I felt less excited by plot, tension and pace, and more engaged with language and mood and place. I started reading more poetry and enjoying it more. I want to say that I learned to read more silently, but also I read with a sense of the mystery of what reading is and how deeply and silently it has shaped our sense of self.

5

Silent Places

So for the three years that followed my Skye adventure I was busy and engaged pursuing these ideas and experiences of silence. But simultaneously and woven into these various forays into the silence and lack of it out there in the world, something else began to happen to me; a more domestic and intimate kind of silence welled up in my consciousness and started to counterbalance this more intellectual research.

One of the things I discovered at this point was that there were bits and pieces of silence woven into the fabric of each day and I began to try to keep an eye out for them and move into them as swiftly and quietly as possible. Some of these moments I had to create for myself – unplug the phone, maintain a pattern of meditation, walk where or when there are least likely to be other people, say 'no' even to delightful invitations to work or social events – but some were just *there*, waiting for me as it were.

Dawn became one of those occasions. I found myself waking earlier and earlier in the mornings. At sunrise, as at sunset, particularly in the summer months, the wind often drops, so that even in very exposed places there can be a period of great calm, especially if the weather is clear. I became attentive to those early mornings, which came so gradually. The stars would fade and the black sky turn indigo. The distance emerged, colourless out of the darkness. The sky would change colour: indigo, grey, cream. The view opened out and away mysteriously. The horizon line like a shadow separated the sky from the moor. The sky would go on changing: grey, cream, peach. Although the sun rose to my left in the east, because of the conformation of the hills, the first sight of it was to my right; the western hills would catch fire first, the sunshine suddenly falling on them in a splash of brightness. The sky would still be changing: cream, peach, white, palest blue. On the moor there were very few songbirds, so this extraordinary silence was not broken by that joyful but insistent clamour, but occasionally there would be buzzards, hunting high, floating against the enormous blue. Sometimes the rising sun would catch them from below and the moth-markings of their under-wings would light up suddenly, tawny gold as they rode the bright air. On some lucky mornings there was an extra bonus: overnight the valley would have filled with a thick mist, which did not rise as high as the cottage, or as the moor the far side of the dale, so I could contemplate the glory of this making of the day, as though above and outside the world, looking out over a shimmering lake of mist, barely stirring in the dawn calm.

Perhaps it was because of thinking so much about creation and the land or perhaps it was simply that living in more silence deepens an engagement with topography and ecology, but in Weardale I found in myself a growing fascination with and love for natural history. There does seem to be a link between what is usually called Nature Writing – that genre of literature which developed in Europe in the late eighteenth century and has been particularly highly developed in the United States, which brings together scientific knowledge and intense careful personal observation and experience – and solitude. Gilbert White, a clergyman and significant naturalist, in Selborne, Hampshire and Thomas Bewick, the wood engraver who grew up in the dales where I now lived, were both fully aware that their habit of solitary walking in the countryside was the key to their powers of observation and their emotional response to what they saw. Henry Thoreau made the connection explicit early on, writing that it was practically impossible to love both company and nature.

In the streets and in society I am almost invariably cheap and dissipated, my life is unspeakably mean ... But *alone* in the distant woods or fields, in unpretending sprout-lands or pastures tracked by rabbits, even in a bleak and, to most, cheerless day like this, when a village would be thinking of his inn, I come to myself, I once more feel myself grandly related, and that cold and solitude are friends of mine. I come home to my solitary woodland walk as the homesick go home. I thus dispose of the superfluous and see things as they are [my italics].[1]

A century later Thomas Merton experienced a similar development. Because of his extensive and continuous journal writing Merton is someone in whom it is possible to see an idea or imaginative commitment growing over a period of time – whereas with most writers we see only their reflections on that growth. As he moved further into his hermit lifestyle he became increasingly conscious of and engaged with the natural history of his silent habitat – the woods of Kentucky, within the grounds of his monastery. Being Merton, he helpfully, if laboriously, spelled it out:

Perhaps we [contemplative monks] have a deep and legitimate need to know in our entire being what the day is like, to see it and feel it, to know how the sky is grey, paler in the south, with patches of blue in the southwest, with snow on the ground, the thermometer at 18, and a cold wind making your ears ache. I have a real need to know these things because I am myself part of the weather and part of the climate and part of the place, and a day in which I have not shared truly in all this is no day at all.[2]

I now found that this was becoming true for me too; I wanted both to see better and to know more about what I was seeing. In some ways there was nothing new in this; although I had, like most British schoolchildren, alas, been educated within a system that maintained the rigorous division between arts and sciences, and I had most definitely been 'arts', during the 1990s I became profoundly interested in certain areas of science – particularly cosmology and astrophysics, palaeontology and some sorts of theoretical mathematics.[3] However, these had been quite abstract ideas; no one gets to look inside a Black Hole slowly, carefully, quietly and then relate the experience of seeing and feeling it to the theoretical knowledge we have about it. This was a new desire – to learn to see what was really going on around me.

There was a more mundane reason for this new fascination. When I left Northamptonshire I had assumed that I would go on gardening, which had met so many of my longings for growth and beauty and knowledge and exercise. Alas, it turned out to be well-nigh impossible to make the sort of garden I wanted to make. This was partly because of the extreme weather conditions – the house was not called Weatherhill for no reason. There is a traditional gardening wisdom that claims you cannot make a proper garden over 250 metres above sea level in the UK and Weatherhill was a great deal higher that that. I am not actually convinced that this is true and I might have found some way of negotiating with the weather had it not been for the rabbits. As Peter Rabbit learned, it is not possible for rabbits and humans to share a garden. I find it hard to describe how many rabbits there were; I could look out of the window and count fifty at a time – they kept the grass beautifully mown, but they mowed everything else you might want to grow. (Except daffodils. Rabbits do not eat daffodils. In fact, there is a range of plants rabbits are said not to eat and I kept sending off for or downloading lists of them, but it was very discouraging. The rabbits and I seemed to have much the same tastes when it came to favourite plants and, moreover, I frequently found that the rabbits had not read the lists.) However, all my attempts to exclude them proved fatuous – the drystone wall surrounding the property was very old, it had fallen and been repaired too often and often not very well, so that its base was too spread out to put in effective fencing. (To exclude rabbits effectively you need to get your wire mesh well underground.) I invited youths with ferrets to come and hunt my rabbits; I invited youths with guns to come and practise on the rabbits. One afternoon we killed thirty-six rabbits and the next morning there were just as many in the so-called garden. I was defeated and gave up.

Instead, I began to walk out away from house and garden, and into the wilderness. Silence had already begun to teach me to listen and hear better, but now I also wanted it to help me to look and see better. Fortunately, Weardale was good country to walk in, high and wild, perfect for meditative hiking and safer for anyone who walks alone. I walked in silence and soon came to recognise that although in the past I had walked and thought, I had never really paid attention.

I had begun to notice this first in Skye; one night there were two red-deer hinds just outside the house; my torch caught their huge eyes staring before they moved off quite calmly. After the next day's walk I noted in my journal:

> I know there must have been a lot of deer out there today, but even though I sat and *looked* I couldn't see them. I'd love to – the big eyes in the dark outside the house have given me longings, as well as the certainty that they are here. Knowing there are deer and not being able to see them makes me wonder about sounds as well: what am I not hearing? Or for that matter not not-hearing? What silences do I miss because I do not hear well enough? Or rather don't listen well enough (hear=see; listen=look). I remember when we went stalking in the Highlands, Alan [the stalker] could see deer where I couldn't, he would keep patiently trying to show me where they were, and then suddenly I would see them, sometimes lots of them, and then not be able to understand how I had failed to see them before. In relation to deer at least, Alan could see and I can't.

Like Merton, and probably related in some ways to where I lived, I began with weather – and particularly with clouds. Clouds are wonderful in so many ways: they are beautiful in both form and colour; they are poetic – their shapes suggesting other things, provoking the imagination; they are prophetic, bringing warnings and promises of what is to come; they are created by complex and various processes, which physics can explain; they have beautiful

names, both scientific and vernacular – cumulonimbus, altocumu-
lus castellanus, cirrus, lenticularis, mares' tails, thunderheads,
mackerel skies; above all they *come*, day after day inexhaustible,
never two quite alike, appearing over the horizon and marching in
long, solemn or playful procession across the sky. They are yet
another of the silent forces around us, announcing in their passage
that silence does have meaning, does have shape and purpose and
something to teach me.

From clouds and other weather phenomena it was not a long
step to insects and flowers. I slowed down enough to watch spiders
spin their webs, although never yet to watch a caterpillar through
the whole process of spinning its chrysalis or a leaf bud unfurl its
first gold-green. In the northern dales, as traditional farming failed
economically and conservation and tourism offered better
rewards, more and more fields were turned back to traditional
management and the wild flowers began to re-establish themselves.
They were a constant source of both joy and interest. One June I
had almost a fight with a good friend who lamented that British
flora was so 'unspectacular'. It was the wrong word, meadow flowers in grass are not spectacular taken one by one, but in their
diversity and modesty and rhythm and detail they are magical. I
wanted to learn to see and know them, especially since I was without a real garden of my own.

But soon what I began to look at most seriously, together with
long views and wide skies, were birds. I became intrigued by
ornithology. At first identifying the birds I saw was a discipline, like
listening to the silences and learning to hear their intonations. To
look for, then to look at, birds I had to be very alert to the present
moment, always in the present tense, the now – that stance
Buddhists called 'mindfulness'. Plants, especially flowers, stay still
while you look at them, even while you find the right page in a *Wild
Flowers of Britain* book and compare the various possibilities – but
with birds it is now, now or they are gone. You have to move quietly
and attentively, always be ready to respond to what presents itself
to you. You have to wait. This sense of waiting in silence became

even more marked when I advanced to sitting in a hide or under a drystone wall and paying attention to nothing in the hope that it would at any moment become a bird, become something.

Of course, birds are not silent at all; hearing them can be as much a means of identifying them as seeing them. The cry of a curlew on the wing or the insistent two-tone call of a cuckoo can be as penetrating and far-carrying as a car horn, but still they somehow inhabit the spaces of silence. You need to be silent to see them, and they come and go as a silent gift.

I was deeply influenced at this point by Annie Dillard's *Pilgrim at Tinker's Creek* – her silent 'stalking', attentive looking and meticulous, beautiful, mindful reporting of what she saw; and what I knew was that I did not look or see with the attentive, open-hearted concentration that she does:

> In summer I stalk. Summer leaves obscure, heat dazzles and creatures hide from the red-eyed sun, and me. I have to seek things out. The creatures I seek have several senses and free will; it becomes apparent that they do not wish to be seen. I can stalk them in either of two ways. The first is not what you think of as true stalking, but it is the *via negativa*, and as fruitful as actual pursuit. When I stalk this way I take my stand on a bridge and wait, emptied. I put myself in the way of the creature's passing, like spring Eskimos at a seal's breathing hole. Something might come; something might go. I am Newton under the apple tree, Buddha under the bo. Stalking the other way, I forge my own passage, seeking the creature. I wander the banks; what I find I follow, doggedly, like the Eskimos haunting the caribou herds. I am Wilson squinting after the traces of electrons in a cloud chamber; I am Jacob at Peniel wrestling with the angel.[4]

I wanted to learn to see as Dillard sees.

Quite soon, delightfully, birdwatching became not a discipline but a joy. The immediate rewards were wonderful – surprisingly quickly the moor became inhabited not by an undifferentiated mob of LBJs ('little brown jobs' – a collective term for all those apparently identical and in fact fabulously diverse small brown birds) but by an exquisite variety of interesting species; by moments of familiarity and equally of surprise and delight. There is a lot to learn; not simply in identifying birds but in reading about their habits and relationships. Birds, like flowers, change with the seasons: in Weardale it was always a thrill, for example, to see the first lapwing coming up from the seashore to nest and brood in the early spring. They come in flocks with their strangely floppy flight, and because their wings are dark above and white below they seem to flicker as they fly. On the ground there is an odd contrast between the beauty of their green and purple iridescent plumage and their ridiculous long wispy crests, which blow out in the wind. They are harbingers of spring: the winter is over, the lapwing are back again.

And birds – well, they are beautiful, swift and free. They fly. As I mentioned in the opening chapter, I have always had a deep fascination with flying. In my imagination, in my dreams and in my fiction, flying – birds, angels, dragons, butterflies, witches, free and graceful in the silent air – has been a central image for freedom and joy.

In Weardale there were short-eared owls. Unlike other British owls, this species is partly diurnal, so I could sit at my desk or in my garden and watch them quartering the moor in long, slow, systematic circles. Like all owls they have deep down-strokes in their flight, but their wings are stiffer than brown owls' so it looked as though they were rowing through the air. They glide in long silent swoops across their hunting ground, balancing effortlessly on the wind. Late on a sunny afternoon I would watch one in its silent flight against the sky for mesmerised hours; sometimes it would move so grandly that its shadow would hunt along the ground below it. All owls have very dense and soft-surfaced feathers, so their flight is unusually silent, even close to. When a short-eared owl is near enough to see in detail it has yellow eyes, set in clear black patches within a paler face; even my usually solemn bird book says it has a 'mean expression', but hunting slowly and purposefully through a long hot afternoon it seems more meditative and elegant than mean. This careful slow search on silent wings is the sort of flying I dream about.

It had always been a fantasy ambition of mine that 'when I got rich' I would learn to fly a small aeroplane (she was going to be called *The Broomstick*). While I was living in Weardale, one of my brothers-in-law earned his private pilot's licence. I asked him to take me up, to experience that promised silence and freedom, over the beautiful flat fields of Suffolk. It was great fun; we swooped over his house and waved to his children in the garden, and we saw the countryside from a new and strangely delightful angle, but silent it was not. It was not just that the engine was both noisy and rattling, it was more that the whole experience was hedged round, as indeed it ought to be, with rules and regulations and communication and busyness. I enjoyed it, but the fantasy died there on the runway and has never come back.

I tried a hot-air balloon too; it was in one sense much better – because a balloon moves at the same speed as the wind that carries it there is no sensation of movement. You look over the side of the basket and see that you are rushing across the landscape, but the sensation is entirely that the landscape itself is gliding away underneath you. The problem, though, was that the sudden roar of the gas burner disrupted all contemplation, and there are again a lot of people, a lot of fuss and a lot of noisy activity involved. Perhaps if one was very rich one could have a balloon of one's own . . .

One summer afternoon two men came up on to the moor immediately behind my house and spread out enormous colourful arcs of cloth. It seemed an unlikely place for paragliding since there was no steep drop or void to leap out into and catch the thermals rising. I went to talk to them – they were 'paramotorists', a new sport, they told me, that added a backpacked motor and propeller to paragliding 'wings' so that they were not dependent on the wind and weather in the old way. They were going to fly home to Newcastle, at a level below air traffic control, so they would be free to go as they chose. They looked extremely charming – somehow old-fashioned, like Daedalus creating wings from feathers and wax to escape from Minos. When they took to the air their legs hung down like crane flies (daddy-long-legs with wings). They circled over the house, took some lovely aerial photographs for me and then buzzed off eastwards; it was the nearest thing I have ever seen to 'real' human flight, but it was not enough, there was no soaring, swooping grace and the engines were too noisy. I gave up – perhaps I should have persevered and tried hang-gliding, which looks wonderful from the ground, but I felt old and stiff and nervous; and also poor – none of these adventures was cheap.

I came to feel that flight, in reality, has proved to be one of the biggest disappointments in the history of technology. For centuries human beings dreamed and created myths and stories about flying. Leonardo da Vinci, along with other scientists and artists, turned his deep creative capacity to thinking about how it might be done; enormous efforts were directed towards achieving what birds and insects do with such ease. That free, weightless movement in three dimensions, like the underwater world, and in addition you can breathe and soar. Free flight is one of the most common subjects of sweet dreams, just as falling is the frequent stuff of nightmares. And yes, we learned to fly; we achieved the dream and it has proved dust and ashes. Ironically enough, everything about human flying is the antithesis of what we dream of. Aeroplanes are noisy, cramped, polluting – they scratch the surface of the blue ceiling and break up the silence of the night. Strapped in like children, herded about like animals, deafened not just by engine noise but also by overcrowded airports and a general atmosphere of pandemonium, and bound by sets of regulations that would be condemned in an ordinary prison, you further have the privilege of doing the maximum possible amount of environmental damage and running the risk of deep-vein thrombosis.

I let the dream go and watched the birds fly instead – and have found myself increasingly reluctant to travel by air.

Then, the last Christmas I was in Weardale, I went to Liverpool to my son's home. Boxing Day was a raw, cold day with a harsh wind blowing in from the Irish Sea. Nonetheless, after the pleasurable excesses of the previous day we both felt in need of some air and exercise. He announced that he knew where we were going and I would like it. We drove north through the city and up the coast. There was a winter-holiday calm and very little traffic; eventually we turned off the main road towards the sea. We had come to Crosby and *Another Place*. Here, for nearly two miles of flat grey beach, Anthony Gormley's hundred identical statues stand with their backs to the shore, gazing out towards the horizon. As the tide rises and falls they are submerged to a greater or lesser extent. Because the installation stretches over a quarter of a mile out to sea the furthest away ones may show only the tops of their heads, or they are drowned. Gormley, the sculptor who created among other works *The Angel of the North*, principally investigates and represents the human body as a place of memory and transformation, often using casts of his own body as subject, tool and material.

Another Place harnesses the ebb and flow of the tide to explore human relationships with nature. Gormley explains:

> The seaside is a good place to do this. Here time is tested by tide, architecture by the elements and the prevalence of sky seems to question the earth's substance. In this work human life is tested against planetary time. This sculpture exposes to light and time the nakedness of a particular and peculiar body. It is no hero, no ideal, just the industrially reproduced body of a middle-aged man trying to remain standing and trying to breathe, facing a horizon busy with ships moving materials and manufactured things around the planet.[5]

That cold Boxing Day the beach was nearly empty. A few other walkers in the distance looked like extra statues. It was huge, monotone and silent. Then my son got out his kite. He had flown a kite as a child and he had told me that he was flying one again, but I had not really paid very much attention. That day he flew a small-ish double-stringed stunt kite. It seemed as though he could make it do *anything* – dance, swoop, soar, dive, drift, loop, hover. It was flight like flight was dreamed of – both under his control and entirely free; silent in the bigger silence; like a bird but tamed to his hand; graceful but leaning on the wind. 'My heart like a bird had escaped from the hand of the fowler.'[6] We flew the kite for hours in that vast silent space; it was too cold and windy to talk, and so for both awe and ease we were quiet and joyful though our hands were numbed with cold and the statues did not turn to watch us; they stood still, staring silently out across the flat grey sea.

I bought a kite myself, although I cannot fly it with the grace and skill that he does. It represented for me a child's joyful dream of flying and I like playing with it, but it never really took over from the birds themselves and their true free flight.

Looking at birds led me into another sort of landscape traditionally associated with silence – islands. Islands feed a romantic dream; from coral atoll to storm-wracked cliff, they represent something deep in the human psyche – aloneness, adventure, silence and, perhaps more subtly, a boundary, a sense of self separate and complete. *Robinson Crusoe* and BBC Radio 4's *Desert Islands Discs*, which has been running since 1942, endure so well because they touch this fantasy. But islands are real too – from Out Stack in the north to the Scillies in the south, from St Kilda far out in the west to the Outer Farnes in the east, Britain, itself an island off Europe, is fringed with smaller islands, ranging from uninhabitable rocks that barely break the surface of the sea to substantial land masses, like the Isles of Wight and Man, and Ireland itself beyond that.

A great many of these islands have distinct ecological profiles of their own and, especially in summer, are homes to colonies of seabirds, who come ashore to mate and breed. Although several of these species are intensely sociable, gathering in their nesting places so densely that one would be hard put to walk between them (on St Kilda there are over 100,100 gannets alone), for obvious reasons they prefer to do this in places least inhabited by humans. Looking for seabirds, ducks, geese and waders took me to some of the most isolated places in the country.

One summer I went to Unst, the most northerly of the inhabited Shetland Isles, the most northerly inhabited place in Britain. This time I went with a friend at midsummer to see, as nearly as one can within the UK, the midnight sun. Even this far north is not far enough to have the sun never set at all – it dipped below the horizon for about twenty minutes. It never grew dark, but the light was very strange and green, and in the magically calm weather we had that week the faded glow of the night gave the still water a ghostly sheen. We rented a tiny cottage right on a pebbled beach, and in the long light evenings Simon would walk up and down the stones singing to the seals, who would pop their heads above the water to hear him and follow him, parallel to the shore about twenty yards out. One evening we watched a school of porpoises running down the bay, arching smooth black backs above the pearly surface. And indeed there were birds, thousands and thousands of birds – delightful and somehow witty puffins, huge powerful gannets diving vertically into the water, slightly sinister-looking skuas, guillemots, and what we came to call the 'diverse divers'.

One reason I had gone was to see golden plover. There were said to be golden plover on the Durham moor but I had never been able to see them. At Hermaness, the bird sanctuary at the northern tip of Unst, they were flaunting themselves on the close-cropped sea-grass; the least attentive ornithologist in the world could not have failed to remark on and identify them. And when I got home I could suddenly see them on the moor too; knowing what I was looking for, looking at, I could see. It was a clear reward for careful searching and attentive looking.

But actually it was not, in the end, the birds that moved me most. It was the islands themselves. Immediately north of Unst, and clinging closely to it, is Muckle Flugga – a deserted rock now, but the lighthouse, fully automated in 1995, still stands as a memorial to the most northerly inhabitant in Britain. And also as a memorial to the dangerous and isolated lives of the lighthouse keepers, whose solitary lifestyle performed rather literally the metaphorical task the hermits had set themselves a millennium earlier – to tend the light in silence and keep the world safe from lethal storms. Muckle Flugga is by no means the only island that used to be inhabited and no longer is – of the 790-odd Scottish off-shore islands fewer than a hundred are populated now and that number continues to fall. Islands are full of sadness, haunted by the ruins of communities that once flourished there. Their silences are new, a consequence of modernity. The most famous abandonment was St Kilda, whose thirty-six islanders were evacuated at their own request in 1930, after two millennia of occupation. In 1697 the inhabitants had seemed 'happier than the generality of mankind as being almost the only people in the world who feel the sweetness of true liberty'. They had a culture, an ecosystem, even a diet that was unique. Now St Kilda has a small population again, of military personnel, but the overwhelming sense there is of beauty and loss and silence, and the brutal ferocity of the wild seas.

Apart from these embattled communities many of the smaller islands have another history and one that appealed to me strongly if romantically. On island after island, the more isolated and far-flung the better – on St Kilda, on the Farnes, on the Shiants, throughout the Hebrides and the northern islands, off the coast of Ireland, around Iceland and possibly even in North America – the traces of hermits can be found. This history is confused and uncertain, but originating in Ireland in the fifth century, there was a well-developed form of Christian spirituality which valued the silent eremitical vocation extremely highly. In Britain the most famous such voluntary exile was Columba, who left Ireland in the mid sixth century and crossed the Irish Sea to become first a hermit and later a missionary and founding father based on the tiny island of Iona, which is just to the west of Mull. His community later spread out across Scotland and converted north-east England as well, but he was by no means unique: over the next several centuries hermits settled alone or in tiny communities all over western Scotland and further afield too.

I went to Islay, a beautiful complex journey itself, more for the hermits than for the birds. The ferry to Islay leaves from

Kennacraig on West Loch Tarbert, halfway down the Mull of
Kintyre. It chugs its way down the long narrow sea loch, then out
to sea north of Gigha. Just before it begins the complicated
manoeuvres that will bring it into Port Ellen on Islay it passes a
spine of rock, a pretty little island, low-lying, barely over a hundred
acres, tucked into the bay where Laphroaig, the wonderful peaty
malt whisky, is now made; it is called Tecsa (or Texa). It is inhabited
only by wild goats and seabirds, and seems to have little to offer
except a good fresh-water source and a number of dry caves. In the
seventeenth century Tecsa had over a hundred people living on it
(oddly enough all except seven of them were Roman Catholics).
Earlier than that, there was a fourteenth-century chapel, which
archaeologists claim is built on an older structure. Even earlier than
that, although it is hard to tell from the physical evidence, the old
chronicles and the place names enable us to be reasonably certain
there were hermits here at least in the seventh and eighth centuries.
There is a legend that St Kenneth, after visiting Columba on Iona,
about eighty miles north over dangerous waters, stopped on Tecsa
on his way back to Ireland. He had absent-mindedly left his pas-
toral cross on Iona and Columba had thrown it into the sea to
follow him; it was cast up on the beach at Tecsa where Kenneth
recovered it. Meanwhile at the other, the northern, end of Islay
there are the remains of a hermitage chapel on Eilean ArdNeimh
(Ardnave) and Islay itself is dotted with yet more tiny chapels and
possibly hermit-inhabited caves.

It is hard to imagine their lives. At the beginning of *Sea Room*,
Adam Nicolson describes the first time he sailed alone from
Harris, itself an island in the Outer Hebrides, to the Shiants, his
group of tiny islands in the middle of the Minch. He had a new
boat, designed and built for this crossing on these waters, he had
maps, a hand-held GPS, radio contact with the coastguard and
good advice – and he was frightened:

> The mind . . . returns to the foolishness of what you have done. It
> was not exactly the vision of the drowning man but I found myself

thinking of the people I love and have loved. Do men drown regret-
ting what they have done with their lives, all the stupidities and
meannesses, the self-delusions and deceits? I was driving blind and
it was not comfortable. I had been in the boat for nearly three hours
and even through all the layers of clothes I was getting cold . . . I
should have been almost on the islands now but I could not see into
the mist bank to the north and east of me . . . I was in a state of
high anxiety. This approach is larded with danger.[7]

Yet these monks, in far smaller boats – tradition says in coracles,
stretched leather on light wooden frames, designed to be portable –
without maps, without even knowing where they were going and
with very little hope of ever returning home, set out to make hermitages in clochans (sometimes called 'beehive huts') and caves on
the remotest islands. Nicholson tells us there were hermits on the
Shiants. These adventures were known in Ireland as 'green mar-
tyrdoms' – to distinguish them from the 'red martyrdom' of being
slain, shedding blood for the faith. To leave home and travel out
beyond civilisation was a martyrdom (the word means 'witness'), a
death of the ego, a self-giving that seems absolute.

We have very little idea now what they thought they were doing,
or why islands were deemed so particularly suitable. Given the mysterious links between the iconography and probably the practice of
eremitical spirituality in Ireland and the Christianity of the
Egyptian desert hermits, I like to imagine that they saw islands in
the barren salt seas as parallel to oases and wells; fresh water in the
desert.

Of course they were seeking silence, but it was from social,
human sounds rather than the pure physical silence of the desert
because, as I learned, British coastal islands are not silent in any literal sense of the word. Along with the other islands I was visiting
I went, too, on a day trip to the Farne Isles, a small group of islands
off the north-east coast, and also now a famous bird reserve. Inner
Farne, beyond but within reach of the monastery at Lindisfarne,
the Holy Island, was where St Cuthbert had his hermitage; he is

the patron saint of Durham Cathedral and an icon of the north-east. As well as wanting to learn how to distinguish between different gulls, fulmars and kittiwakes, I wanted to feel Cuthbert's silence on the eastern rim of his world. There is a connection between these two interests. Cuthbert, who had resigned as both bishop and abbot to return to being a hermit, issued regulations to his monks for the special protection of eider ducks, which is why these birds are still called 'Cuddy Ducks' ('Cuthbert's ducks') in the north-east of England. However, although it was a clear calm day, I've seldom heard such a racket in my life. The volume of cacoph-onous din set up by the thronging bird life on the islands was stupefying. The terns were nesting – and were both restless and tur-bulent. Moreover, terns dive-bomb people who they think may be threatening their nests aggressively enough to draw blood. Gulls were shrieking and there was a constant mewling, squawking and screaming. And under and through all that there was the never-ending sound of waves breaking in different rhythms and patterns. I realised I could never find my own silence on an island.

Yet this was Cuthbert's silent paradise. It seemed so inappropri-ate for a hermitage that later I rang up the Royal Society for the Protection of Birds to see if anyone knew whether the terns had nested on Inner Farne in the seventh century. I could not believe that anyone could have found it a place of silent retreat and won-dered if the terns had arrived later. The information officer did not know the answer, though he was very helpful. But thinking about it now, they cannot have been there in Cuthbert's time because terns (whether miraculously silenced or failing to disturb Cuthbert's prayer) are exactly the sort of detail that Bede would have included in his *Life of St Cuthbert* had there been any. He does mention eider duck and ravens, so it seems unlikely he could have resisted a blood-drawing tern if he could have got away with it.

We do not know very much about the spiritual theology of these early hermits. Their lives are lost in legend and story, their physical markers faded or wiped out by the wildness of the places where they dwelt. We know more about Cuthbert than about many of them because Bede knew and loved him personally, and wrote about him at length, but what interested Bede is somewhat different from what interests me. So, for example, Bede records that Cuthbert would pray all night standing up to his neck in the frigid waters of the North Sea and, indeed, that when he emerged otters would come and warm him with their tongues and fur. This combination of the ferociously ascetic and the miraculous engages Bede, for what he is writing about is an ultimate form of something so obvious to him that he never says anything about what Cuthbert thought he was trying to achieve, nor about the content of those prayers.

It is not until rather later, from the tenth to the twelfth centuries, that we begin to get accounts that attempt to explain what the island hermits were seeking, in the beguiling poetry of the Irish monks:

Delightful I think it to be in the bosom of an isle, on the peak of a rock, that I might often see there the calm of the sea. That I might see its heavy waves over the glittering ocean, as they chant a melody to their Father on their eternal course. That I might see its smooth strand of clear headlands, no gloomy thing; that I might hear the voice of the wondrous birds, a joyful tune. That I might hear the sound of the shallow waves against the rocks; that I might hear the cry by the graveyard, the noise of the sea. That I might see its splendid flocks of birds over the full-watered ocean; that I might see its mighty whales, greatest of wonders. That I might see its ebb and its flood-tide in their flow; that this might be my name, a secret I tell, 'He who turned his back on Ireland.' That contrition of heart should come upon me as I watch it; that I might bewail my many sins, difficult to declare. That I might bless the Lord who has power over all, heaven with its pure host of angels, earth, ebb, flood-tide. That I might pore on one of my books, good for my soul; a while kneeling for beloved heaven, a while at psalms. A while gathering dulse from the rock, a while fishing, a while giving food to the poor, a while in my cell. A while meditating upon the Kingdom of

heaven, holy in the redemption; a while in labour, not too heavy; it
would be delightful![8]

Islands are 'delightful' not just to hermits, but to many other
more modern people as well. In 2003, indeed, a four-acre island in
the Outer Hebrides came up for sale; it had a ruined cottage or
bothy in a small cove at one end and wonderful views over a broken
cliff and beach coastline, other tiny islands and the vast sea. My
brother-in-law and I talked about buying it. I would rebuild the
bothy and live there alone and later, when he retired, he would
build a house at the other end. It was a daydream, really, and we
both knew it. When I confronted the complications of power generation and motorboats, when I faced up to the long, long dark of
the winters and the enormous distance and solitude, I quailed – to
say nothing of the fact that my sister had no enthusiasm at all for
the project!

And underneath those practicalities was a growing certainty that
although I was entranced by the islands and felt their desolate loveliness deeply, they were not my place. The endless movement and
sound of the sea was not my silence; the low-lying islands and flat
expanse of ocean did not, for all its charms, offer me that lift of
land and sense of space that the moors did. I knew, too, that I
would feel contained and restricted within an island's boundaries;
that I would miss the long walks, the physical sense of the land
being wider than I could encompass. The sense of ownership, of
being 'monarch of all I survey',[9] was not as important to me as my
sense of freedom, my right to roam.

What this little fantasy did make clear to me, however, is that
what I was doing during the three years after my adventure into the
complete silence of Skye was exploring the various terrains of
silence, in both culture and wilderness, and finding everywhere the
same 'delight' as the Irish poet found. It is hard to write about without it all sounding restless and unsettled, but I kept coming back
from these various forays to my house on the moor and brooding in
solitude and silence over what I was discovering. And one of the things

I discovered was that there was a traditional territory of silence that I was avoiding; and I was avoiding it because I was frightened.

I was scared of forests.

I am not alone – I know a good number of other people – bold walkers of high hills or those happy to sail little dinghies in tidal waters alone, both surely far more dangerous activities in physical terms – who do not like to be in forests, who are scared or freaked out by them. Some of this discomfort is probably related to the unnatural 'dead' atmosphere of most of the forests we know – the huge monoculture stands of Sitka spruce (*Picea sitchensis*) that squat dark and ungainly over so much of the wilder countryside of Britain. Sitka spruce, favoured by commercial forestry between the world wars because of its fast growth, is native to Canada. Although it flourishes in Britain, it does so at a considerable eco-logical price: native oak trees have been found to support 284 species of insect compared to the Sitka spruce's 37. Fewer insects mean fewer birds and fewer birds means less botanic diversity that in its turn reduces zoological diversity. The trees are planted in straight rows, often very close together, and the huge ploughs that cut up the earth to make planting possible leave broken, haggy ground and often deep drainage cuts of sour water underneath the trees; old field systems and agricultural holdings were stripped out to create the plantations – these plantations really are 'dead' in quite a technical sense.[10]

But, together with this discomfort, there is a more chthonic fear; forests are what Freud called *heimlich unheimlich* – they are uncanny. Inside most of us post-Enlightenment and would-be rational adults there is a child who is terrified by the wild wood.

> Everything was very still now. The dusk advanced on him steadily, rapidly, gathering in behind and before; and the light seemed to be draining away like flood-water.
>
> Then the faces began . . .
>
> Then the whistling began . . .
>
> They were up and alert and ready, evidently, whoever they were!

And he – he was alone, and unarmed, and far from any help; and the night was closing in.

Then the pattering began . . .

And as he lay there panting and trembling, and listened to the whistlings and the patterings outside, he knew it at last, in all its fullness, that dread thing which other little dwellers in field and hedgerow had encountered here, and known as their darkest moment – that thing which the Rat had vainly tried to shield him from – the Terror of the Wild Wood.[11]

Once upon a time the forest went on for ever. It is almost impossible to imagine now how continuous that forest was. In Britain the wide sweep of the downs was all forest and it ran pretty much unbroken except for the chain of naked heights along the Pennines north through most of Scotland. Every seam of coal underground represents a fallen petrified forest. In Continental Europe it was much the same: from the Mediterranean almost to the Arctic circle, except where the mountains, tundra or bog made the land so inhospitable that even alder and scrubby half-horizontal birches could not gain a roothold, the forest created a huge unimaginable sweep of silent danger. Human beings had to hack out small corners to set up home – usually clinging to the fringes, huddled on coasts or beside rivers, going into the forest as seldom as possible. Forests are enormous but they give no sense of space, because you are always in the tiny bit of forest you are in – you cannot see out. When in the eighth century Boniface went into the endless forest, which ran away beyond the Rhine through Germany, Poland and into Russia, to convert the pagans, almost the first thing he did was summon Anglo-Saxon Benedictines to set up monasteries and start singing in the silence. This was a silence that he knew needed breaking.

I knew there were wolves in the forest; there were witches in the forest; there were demons. I was haunted by the silence of the forests, which is the silence of the fairy stories. These northern European stories have their roots in the silence of the forest and are as ancient and tough as the Wild Wood itself. I did not like the idea that there was a whole silent terrain that I had not visited because I was scared. Moreover, these stories had been my territory as a *writer* for a long time; a great deal of my fiction, and especially my short stories, have been retelling the ancient tales, trying to pull them into the modern world and face up to what they tell us about ourselves. Thinking now about silence I had to accept that, along with feminist reinterpretation and my desire for fiction that explores universal human themes, I had been writing my own fears, my own darkness and my own profound sense that violence and beauty, risk and joy, are inextricably tangled together; and the roots lie in the forests.

I decided that I needed to challenge my fears and experience the forest and its fairy stories. The primeval forests of Europe are not monotone, and once upon a time the diverse habitats must have merged into each other smoothly from the most northern birch and alder scrub forests of Scandinavia southwards to the Via palm forests on Crete. Now, however, they tend to come in smaller and more discreet patches. I should perhaps have gone to the Reinhardswald – the great oak forest between Kassel and Göttingen in Germany. Jacob and Wilhelm Grimm, who published their first collection of *Märchen*, a better name for such tales than the English 'fairy stories', in 1812, were professors of linguistics in Göttingen and it was here that they recorded the 800-odd local folk stories, which have become the core texts of northern European childhood. There is now a 'fairy story route', a long-distance walking path, through the area, leading to Sababurg Castle, Sleeping Beauty's palace, where in the tale total silence reigned for a hundred years.

However, I found I did not want to be away for so long, and – just as I had avoided specifically religious communities when I went to Skye – I did not want my experience of the forest to be mediated too directly through a tourist-inspired interpretation. Moreover, my experience is that travelling in a country where you do not speak the language increases both the need for and the effort of communicating. Instead, I decided to go north into one of the few remaining stands of the Great Caledonian Forest, which once covered over 15,000 square miles of Scotland. There is very little of it left now and it is hard to imagine how it must have stretched on and on beyond imagination. In the north and east of its range the forest is dominated by Scots pine and in the damper west by sessile oak; but for people who have only known the modern plantations it is difficult to realise how diverse and rich the ecosystems of the forests are; 'dominated' should not suggest any exclusivity; the ecosystems of ancient forests are rich and diverse, with a huge variety not just of trees, but of other organisms. In Britain alone there are over 600 species of moss and as many again of lichen.

The Caledonian Forest has its own shadowy literature, particularly in the Welsh tales. Merlin, King Arthur's magical counsellor, retreated to these woods in his madness after the battle of Arfderydd. The Caledonian Forest was, from a southern perspective, associated with madness and magic. The terror of the wild wood is older than the oldest stories, and they have grown out of it.

Now there is less than 1 per cent of the original forest, reduced to thirty-five small patches. I chose to go to Glen Affric, one of the more substantial of these remnants and famous for its isolated strange beauty – an ancient band of wood along the side of the loch and the huge ferocious hills above. It is hard to describe the isolation and harshness of the surrounding country, which somehow makes the closed-in feel of the forest itself even more intense. Among other things Glen Affric boasts the most isolated youth hostel in the country – it is eight miles from the nearest road and you are advised not even to attempt to go there without detailed maps and a compass. I was more self-indulgent, though, and stayed outside the glen in rather cosier conditions.

I walked and sat in the forest for three days. Underneath the towering scots pine there was a range of smaller scrubbier species – rowan, alders, birches, aspen, hazels, junipers. The ground under the small trees was lumpy and mossy. Some of the mosses were a vivid, even virulent green, and gave way under my feet in unexpected directions; there were clumps of fern-like fingers. Unlike a forestry plantation, there is a great deal of variety in an ancient wood – single huge pines, surrounded by lower scrub or dense thickets of spindly tangled growth, carrying a lot of skinny dead twigs. Very tiny, very fast, crystal-clear burns rushed through. The trees were draped in flowing lichen. Lichen itself is a strange life form – a not fully understood symbiosis of plant and algae, and it comes in innumerable forms – those close-clinging yellow patches on damp rocks are lichens, the rough orange skin that clings to tree trunks are lichens and so are the long grey strands that hang down over the little burns in the ancient woodlands. They look like cobwebs or spiders' webs but are heavier, denser than either.

Beside a burn, in front of the moss-covered remains of an abandoned stone wall, I saw a weather-beaten notice that said, 'Tress Cutting is Prohibited'. For a few startled moments I thought this referred to the lichen, though sadly closer examination revealed that it only said 'Tree Cutting is Prohibited'. I liked the idea of the trees as ensorcelled maidens with lichen hair, now grey with age and stirring gently in the breeze. It was very beautiful and very spooky.

It was very silent, too. I knew, sitting there, that I had been right to be scared. This was primal landscape and full of silent shadows of menace, the menace of being lost, magical-mad like Merlin, swallowed up into something wilder, bigger and infinitely more ancient than myself. In my mind I could hear the ghost wolves howling in the hungry winter. There is a current debate about the reintroduction of originally indigenous species into these surviving woodlands and the wild area around them; and while almost everyone would desire the windflower, the one-flower wintergreen, to be dancing again here, there is an almost atavistic resistance to reintroducing wolves. Before I went to Glen Affric I had been fairly simply pro-wolf, persuaded by the argument that they would prove the most effective way of managing the excessive red deer population that denudes and destroys the forest itself, and conscious that the prejudice against and consequent destruction of wolves was almost completely unfounded. But sitting there looking slightly edgily at the treacherous moss hags, the strangely distorted trees, the somehow sinister stillness of the loch itself and the lichens, which might at any moment reach out their cold crinkled fingers and touch me damply, aware that immediately around me was dense silence into which I could not see and in which anything might lurk concealed, I had a deep sense of relief that there were no wolves.

The silence of the forests is about secrets, about things that are hidden. Most of the terrains of silence – deserts, mountains, oceans, islands, moorland – have austere but wide views. They are landscapes that can be appalling in their openness, but at least you can see what is coming. The wide sky is bright above you, the clouds give you warnings of approaching weather and the land sweeps away into the distance. But the silence of the forests hides things; it does not open them out but closes them off. Trees hide the sunshine; and life goes on under the trees, in the thickets and tanglewood. Forests are full of surprises. It is not strange that the fairy stories that come out of the forest are stories about hidden identities, both good and bad. The princess looks like a goose girl, but the wicked stepmother looks like a beautiful queen. In the Grimms' version of Cinderella the infamous 'Ugly Sisters' were not ugly – they were, indeed, 'beautiful and fair of face, but vile and black of heart'. Snow White's murderous stepmother was 'the fairest of all'. The wolf could disguise himself as the sweet old granny.

The forests do not generate the huge god of the desert, nor the partisan, passionate, sexually active deities of the Greek mountains and islands. They produce little fragmented stories, of magic and human courage and dark plots, stories of secrets and silences. Over and over again in the old stories there is a silence: mysteries; hidden names; concealed identities; things not told, withheld, cloaked by silence. These tales have oral roots, so each time they are told they are told for a slightly different purpose. Do you want to soothe your baby towards sleep? Warn your child against wandering? Inspire your teenager to enterprise? Amuse your sulking adolescent with a thrilling horror? Console the elderly or even get rid of your unwanted lover? You tell them a story and the story, like the forests it came out of, shifts to your need.

We know now that the Grimm Brothers themselves, despite their linguistic and 'scientific' intentions, shifted the stories, made them more Christian, more family-orientated; they emphasised the good but absent father (theirs died and it changed their lives from idyllic to penurious overnight) and the cruel malignant stepmother, who seemed under pressure to have changed from the sweet warm mother of their infancy. Bruno Bettelheim in his immensely influential and suggestive *Uses of Enchantment*[12] sees the stories as offering liberation to boy children.* I see them as offering empowerment to women. You can make of them what you will – they are shape shifters. We do not know where the stories came from, their roots are truly buried in silence. There is not and cannot be a single easily pinned-down meaning to fairy-story silence. It is more honest, perhaps, to recognise that there are a number of different sorts of silence in the forest.

There is the silence of secrets; the things that must not be told. In the stories this 'secrecy silence' has a very straightforward narrative function – it keeps the story going, allows things to develop, plots to work themselves through, babies to grow up into princesses. So characters in fairy stories are frequently bound to preposterous oaths not to tell, to keep silent about whatever has happened to them. In 'The Goose Girl' the princess has everything taken from her – her magical horse, her royal status and her princely fiancé – by her wicked servant, while she herself is driven out to keep geese. The whole story here depends on the princess keeping the oath that she was forced to swear 'by the clear sky above her' not to tell anyone about the maid's behaviour. Since virtuous characters in these stories keep their promises regardless of the cost, the teller of

---

* Bettelheim's clinical speciality was in autism. As was fashionable at the time, he endorsed the theory of the 'refrigerator mother' – autism was caused by withholding mothers. No wonder he found the Grimms' wicked stepmothers and ice maidens so meaningful.

the tale is now free to devise a complex narrative by which the truth is exposed without the princess breaking her word. In reality she has only to say, 'I am a princess and this woman is my wicked maid' and the whole story is resolved.

But I sense there is something more going on in this particular structure than simply a cunning plot device. These sorts of promises are nearly always extracted from younger people by adults who wish to oppress them in socially unacceptable ways. It is hard not to feel here something of the darkness of sexual abuse, in which the child is bound by the complicated mixture of shame and fear not to tell, and indeed can repress those memories so effectively as to be 'dumb' about them – the child not only does not speak, but cannot speak, and sometimes may not even remember. Remember in its literal origins means to put something back together again, to make it whole, to rejoin the members or parts into a single unbroken form. Psychotherapy in these cases urges patients to speak, to tell a story not just about events but also about the way the events were silenced.

There is also the silence of renunciation, often of penance. In these stories the young protagonists go or are driven into the forest. There they meet a hermit, or an old wise woman, who very often turns out originally to have been a warrior or princess. Either through choice or as punishment they had exiled themselves in the forest – and in silence learned wisdom. Now they can understand the language of the birds, or have a mastery of herbs and healing, which they use to assist and serve the young. The ancient custom of keeping a night vigil alone in a church before major life events – like setting out on a quest or crusade, or even being made a knight – might derive from these stories. Nor is it only men who retreat into silence to expiate past sins and emerge not merely absolved, but with a new depth of knowledge. Guinevere and Maid Marian both become nuns. Sleeping Beauty is consigned to the absolute silence of sleep as a punishment for her parents' pride and forgetfulness – first they failed to invite all the magical powers to the child's christening and then they thought they could circumvent a curse. She sleeps for a hundred years while the thorns grow thick around her and the whole castle is silent with her. But she is awakened to love and joy when she has served her turn. In the face of oppressive power, silence is often a sound strategy, at least in the short term.

There is another related but different sort of silence in these stories. It is always perilous to tell of fairy things. If the hero or heroine comes by fairy knowledge – help or riches or simply good luck – they must never tell where these good things came from or they will vanish. Sometimes the fairy folk coerce silence by terrible vows or threats. Sometimes they even seal characters' mouths and make them dumb so that they *cannot* speak. This sort of silence trickled out of the stories and into 'real life'. In several witch trials in Scotland in the early seventeenth century this silencing comes up in evidence: Elspeth Reoch's fairy lover made her

> be dumb for having teached her to see and know anything she desired. He said that if she spoke gentlemen would trouble her and [make] her give reasons for her doings . . . and on the morrow she had no power of her tongue nor could not speak . . . wherethrough her brother [hit] her with a [bridle] until she bled, because she would not speak and put a bow string about her head to [make] her speak. From the which time she still continued dumb.[13]

Scottish witches had much more exotic and florid experiences of the devil's works than English witches. This probably has less to do with Celtic versus Anglo-Saxon imaginations and more to do with the fact that Scottish law allowed witches to be tortured in more extreme ways than English law did. Isobel Gowdie told her court a spell for flying and assured them that it was easy; Elspeth Reoch was given Knowledge and bound to silence. We now know that 'evidence' given under torture is extremely unreliable and these trials offer older proof of that. In such witch trials I think we see women under intense and painful pressure drawing on stories from their communities in order to have something to say.

A great many fairy stories are about someone's true identity. You may look like a goose girl; you may be so filthy and ill-kempt, through poverty or neglect, that they call you Cinderella, but truly you are the princess – and the evil servant or stepsister who has usurped your rightful place will be exposed. Related to this there is also a very specific silence about a person's true name. In the *Earthsea Trilogy* Ursula le Guin picks up on this particular silence: to know people's or things' true names gives you power over them. The art of magic is the art of learning true names and how to use them. Le Guin did not invent this – it is embedded in a great many cultural myths and stories: if you know a person's real name, you know their true identity, for good or bad, and you have power over him or her. 'Rumpelstiltskin' is a very well-known European version of this sort of silence. The imp or minor devil who bails out the heroine by spinning her straw into gold – a task laid on her, incidentally, only because of her own lies – does so in exchange for her first child when she has one. The straw is spun, she marries the prince and she has a baby. The imp returns to extract his wages, but she strikes a bargain with him: if she can discover his real name the pact will be voided. Through an odd mixture of chance and endeavour she does indeed succeed – she tells him his name and he vanishes in a puff of smoke. Identity, these stories suggest, must be guarded and cherished.

The idea of trial by silence is very ancient: it emerges in folklore and religious ritual from almost every culture. The aboriginal boy must undergo an initiation of silence-in-the-wild to become a man, while on the other side of the world the squire and the novice must pass through a night of silent vigil, the tall columns and vaulted roof rising above them like trees, to achieve their high status as knight or monk.

Trials are the stuff of fairy stories. Quests, both outward into the unknown world and inward into the protagonist's moral being, are basically trials. Only the worthy can prove they are worthy. Only the *real* princess can feel the pea through all those mattresses. Unlike myths, fairy stories are never about transcending nature, but about uncovering – discovering – an already existing identity. The function of trials is to uncover the truth: this is why trial by combat between two men was deemed capable of determining a woman's sexual fidelity; why trial by water could prove whether someone was a witch; or indeed trial by jury can infallibly expose a criminal. Etymologically 'trial' derives from 'try', not in the sense of 'attempt', but in the sense of 'test' – to try out a new car, or try on a new frock.

Perhaps the best-known European fairy story dealing with 'trial by silence' is 'The Six Swan Brothers'.[14] Here the nameless heroine's six brothers, betrayed by their stepmother, are turned into swans and she voluntarily undertakes a trial by silence to release them: she will be silent for seven years. She is bound neither by a forced oath nor by being struck dumb – she chooses to be silent freely and with love as her only motive. She also has to make them each a shirt out of starwort. This is deeply mysterious because starwort is a leggy wild flower with tiny petals and not particularly fibrous stalks; it does not seem possible to make thread out of starwort. The only clue I can find to the meaning of this strange task is that starwort, in some parts of the country, is called stitchwort – probably because, as an infusion, it was believed to heal 'stitches', the kind that stab you in the side if you run too far or fast. The pain, the endurance of pain and the difficulty of the task all come together here – although I don't know if the twinning works in German whence the story originally comes.

She sits in a tree, like a bird, completely silent and sewing the shirts. A king finds her there, woos her, takes her to his palace and marries her, but still she does not speak. Her wicked mother-in-law steals her newborn babies, smears her mouth with goats' blood and eventually persuades the husband that his silent wife is a witch and has eaten their children. She does not defend herself. She must be burned. She is led to the stake, the almost finished shirts carried neatly over her arm – and at the last moment the air is filled with swans, they swoop down, put on the shirts and are restored to human form. She is free to speak, she tells her story and all is well,

save that one shirt was unfinished and the youngest brother must
go through life lopsided, with a swan's wing instead of his own left
arm.

This is a very strange story. Surely a woman is not *meant* to love
her brothers more than her husband or her children? In
'Rumpelstiltskin' the 'heroine' is let off her Faustian bargain simply
because mother love is allowed to override justice; she is freed from
a promise because she is a mother. This is a much more normal
approach to mothers and their commitments. If fire tests courage
and water tests purity, what does silence test? Not love certainly.
The boundaries of the self, perhaps.

Integrity. Together with vigils and trials by silence go fasting and
trials by hunger. The silent hermits are fiercely ascetic. Taboos
about food and taboos about words are often closely related.
Persephone must not eat while in hell; she must keep her mouth
shut, or she will be claimed by death for ever. None of this is
surprising: our mouths are one orifice over which we might seem
to have control. To speak is to give not just secrets, but our selves,
away. Not to speak, then, is to be self-contained, autonomous, adult
and, by implication, chaste. Trial by silence tests integrity.

Going to the forest did not cure me of being scared of it, but it
taught me that the terror of silence was complex and the struggle
to engage with it and understand it was beautiful as well as dark. I
came home from Inverness somewhat enchanted myself, and more
aware than ever that the long shadow of the wild wood plays an
essential role in our contemporary negative attitudes to silence.

Looking back at those three years in Weardale, I see them as a
kind of novitiate. When a would-be nun (or monk of course) enters
a religious order she is first a 'postulant', a person 'postulating' or
proposing that she might want to join. A postulant takes no vows
and makes no commitments. If this works out well on both sides,
she then becomes a novice. A novice is a new nun in formal training; as well as participating in the life and practice of the order she
is taught – about prayer, about the theories behind it, and about the
history of monasticism and her own chosen version of it; in a sense

a novice is an apprentice – she is learning the skill of her life work in both theory and practice. In Weardale I was a silence novice, studying the practice and history and theory of silence.

When I moved to Weardale I did not fully realise this – I thought it was a new beginning that would go on for the rest of my life, but in fact it turned out to be more of a pause. Even as silence is undermined in so many ways in the contemporary world, there remain tiny puddles of it in most people's lives, pauses in the stream of sound, which they value though do not usually call silence. A common example is a hot bath at the end of the working day, whether or not accompanied by a drink. 'Unwinding' is a popular term for these little silences, suggesting that one does get wound up by the noise of daily life, and just under the level of consciousness one knows that incessant social activity can deplete as well as nourish the self. I have come to see Weardale as just such a pause.

A pause is a rather nebulous little whatsit, somehow, and hard to get a grip on. But certainly in a pause there is anticipation. Musical notation has proven better than spoken language at encoding small silences: here a silence is called a 'rest' if it is a precisely measured stoppage (half-beat; a beat, a bar) but a 'pause' if it goes on for an imprecise amount of time: they're written differently on the staves. Language has lots of vocabulary for different small silences, but no way of showing how they fit into the hubbub of words around them: pause, stop, rest, end, caesura, hesitation, lacuna, delay. In defining 'pause' the OED rather favours 'hesitate' in the examples it gives, but 'hesitation' suggests a kind of fumbling whereas to me at least 'pause' does not; it is difficult to imagine a 'serene hesitation'.

The one most obvious thing about a pause is that it doesn't go on for ever. To *be* a pause it must sooner or later, and probably sooner, be broken; whereas with a 'stop' or an 'end' there is closure. It isn't just that a pause doesn't go on for ever – it is that we know it isn't going to. It is building up to something. Presumably this is how comic 'timing', the famous pause-before-the-punchline, functions. The comedian creates a little silence to give the audience time to want to know what the punchline will be, time to intensify their desire. But they do have to know there will *be* a punchline – they have to be 'trained' in the genre codes of stand-up comedy or it isn't going to work. If the pause goes on too long the anticipation evaporates, into anxiety or boredom or over-anticipation.

In *Le Plaisir du Texte* Roland Barthes, the French literary theorist, argues that contemporary literary forms require 'closure'; but that the satisfaction of closure (full-stop endings) deprives readers of the 'bliss' of the opening-out ending. Presumably he wanted works of literature to *end* with a pause. And T. S. Eliot described poetry as 'writing with a lot of silence on the page'. Did he mean writing with a lot of *pauses* on the page, since the poet is going to start a new line at any moment?

The only use of pause to mean a *permanent* ending that I can think of is 'menopause'. While I was considering this odd euphemism, I noticed with ironic amusement that the American word for a full stop is a period.

In this pause I learned a lot of things, external and internal, many of which were entirely unexpected. The biggest surprise was the realisation that there were so many different sorts of silence. My assumption had been that silence was going to be monotone; that all silence would be somehow the same and however one came by it, the end product, as it were, would be very pure, very beautiful but somehow flat, undifferentiated. Skye and the flotation tank had begun to teach me better, and now I was finding more and more complexity. The more silences I looked at, the more silent places I went to, the more I became aware that there were dense, interwoven strands of different silences.

Even at the physical level there is a huge variety. The BBC's radio sound archive has tapes of a remarkable range of different silences – 'night silence in an urban street'; 'morning silence – dawn, the South Downs'; 'Morning silence – winter moor'; 'Silence, sitting room' – 'garage' – 'large hall' – 'cement bunker' – 'beach'; and so on; and even so most radio producers prefer to go out and record their own version of silence for their specific programmes. This is partly because in fact it is practically *never* truly and completely silent, at least within the earth's atmosphere, but it is also because these different silences have different emotional connotations.

Beyond the purely auditory experience there is an even greater range; there are emotionally different silences and intellectually different silences too. I have come to believe that while sound may be predominantly a brain phenomenon, silence is a mind event. The experience of silence is more tightly bound up with culture, cultural expectation and, oddly enough, with language than the experience of sound is. Chosen silence can be creative and generate self-knowledge, integration and profound joy; being silenced (a silence chosen by someone else and forced upon one) can drive people mad. It is possible to experience external silence without any sense of interior silence and in a few cases the reverse. Catherine of Siena, the Italian mystic, was famously able to maintain a conscious awareness of her own interior silence while pursuing an eloquent and complex ambassadorial role about the politics of the papacy. Silence is multifaceted, a densely woven fabric of many different strands and threads.

This was helpful to my conviction that silence was not simply a deficit or lack, an absence of sound (or speech or noise). It seemed to me that if silence were simply a negative event, a blurred absence of a great reality called sound, then it could not have specific qualities of its own, no pitch, volume or tone and no reverberations. But increasingly all my experience suggested that silence does indeed have these qualities, or at least qualities close to and comparable with these. 'A scary silence' and 'a holy silence' are crude examples; but I learned to tell when it had been snowing in the night by the quality of the silence, even more than the light, when I woke up – snow silence is different from wet silence or sunny silence. Silence can be calm or frightening; lonely or joyful; deep or thin. Certainly silence seems to have reverberation – the silence in the sensory deprivation pod and the silence at Throstlehole *felt* very different.

I found it quite daunting to discover that silence was so complex and asked such difficult questions of me. But I also found it fascinating and deeply engaging. There was, and there remains for me, something deeply mysterious about the fact that there are different kinds of silence. I find comfort in Georg Cantor's elegant mathematical proof that infinity comes in different sizes. Both philosophically and mathematically this was deeply shocking (it made Wittgenstein extremely cross) – but nonetheless it is now generally accepted. If there can be different sizes of infinity, of course there can be different volumes of silence; and indeed, I now hope there may be whole symphonies of silence.

6

Desert Hermits

During these years in Weardale I grew deeply contented. I lived in a place of extraordinary wild beauty. I was fit and well. I had all these fascinating things to think and learn about. I was never lonely and never bored. I had enough satisfying work to do. I felt my prayer life and my theological understanding were developing, and moving forward in ways that seemed both natural and exciting. I felt I was creating a way of living, freely and silently, that might be useful to a noisy world as well as to me personally. Above all, I enjoyed the sense of exploration, and possibility.

Then I noticed something shocking. I had come to Weardale for four conscious reasons: to study and think about silence, to find out if it was delightful to me, to deepen my prayer life and to write better. I was indeed doing and enjoying all the first three, but I was not, in fact, writing. Or, to be more precise, I was not writing any fiction and certainly not of the kind I wanted to write. When I had come north it had been with a sense that the stories were not *enough* – I wanted to dig deeper into them, to pull more out of them. It had not occurred to me that I would abandon them, nor they me. The desire to write, to tell stories that pull my thoughts and emotions together, has been something that I have lived with and found integral to my sense of well-being, even of identity, for as long as I can remember. Now quite simply *stories* did not spring to mind; my imagination did not take a narrative form. I had in a peculiarly literal way 'lost the plot'. I found this disturbing.

More to the point, I could not understand what was happening. When I set out on my journey into silence, I had a very well-embedded assumption. I was a writer and a pray-er; through a disciplined practice of silence I would get better at both.

It is a commonplace, almost a cliché, that silence and solitude are good for the creative artist and particularly for writers: 'the world is too much with us', we need privacy and peace, and a minimum of interruption because 'solitude is the school for genius'. Equally, it is very generally held, in almost all religious traditions, that silence (in larger or smaller doses) is necessary to the aspiring soul. This belief is not confined to monotheistic faiths and even the most communitarian traditions, like Judaism and Islam, have a silent tradition and core narratives about withdrawal into solitude and silence as a precursor to hearing 'the voice of God' and being enabled to take radical action.

So it had seemed perfectly reasonable to me that I could go and lurk up on a high moor, put in the disciplined practice of concentration and meditation, and thus become *both* a better, more prolific imaginative writer *and* more safely and intensely engaged in the life of prayer.

To put it at its simplest I was now being proved wrong.

Luckily I had already become aware that there are lots of sorts of silence. This gave me an idea that there might be something profoundly different between the silence of the hermits and the silence of creative artists. I started to read more attentively the attempts of both groups to describe what they thought their silence was *for*. What I began to see was that the two projects are, in a number of ways, inherently contradictory. Here are two quotations from famous silence practitioners. Both quotes are from personal letters, rather than published text, and I do not think that this is mere chance.

> You said once that you would like to sit beside me while I write. Listen, in that case I could not write at all. For writing means revealing oneself to excess, that utmost of self-revelation and surrender . . .

that is why one can never be alone enough when one writes, why
there can never be enough silence around one when one writes, why
even night is not night enough.[1]

And:

We must cross the desert and spend some time in it to receive the
grace of God as we should. It is there that one empties oneself, that
one drives away from oneself everything that is not God and that
one empties completely the small house of one's soul so as to leave
all the room free for God alone. . . . It is indispensable: the soul needs
the silence of it, the inward retirement, this oblivion of all created
things.[2]

The first is by Franz Kafka in a letter to his fiancée (perhaps not
altogether surprisingly they were never married). Kafka was a
Czech-born Austrian of German-Jewish parents, much influenced
by the pre-existentialist theology of Kierkegaard, who saw social life
as a continuous assault on the individual by a pointless and irrational society. He was hypersensitive and deeply introspective. Here
he clearly sees silence as a means to strengthen his ego, by protect-
ing it from social pressure, with a view to establishing an authentic
self or 'voice' in which to write, and as a way of developing and
experiencing personal fulfilment.

The second quote is from Charles de Foucault to a friend. De
Foucault came from a prosperous military family, minor members
of the French nobility. He served in the army until he experienced
a profound spiritual awakening. He first joined the Trappists, but
found the fairly extreme asceticism of the order inadequate to his
personal creed of self-immolation. Eventually he was dispensed
from the order and became a hermit in the Sahara Desert, where
he was murdered, in 1916, by Tuareg nomads. It is evident that he
saw silence not as a means to shore up or strengthen the boundaries of the ego, but to dismantle them – for an extreme act of
'self-emptying', or cosmic merging. The concept of 'fulfilment'

would have been repugnant to de Foucault, filled-fullness and self-emptying being rather precisely opposites. His entire purpose seems to have been the destruction of his ego through radical self-denial.

It is interesting how much these two have in common in one sense. They both saw silence as integral to their life's work. They both come from a similar historical period. They are both using the same genre, the personal letter, to discuss the same issue. They both use surprisingly similar imagery. Of course, rather than comparing them in this way, I could equally contrast them by other sets of identities – by race, class and, indeed, by emotional history: Kafka constantly dreading being overwhelmed by his father; de Foucault fatherless from a very young age. I have quoted them because of their unusual clarity about their intentions, which exposes the radical distinction between them. It is quite difficult to find many quotations as direct as this from those whose sense of self is simultaneously constructed and buried in silence.

However, I am certain that neither Kafka nor de Foucault is unique. I could similarly compare and contrast Virginia Woolf's *Room of One's Own* with Catherine of Siena's 'little secret room' or 'hermitage of the heart'. The vocabulary and imagery are markedly similar; the projects are radically opposed. Woolf seeks solitary space in order to escape from the social pressures on women and establish a secure identity and voice; Catherine seeks the same space in order to empty herself of ego and merge her identity with, lose her sense of self in, her God.

So a new and, I have to say, painful question developed for me, coiled within the pleasure and excitement of my growing silent life. Is it possible to have both – to be the person who prays, who seeks union with the divine *and* to be the person who writes, and in particular writes prose narratives? I was very much aware that I have always believed that silence, and particularly silence in 'nature', was supposed to stimulate both artistic creativity and religious spirituality. That was not what I was experiencing.

Increasingly, I felt that there were, or seemed to be, two different sorts of silence, which required very different techniques. In prayer one is trying to empty oneself of ego; pour oneself out, become permeable, translucent, empty, open to the transcendent; whereas in the act of making art one needs the silence to focus all one's capacity, to shore up or strengthen the ego. I began to understand more seriously what George Steiner had meant when he described artists as 'rival creators'. I had always thought that this was rubbish – and that God wanted us, rather, to be co-creators. I was learning, with different degrees of acceptance, frustration, willingness and resistance, that I could not *be silent* and at the same time be creating new words and new worlds. Silence has no narrative. Silence intensifies sensation, but blurs the sense of time.

I began to feel that this meant, or might mean, that I had to make radical choices about who I chose to be. Could I be happy to give up writing? Could I be contented with a more active and businesslike kind of religious practice? The answer to both questions, most of the time, was 'no'.

I had a problem.

So I decided to try to dig down to the roots of these two very different silences and try to understand them better. Because I had found the atmosphere of specific places so helpful in my earlier searches I decided I would make two more journeys: one to the desert, which the Christian hermits of the third to sixth centuries had used to explore radical silence as a means of getting closer to their God; the other to the mountains, which had proved so important to the writers of the Romantic Movement whose ideas have so deeply informed contemporary understanding about what it means to be a creative artist.

I went to the Sinai Desert first, because that is the older of the two strands.

Geographically, Sinai is a part of the vast belt of desert that runs from the Atlantic across the top of Africa (the Sahara) into Saudi Arabia and, curling northwards, along the eastern side of Jordan into Syria and Iraq. The part of this chain of deserts that lies between the Nile and the Euphrates is the wellspring of Judaism,

Christianity and Islam, the monotheisms of the 'Children of the Book', which are sometimes called the 'Abrahamic faiths'. In this shared story Abraham and Sarah came out of Ur of the Chaldees, an ancient city on the Euphrates about 150 miles south of modern Baghdad, trekked along the northern edge of the desert to Haran (in Syria), then south through what is now Israel, into the Negev in the north-west of the Sinai peninsula and down into Egypt, and finally back through northern Sinai to the land of the Canaanites, now Israel and Palestine. Somewhere in this vast, bleak journey the idea of a God who was almighty but nameless, who could not be bribed, who was not tied to any place or temple, who could be met directly and personally, who would speak to His people, began to take root.

Generations later, so the story runs, the young Moses, fleeing justice (perhaps the very first nationalist to begin as a terrorist and end as a patriarch) after murdering an Egyptian overseer, encountered God in a burning bush at the foot of Mount Sinai. Inspired by this vision, he led the Hebrews out of slavery in Egypt and into this desert for forty years until they finally arrived in the 'promised land', which was also the land of their ancestors. In the desert the Hebrew migrants experienced a harsh purification, a total dependence on their God and above all a direct and abiding encounter with the divine. On the summit of Mount Sinai God gave Moses the tablets of the law. So crucial was this understanding of the desert as the place where God could be found that Jesus and Muhammad, seeking, centuries later, to move the religious tradition forward, both withdrew into the desert to prepare themselves for their missions.

Everyone who has written about the desert, from the hermits themselves right through to modern tourists, speaks about the density of desert silence. Gertrude Bell, the British traveller who was to become such an important figure in the political development of the Middle East after the 1914–18 war, wrote to her father during her first desert journey:

Shall I tell you my first impression – the silence. It is like the silence
of mountain tops, but more intense, for there you know the sound of
the wind and far away water and falling ice and stone; there is a sort
of echo of sound there, you know it father, but here nothing . . .
silence and solitude fall around you like an impenetrable veil.[3]

It was this silence that I wanted to taste. I joined a desert retreat
organised by Wind, Sand and Stars, 'which offers an opportunity
to spend a week in one area, meditating in the space, silence and
beauty of this ancient place'.[4]

Getting into the desert was an unusually fretful and noisy experience. I flew to Sharm el Sheik, the tourist resort on the south coast
of the Sinai peninsula. All the irritation with flying that I had developed over the previous years was given appalling confirmation – an
overfull plane of happy families en route to a beach holiday; the
particularly stressful noise of human voices speaking at high volume
in a language I could not understand; an intense cacophony of offi-
cious incompetence at the airport. The flight was late, too late for us
to proceed to the proposed campsite for the first night. There was a
din of meeting too many new people in the dark and not knowing
quite who anyone was; a restless night, a hectic dawn reorganisation; a long drive in a crammed jeep over bumpy roads.

And then we were in the desert.

The jeep engine was turned off and we transferred to camels.
Once I got used to it, I found the gait of my camel oddly soporific,
slightly like being in a small boat on a calm sea, a steady rocking
sensation. A camel does not need much steering or much attention
at all, really, very different from a horse. It was hot and I rocked
there under the bright sun. The sky was white, too dazzling to look
at, and gradually the silence of the desert took hold and overwhelmed me. I sat on the camel swaying passively with it, losing any
sense of time and distance.

Sinai is not a sand dune desert – it is a rocky, mountainous desert.
I have never been anywhere so beautiful and so harsh. Our campsite was called the White Wadi: a flat semicircle of very white sand,

sprinkled with smaller black stones and protected on three sides by sharp irregular escarpments. The cliff-like formations jutted out into the wadi, and down them flowed steep streams of sand that moved and flowed like water when I tried to walk up them; from a distance these falls of sand looked like glaciers.

A very long time ago the whole area was under the sea, a warm, shallow ocean. The rocks are sandstone laid down in narrow layers of sediment. The same slow inexorable movement of the earth's tectonic plates which pushed up the Alps lifted the Sinai peninsula out of the water like a monster lumbering out of the depths, shaking the water off its rough coat. Once the sea had gone and the rocks dried out, the wind wrought the sandstone, eroded it into grotesque beautiful forms, stained in places with vivid iron drippings; in the camp it seemed sometimes as though we were surrounded by great dead beasts, the escarpments their ancient bones. The same wind ground it down into sand, the finest, whitest sand I have ever seen. There are other rocks too – baked basalt, far more resilient and left behind as black patches in the white.

This part of Sinai had a harsh, even cruel, beauty, 'a dry weary land without water'. At first sight it seemed completely barren, even dead – but each morning in the smooth sand there would be tiny footprints running often right up to my sleeping bag: scorpion tracks; they were there though I never saw one. Here for a week I sat each day perched up on the escarpment, in a cleft in a rock, almost a cave, for protection from the sun, looking out over the desert camp, and thinking about silence and prayer. Below me was a long view of the flat desert floor, and the sharp cliffs of rock seemed to rise directly from the sand and ascend vertically. Above me was the blue sky. Once, late in the morning, I saw a single bedu, in long dark clothes and a black head covering, appear at the furthest limits of my view, probably over three miles away and walking steadily towards me across the sand. Eventually the cliff that dropped below me hid him. He had the quality of a dream and may indeed have been one. Once I saw some type of crow floating effortlessly over the camp, watching sharply; very occasionally there were tiny birds, swift and eager as swallows, which flew with sudden grace through the broken rocks. Apart from that there was nothing; a huge hot nothing. It was the deepest silence I have ever known. There was nothing to hear.

It was hot and it was silent. I began to experience for the first time that mysterious 'song' or 'sound of silence'. There is a problem describing it, because it does feel like an aural experience, you do hear it, but I think it is in fact the absence of anything to hear. John Cage thought that it was a physical sound and it proved to him that silence did not exist:

> For certain engineering purposes, it is desirable to have as silent a situation as possible. Such a room is called an anechoic chamber, its six walls made of special material, a room without echoes. I entered one at Harvard University several years ago and heard two sounds, one high and one low. When I described them to the engineer in charge, he informed me that the high one was my nervous system in operation, the low one my blood in circulation.[5]

It was this experience that inspired *4′33″*, his 1952 composition in which a pianist sits at a piano and does not play it for just over four and a half minutes. Cage's point was that anyone listening properly would have heard sound in the concert hall. It is these sounds, unpredictable and unintentional, that constitute the music of this piece.* Cage appears to have accepted his 'engineer's' explanation without any questions. He writes several times about this key experience and in later repetitions drops all reference to the engineer's opinion and presents the explanation as though it were an accredited scientific fact, but other people hear it differently and are less certain that it is in fact physical sound at all. In his book about deserts, *Grains of Sand*, Martin Buckley writes:

* As a rather delightful footnote, in 2002 British songwriter Mike Batt released an album containing a track called 'A one minute silence', credited to himself and John Cage. The estate of Cage launched a lawsuit against Batt, claiming it infringed the copyright of the earlier Cage work. Sadly the case was settled out of court for a large undisclosed sum, but it raises the interesting question of what a copyright in silence might conceivably be.

> Short of a vacuum, true silence requires the absence of friction of
> air upon object – the emptiness and stillness found only in the desert.
> Hovering over the binaries of dust and sky, dun and blue, shade and
> sunlight, silence eventually becomes a sound itself: a sibilant blood
> rush in your ears.[6]

I have discussed this very peculiar and distinct sound with a good
number of people who have spent time in silence. Almost everyone
agrees that it is *there* – very low volume, continuous, and (usually) two
or more toned, exactly as Cage describes it. You can only experience it at very intense moments of physical silence. I don't know
what it is. No one seems to know what it is. It is the voice of God. It
is minute particles caught in the inner ear. It is the consequence of
there now being so many people in the world making so much noise
that there is nowhere to escape the last dying reverberations of
human sounds. It is the spinning of the universe, or the slow crawl
of the tectonic plates deep underground, moving at about the speed
that fingernails grow. Although I first encountered it in the Sinai
Desert this strange effect can happen anywhere that there is profound enough silence, still air and someone paying attention. I still
find something thrilling about it too.

Up in my desert eyrie I had another potentially more dangerous
experience. As the day wore on just as silently and ever hotter, I
would find myself slipping into a kind of lassitude that made the
effort to do very simple things, like drinking, feel immense. It was
a strange, dreamlike state, in which nothing seemed important or
worthwhile, without it feeling particularly horrid or alarming. I
understood with gratitude why Matt, our excellent desert guide,
had gone on and on – *ad tedium* – about how important it was
to keep drinking and nagged about quantity: because he had done
enough to override my lassitude, in that respect at least. But at one
point, as the sun moved round, my legs weren't in shade any more.
I sunburn easily and badly, but even though I knew they would
burn, possibly dangerously, and before long the rest of me as well,
I still looked at my legs in the sun dreamily, thinking, 'I must move,'

but not quite finding the energy to do so. When I described this to Matt, he said, 'desert lassitude' – that it was very common and dangerous. He felt it was a response to solitude and heat that is similar to snow sickness.

That day in Sinai I was protected from any serious consequences by the fact that I had to report back to the camp for supper – and, to the great inconvenience and annoyance of others, would have had to be found and fetched back if I had failed to appear. This realisation did make me wonder if one element in the gradual adoption, in the West, of community (cenobitic) models of the monastic life in preference to solitary hermits was precisely to protect the individuals, not from ravening beasts or the incursions of barbarians, but from this interior movement of the self as it becomes emptier, less precious, less well boundaried and less adjusted to survival. Disinhibition and loss of clear boundaries would be more likely to be fatal in the desert than almost anywhere else.

I spent a great deal of each day, from the breathtaking rose-coloured dawns right through the long hot silence of midday, sitting up there and trying to think about silence and prayer.

There is a tendency today to assume that prayer is primarily a private and interior activity, as opposed to 'organised religious ritual', or 'rote prayers'. But all the anthropological evidence suggests that first of all prayer was communal and ritualised, and the development of silent meditation or private prayer comes much later in all cultures. The earliest account of silent prayer that I have found rather makes this point. It occurs in the Hebrew Scriptures:

> Once upon a time there was a man from the hill country of Ephraim, called Elkanah. He had two wives – Peninah and Hannah, who had no children. Each year the whole family went up to Shiloh, where Eli was priest, to worship the Lord of Hosts and make the ritual sacrifices. Year after year, Peninah used the occasion to taunt, provoke and irritate Hannah about her infertility. Hannah was so upset that she wept and refused to eat, even though Elkanah would treat her tenderly and ask, 'Hannah why are you weeping? Why is

your heart so sad? Am I not more to you than ten sons?' But Hannah was not comforted and left the family group, deeply distressed, and went off on her own into the temple to pray. As she prayed Eli watched her. Hannah was speaking in her heart; only her lips moved and *her voice was not heard; therefore Eli took her to be a drunkard.* Not surprisingly Eli reprimanded her, but she replied, 'I am a woman sore troubled. I have been pouring out my soul before the Lord.' Eli, clearly moved, told her, 'Go in peace, and may the God of Israel grant your petition.' Then Hannah left the Temple and was sad no longer. The following year she gave birth to a son, whom she called Samuel.[7]

This is a very ancient story – probably originally eleventh century BCE, but it is worth noting that it continued to be curious enough for the later editor, who put the Books of Samuel into their present form after the fall of Jerusalem in 586 BCE, to keep it in – obviously silent prayer did not take off with quite the speed one might now expect.

It is a story set in a culture that values the word and the community so highly that silence has very little positive role in classical Judaism. When I talked to Christopher Rowland, Professor of Biblical Studies at Oxford University, about silence in the Hebrew Scriptures, he felt that for that community silence was a negative thing, a lack or absence, indeed, and so of little or no cultural interest.[8] In this culture to be alive is to be speaking – the dead in Sheol are silent. The faithful speak to God and God speaks to them directly, or through messengers ('angels') and through the prophets. It is not that Judaism lacks mystical or visionary insight, or denigrates intense personal union with God; it is more that the accepted form and expression of this inner authority was prophecy and poetry, rather than silent contemplation.

One might expect a society that formed its spirituality in the silent desert, and which forbids itself visual representations, to need and value language especially highly. In such a context words take on an additional weight and significance, and silence poses a particular danger. Perhaps it is not surprising that in the Hebrew Scriptures 'silence' signifies more than simply our modern quietness and comes to mean total ruin or destruction, subjection, death and the grave. The direct Word of God, and the authorised record of it in the law and in history, is essential to the life of the community. In such a culture the great terror is that God will fall silent:

> 'Behold the days are coming,' says the Lord God, 'when I will send a famine on the land; not a famine of bread, nor a thirst for water, but of *hearing the words of the Lord*. They shall wander from sea to sea, and from north to east; they shall run to and fro to seek the word of the Lord, but they shall not find it.'[9]

Yet at the heart of Judaism is the Great Silence. The name of God is not spoken. Even God does not break this silence: when asked for a name, God only said, 'I am who I am.' Once a year, in awe and solemnity, the High Priest in the Holy of Holies in the Temple in Jerusalem spoke the name of God. Even that has been silenced: the name was written down in consonants alone, but obviously a word cannot be pronounced unless its vowels are also known. After the destruction of the Temple by the Romans in 70 CE there was no place in which the name could be spoken and – somehow – the way to speak it got lost, silenced in a new way.

This is one silence that was not broken. It is a taboo so deep that it was not even inscribed in the law. But there is an ancient tale about speaking the name of God. When God first created the world, he created human beings 'in his own image; male and female he created them' (Genesis 1:27). Later, after many things and for many reasons, the Lord God said, 'It is not good for man to be alone,' so He took one of Adam's ribs and made Eve from it, to be 'bone of Adam's bone and flesh of his flesh' (Genesis 2:18–23). There is a myth, however, to fill the obvious gap. The first woman, the one made directly in the image of God and equal of Adam in every way, was called Lilith. She refused to be subservient to him – some versions tell that she refused to lie underneath him when they had sex, while he felt his status required the missionary position – and the couple fought. Outraged, she named the unnameable name and it gave her power. She flew out of Eden and down to the Red Sea coast where (untouched by the Fall and therefore immortal) she lives for ever, sustained on the flesh of her own children, which she conceives alone, giving birth every morning and consuming them before nightfall. She is the screech owl and newborn babies must be protected from her rapacity and enmity with amulets and charms lest, not satisfied with her own offspring, she tries to consume and destroy yours. Power and peril, male and female seem well balanced in this story. But the central silence is protected by threats as well as by promises.

This unnamed God is known not through silence but in the ongoing story of the community and through his own direct spoken word. When asked for his name, God first said, 'I am who I am,' but then added, 'The Lord God of your fathers, the God of Abraham, the God of Isaac and the God of Jacob . . . this is my name for ever and thus I am to be remembered throughout all generations' (Exodus 3:14, 15).

Very early Christianity did not break with this tradition. Although the Gospels record Jesus's forty-day fast, presumably in silence, and his temptations in the desert, and although they describe him on occasion going off to the hills to pray alone, when his disciples asked him to teach them to pray, he did not instruct them in meditation techniques nor urge interiority and silence; instead, he immediately gave them a formalised set of words, clearly designed to be said out loud and communally. (The Lord's Prayer is in the first person *plural*: 'our', 'us' and 'we'.) Nor in his epistles, which instruct the new Churches around the Mediterranean in great detail about the life in Christ, does Paul seem give any attention at all to what we would now call 'spirituality', the silent and interior practice of personal prayer. The attitude that insists that the practice of Christianity is centrally the disciplined worship of the community and works of charity and justice has continued ever since. 'And whose feet will you wash?' asked Basil the Great testily as yet another member of his community headed off into the desert to become a hermit. It was a major plank of the Reformation, but also of the Counter-Reformation, and is still embedded in a great deal of contemporary theology.

So it is not entirely clear *why*, from the middle of the third century, Christians began to go into the desert, initially around Egypt and east of Jerusalem, and develop an intense spirituality based on rigorous asceticism and particularly on silence. Nonetheless, for the next several centuries they did so in surprising numbers. The extremity of the desert and eremitical life is as far as one can possibly go – so they went.

The simplest explanation is that the end of active persecution by the Roman state provided a challenge to a Church that had seen martyrdom as the noblest expression of faith, not just because dying for a cause is always effective, but also because being martyred was imitating the life of Jesus. The extremes of the ascetic life were a response: create something as difficult and disagreeable as dying and you too can be as heroic as the martyrs were. While this is generally viable, it does not explain why *silence* became such a central form of asceticism. There are lots of other more spectacular disciplines, as the early Church set out to demonstrate. Rowan Williams, the Archbishop of Canterbury, has suggested that early Christian spirituality was highly experimental: sit on a pillar, nest in a tree, live in a desert, dance, study, fast, don't speak and so on – *and see what that does for your interior life and your relationship with God.* In the light of the actual physical and psychological effects of silence it seems reasonable to suppose that silence emerged as an effective instrument for inducing profound experiences, and for lowering the barriers between the self and the Other – the resurrected Christ.

Peter Brown, in *The Body and Society*, has suggested that some of the impetus towards Christian chastity and virginity (now interpreted mainly as body hatred and dualism) in fact arose partly from a radical refusal to participate in or support the Roman Empire. For women virginity meant childlessness and refusing to have babies was a clear way of expressing contempt for the system, especially as the

Empire had a worrying population shortfall. If this is correct, it might be worth remembering that public speaking (rhetoric) was another key citizens' duty and the central focus of a Roman education: silence, like virginity, was a critical stance.

In any event, in a surprisingly short time this new faith threw off the aura of faint suspicion in which silence had been wrapped and adopted it with enthusiasm. It is hard now to understand what a profound and radical shift this idea of silent and interior prayer was.

Each day, I took up into the rocks with me Helen Waddell's translation of *The Sayings of the Desert Fathers*, a collection of the things that hermits said about the eremitical life, which were collected by various contemporaries and became immensely influential in the Church for many centuries; and *The Life of Antony*, by Athanasius, a pugnacious bishop and politician who nonetheless wrote an immensely moving account of Anthony's life. I tried to sit still and listen to these accounts in the silence of the desert itself, and think about their experiences and how they might relate to my own.

It is tricky to do this honestly, because these writers had such a very different mindset from mine. Two particular differences get in the way of a straightforward comparison between a modern silence seeker and Anthony. The first is that his culture on the whole had very few problems with asceticism and physical penance. The kind of ascetic practices we might see as self-hatred or even masochism, were seen – following Paul in his epistles – not so much as penitential but as training, as for an athlete or soldier; and training for a prize well worth winning. We now believe that fasting and sleep deprivation, for example, produce some very particular physiological results that have little or nothing to do with holiness as we understand it. We would probably diagnose a substantial number of the famous and highly regarded saints of this tradition as suffering from 'eating disorders'.[10]

The second difference is the very straightforward belief in devils – or demons or Satan himself. This went way beyond a belief in the 'forces of evil' as an abstraction and pre-dates the Augustinian idea that people have a predisposition to sin and a split, divided will. This belief meant that effects like auditory hallucinations, boundary confusions and a consciousness of risk have a totally different meaning and value. Of course they were all at risk – there is nothing that stirs up devils so much as watching a hermit trying to control his or her passions. The demons were continually there, malignant, assiduous and cunning.

Even when I was able to recognise these differences, there remained a sense in which the sources we have for the hermits of the desert are, in modern terms, ideologically contaminated. Athanasius's beautiful and moving 'biography' of Anthony, for example, was written in part for political reasons. Athanasius was well aware of Anthony's immense popular prestige. It was crucial to him to demonstrate that Anthony was a rigorous anti-Arian in order to mobilise popular enthusiasm for his own lifelong struggle against this widely received Christological heresy. However, it is well-nigh impossible to work out anyone's academic theology if he lives in complete silence and never says anything. Athanasius manages, rather cleverly, to present Anthony as silent all the time *except when he was sounding off about orthodoxy*. For this cause he was apparently always willing to break his silence, even to leave the desert and come to Alexandria and speak out. Of course this may be exactly and precisely true, but knowing Athanasius (*contra mundum* they nicknamed him: 'against the world', 'against everyone'), one can't help having some doubts.

Modern biography – trying to discern and then explain the true inner life or nature of a famous person – did not develop as a literary form until the Enlightenment.[11] Augustine's attempts to write autobiography in the modern sense in *The Confessions* were extremely ill-received by his contemporaries. Athanasius, like other commentators on the early saints, was not attempting biography in the sense we would understand, but hagiography (writings about the lives of holy individuals), a separate genre with its own codes. One of the 'rules' of hagiography, at least until the nineteenth century, was that the saints should be exceptional and extreme in whatever way of life they are engaged with. Their sins prior to repentance are always the worst the writer can think of; their penances eccentrically abject; their virtues miraculous in their intensity. Christian hagiography dotes on penitents (ideally young beautiful females whose sins have been sexual); Buddhist 'hagiography' seems to prefer rich, nobly born young men. Practically no one in this literature goes off to be a hermit because they think they might like it. They are driven – at best by a desire to atone for hideous sins, but failing that by a fierce and painful renunciation of a sinful world.

The life of St Mary of Egypt (seventh century, from an oral tradition) provides an early model for this sort of narrative. Zozimos (fifth century CE), himself a famous ascetic, used to spend Lent in the desert; there by chance he met a woman, naked but wrapped in her own hair. She told him that at twelve she became a prostitute, not for money but for 'unbridled lust'. (I find this detail intriguing. A modern morality would tend to treat taking money for sex as more sinful than indulging genuine sexual desire. I am not sure when this shift in consciousness took place.) At twenty-nine she took a pleasure cruise to Jerusalem, which she paid for by selling sex to the sailors. However, once there she was miraculously unable to enter the church. An icon of Our Lady taught her that this was because of her sins – so she instantly repented and rushed out into the desert, where she had lived for the last forty-seven years on 'what this wild and uncultivated solitude afforded', before Zozimos stumbled upon her. She had lived in complete silence for all this period and had undergone agonising temptations and equally agonising mortifications, and now her 'mind was restored to perfect calm'. She had been taught the Scriptures directly by God, as she could not read. She asked Zozimos to bring her the sacrament,* which he did once, but when he came back again the following year he found her dead

---

* It is necessary, of course, that her silence be broken in this respect – since if she has never received any of the sacraments she can't technically *be* a saint. This is a good example of the sort of pressures that hagiography is working under. As well as extreme penance you also want scriptural knowledge, a sacramental life and some miracles – note the lion.

and a handy lion helped him bury her. This is an exemplary hagiographic account and it reveals some of the problems in discussing the tradition of silence.[12]

Nonetheless, with all these caveats in place, I wanted to brood on the contemporary accounts of the hermits in the hope of understanding this desert spirituality better. I chose *The Life of Antony* because Anthony is seen as the founder of the monastic tradition and the first of the Desert Fathers. He was not the first individual to experiment with silence as an aid to spiritual growth – we know that he himself sought instruction from some already practising hermits – but partly, indeed, because of Athanasius's hagiography, his influence and importance, both in his own day and in the development of Christian monastic life ever since, cannot be underestimated.

Anthony was born in Egypt and, while still quite young, sold all his possessions and started to live as a hermit. Subsequently he barricaded himself into a ruined fort in the desert west of the Nile for twenty years in total solitude. (His friends posted him food through a small aperture.)

Adam Nicolson, drawing on his own experiences in the Shiants, comments on the early stages of Anthony's spiritual development:

> All the solitaries of the past have lived with that intense inner sociability. Their minds are peopled with taunters, seducers, advisers, supervisors, friends and companions. It is one of the tests of being alone: a crowd from whom there is no hiding . . . A hermit will force himself to confront that crowd of critics. The followers of the great St Anthony, the third-century founder of Christian monasticism, who immured himself for twenty years in the ruins of a Roman fort in the Egyptian desert, could hear him groaning and weeping as the demons tested him one by one.[13]

After twenty years, however, his friends and admirers broke their way into Anthony's fortress and forcibly ended that phase of his silence. They were surprised to find that he was neither emaciated

nor mad, but fit, well and serene; 'his mind was calm and he maintained a well-balanced attitude in all situations', although he
manifested 'an aura of holiness'.

He then moved to the eastern desert and spent the next period of
his life training and supporting other would-be hermits, teaching,
healing and developing his ideas on silence and self-discipline. He
was illiterate so he has left us no first-person accounts or theology,
but he was widely quoted and his thoughts were recorded by a
number of his disciples and visitors. However, 'the arrival of so
many people was a nuisance to him for they deprived him of the
silence he desired', so he persuaded some travelling merchants to
take him with them deeper into the desert.

> After a journey lasting three days and nights they came to a very
> high mountain at the foot of which flowed a spring of sweet water;
> on a small strip of flat land encircling the mountain there grew a few
> untended palm trees. Anthony fell in love with this spot. He accepted
> some bread from his fellow travellers and he remained alone on the
> mountain. He lived there as though he recognised that place as his
> own home.[14]

Although he made an occasional trip back to his settlements, and
received visits and supplies from his brother monks, 'he was pleased
to be able to live in the desert by the work of his own hands, without troubling anyone else'. And he died there aged 105.

This pattern – first a long period of discipline and asceticism, followed by a teaching stage and ending with a second gentler
withdrawal – is a very common trajectory, not only in Christianity,
but in many religious traditions. Buddhist monks may not take a
permanent vow of silence because, if they are successful in finding
enlightenment, they will have an obligation to teach others their
way. Nonetheless, reading about the final phase of Anthony's life
on his Inner Mountain, as it came to be called, while myself sitting
on a mountain in the desert, moved me deeply. It opened up a kind
of longing, a first awareness that Weatherhill was not going to be

enough – that I too was looking for an inner mountain and possibly even a self-emptying that would make that possible.

As I have indicated, Athanasius was not a sweet or compliant man himself – he was an energetic, argumentative and fairly unscrupulous ecclesial politician with a remarkable lack of humility. Yet even allowing for the fact that he wanted Anthony's prestige for his anti-Arian campaign, it is impossible to read *The Life* without realising that he saw in Anthony, whom he had met, great warmth, sanity, serenity as well as courage and self-mastery. Athanasius liked Anthony. I began to agree with Athanasius; I was encountering an extraordinarily attractive individual – wise, self-ironic, generous, integrated, happy; at peace with himself and with his fellow human beings. This was holiness; not simply a consequence or effect of silence, but the fruit of silence. Suddenly the unspeakable harshness of his life, the disciplines of silence, the long struggle to destroy his ego and empty himself of self, made a new emotional sense. I wanted to be more like Anthony.

Anthony started a major movement. I am not here going to explore the whole history of Christian hermits or silent spirituality; the ground is well covered already.[15] But, briefly, during the next three centuries, thousands of Christians moved into the Egyptian and Syrian deserts to become hermits. Two different traditions emerged, although there seems to have been little dispute or competition between them. The hermits were either eremitic (solitary) or cenobitic (community based). Both these approaches to silent prayer spread fairly quickly throughout the Christian world; before Benedict established the formal basis for monastic communities in Italy, there were hermits on Mount Athos from at least the fourth century and John Cassian, who trained in the Egyptian desert, had founded a community in France in the early fifth century. Although communities are likely to leave more enduring footprints, we can be certain that there were also solitary hermits in the Sinai Desert, all over the near Middle East, in Greece, Italy, Spain and, remarkably quickly, even in Ireland. The Islamic conquest of Roman Syria, Palestine and Egypt in the mid seventh century inevitably speeded up this dispersal.

On the whole the desert hermits did not write much about their theological thinking – indeed, they did not write much about anything, even those of them who were literate. Most of what we know about their lives and their intentions we know at second hand, through extremely popular and widely disseminated collections of their 'apothegms', their 'sayings'. These were often responses to questions that visitors asked them, and were frequently ascribed to the most famous of the hermits, or presented as something 'an Old Man once said'. In the 1930s Helen Waddell, the poet and scholar, translated and edited various collections of the apothegms as *The Sayings of the Desert Fathers* and they have since become fairly widely known in the English-speaking world.

Waddell's collection read very immediately and freshly in Sinai. There is a lapidary quality to many of the sayings – as though they were tiny gifts given to the reader to think about and use, rather than a sustained argument. Of course, not all of them are about silence; this desert spirituality was about various ways of emptying oneself of pride, of ego, of desire for anything except God. But silence was a basic requirement for that self-exploration and self-discipline, the more intense the silence the better:

> At one time Abba Arsenius* came to a certain place and there was a bed of reeds, and the reeds were shaken by the wind. And the old man said to the brethren, 'What is this rustling?' and they said, 'It is the reeds.' The old man said to them, 'Verily if a man sits in quiet and hears the voice of a bird, he hath not the same quiet in his heart: how much more shall it be with you, that hear the sound of these reeds?'†

---

* Abba is an Aramaic word for 'Father' and was what Jesus called God. It became an honorific title for hermits, especially those who acted as teachers to neophytes. From here it evolved into its modern English form, 'Abbot' (the head of a monastery) and the French *Abbé*, and is the etymological reason why collectively the hermits are known as the 'Desert Fathers'. I tend to avoid this expression and use 'desert hermits' when possible because 'Father' can obliterate the fact that there were women desert hermits too.

† It is curious that when Henry Thoreau described his ambition to live in silence, he wrote in his *Journal* in 1841, 'I want to go soon and live away by the pond where I shall hear only the wind whispering among the reeds.' His silence was very different from Arsenius's.

Some of the other Sayings about silence that particularly touched me in Sinai were:

Who sits in solitude and is quiet hath escaped from three wars – hearing, speaking, seeing: yet against one thing shall he continually battle: that is, his own heart.

A brother told Abba Sisoes, 'I want to control my heart but I can't.' The Abba replied, 'How can we control our hearts when we keep open the door of our tongues?'

Just as if you leave the door of the public baths open the steam escapes and their virtue is lost, so the virtue of the person who talks a lot escapes through the open door of the voice. This is why silence is a good thing; it is nothing less than the mother of wise thoughts.

Stay in your cell; control your tongue and your belly and you can be saved.

Not all quiet men are humble, but all humble men are quiet.

John Cassian's writings are slightly different from the Sayings, although some of them are included in Waddell's anthology. He was writing *about* the desert hermits in order to help his new monks in France. He is often therefore much more explanatory than the hermits themselves. He gives an account of why the desert was so central to the eremitical life:

We could have built our cells in the valley of the Nile, and had water at our door . . . We are not ignorant that in our country there are fair and secret places, where there be fruit trees in plenty and the graciousness of gardens, and the richness of the land would give us our daily bread with very little bodily toil . . . But we have despised all these; we have joy in this desolation, and to all delight do we prefer the dread vastness of this solitude, nor do we weigh the riches of your glebe against these bitter sands . . . He who keeps an anxious watch over the purity of the inner man will seek those places which have no rich fertility to seduce his mind to their tilling, nor beguile him from his fixed and motionless abiding in his cell to work that is to be done under the sky, whereby his thoughts are emptied out in the open, and all direction of the mind and that keen vision of its goal are scattered over diverse things. This can be avoided by no man, however anxious and vigilant, save he shuts in soul and body together. Like a mighty fisherman perceiving his food in the depths of his most quiet heart, intent and motionless he catches the swimming shoal of his thoughts; and gazing curiously into the depths as from an upstanding rock, judges what fish a man may wholesomely draw in, and which he may pass by or throw out as bad and poisonous.[16]

Yet in all this rigour and silence and mortification and denial the hermits consistently demonstrate a buoyant tender love, for God and for each other. More important even than discipline and penance was care for the weak and the great hermit virtue of hospitality. As many of the apothegms speak of this as speak of the harsh fasts, long vigils and weary hours of pointless work. Waddell writes at length of the 'heartbreaking courtesy' of the desert hermits, their profound belief in hospitality and gentleness and generosity.

The desert hermits, and all those since who have pursued this form of spirituality, have known that it will be hard. They say so frequently, even as they urge patience, courage, the refusal to judge and the virtues of fortitude, endurance and humility.

Sore is the toil and struggle of the unrighteous when they turn to God, and afterwards is joy ineffable. For even as those who would kindle a fire are beset with smoke and from the pain of the smoke they weep, and so they come at what they desired. Even so it is written, 'Our God is a consuming fire': and needs we must kindle the divine fire within us with travail and with tears.

The cell of the monk is the furnace in Babylon – but there the three young men found the Son of God.[17]

This sort of prayer is based on the idea that self-emptying, loss of ego, handing one's whole self over to God, in prayer and in practice, is the key not just to some future post-death 'salvation' but to an essential happiness and well-being now; empty of self they hoped to be filled with God. To this end the desert hermits set about humbling their pride, liberating themselves from their slavery to desires, training themselves by rigorous self-discipline. Their means to this end was a level of asceticism which can seem masochistic or even deranged. But as they understood it, the disciplines and rigours of this life set them *free*: free from the bondage to habits, to pointless desires and to the weakness of the will that Paul summarised so neatly: 'That which I would do I do not do and do I even that which I would not do.' Free to lose ego, lose identity, strip naked before God and be loved.

And at the heart of this discipline was silence; first external silence, fleeing the pressures of the social; then internal silence, peace of heart and mind, which could only come from the generous giving away of the self backed up by very hard work. And, beyond that, they hoped they might encounter the silence of God. This is what has since been called 'apophatic prayer' or the *via negativa*. Practitioners, knowing that no images or words can begin to measure up to the immense infinity of the divine, stop trying; they banish all images, thoughts and feelings, all words, and seek only to be absorbed in the void, or, in the words of the very lovely fourteenth treatise on apophatic prayer, to enter the 'cloud of unknowing'.

In some ways this sort of spirituality has a great deal in common with Buddhism. Nonetheless, I sense that there is a difference of intention between Buddhist and Christian silence. Buddhist silence seeks beyond the personal – seeks to end desire and, indeed, to end all things, to escape from the wheel, from the cycle of return, and to merge completely into the one world spirit – variously expressed as Nirvana, Enlightenment or Buddha-mind. Christian silence seeks an openness to the divine that is personal, in Christ who 'emptied himself of all but love'. Self-emptying kenotic love is therefore a fulfilment of the true self, which, traditionally, is held to have the capacity to rejoice eternally without losing specific personality. Moreover, Christianity believes that the world is real and redeemable – and that therefore 'personality', as part of that whole, is sustainable. Buddhism believes that the world is 'illusion', not real – it and all its grief are shadows and delusion from which we can, through undeceiving ourselves, escape. I think these are different freedoms, although the way of arriving there is so similar.

The influence of the hermits is hard to exaggerate. The desert experience, the disciplines of asceticism and the annihilation of the ego in silence created an aspiration and understanding that has run as a thread throughout the history of Christian spirituality. Religious orders of many different kinds have endeavoured to recreate the conditions of the desert in communities of prayer. And parallel to them, private individuals, more hidden and often effectively invisible, have pursued the same end as hermits or solitaries.

It is a tradition still alive today. But it is becoming profoundly counter-cultural, especially in the West. It is not really part of a modern mindset at all – this ruthless self-destruction. Sometimes Charles de Foucault's voice seems to come from a previous universe, even though he lived beyond the first decade of the twentieth century. Some of this is because of his curiously French imperialist and military ethic, which emerges particularly in relation to 'his natives', the Tuareg. But more than that it comes from the way he seems to have, as Peter France puts it,

> looked for opportunities for self-abasement, for abnegation. This was not a part of the life of Nazareth and it can easily be seen as a sign of psychological disorder. Many of the saints have displayed this need for abjection, for mortification, which stems from their meditations on the Passion of Christ . . . Those who choose to imitate him have often pursued the imitation into areas of mortification which helped them to identify with him . . . [Charles's] conduct can only be understood in this light.[18]

Two other modern exponents of this ruthless silencing spirituality are Thérèse of Lisieux and Simone Weil. It feels strange to me to link these two radically different women in this way. Thérèse Martin was a petit-bourgeois French provincial girl who became a Carmelite nun at the extremely early age of fifteen and died of tuberculosis at twenty-four. She also, rather unexpectedly, wrote one of the best-selling religious books of the twentieth century – *L'histoire d'une âme* (*The Story of a Soul*), which was published posthumously in 1899. She was canonised in 1925. Simone Weil was a French-Jewish intellectual, brought up in Paris. She was deeply involved in anarcho-syndicalist politics and Marxist theory. She went to Spain in 1936 to fight with the International Brigade. After 1938 and a profound mystical experience, she turned her attention to religion and especially Catholicism, although she was never baptised.[19] In 1942 she came to London to work with the French Resistance until she, too, was diagnosed with tuberculosis. She died in 1943. The coroner's verdict was that 'the deceased did kill and slay herself by refusing to eat whilst the balance of her mind was disturbed'.

On the whole, for most progressive twenty-first-century liberals, Simone Weil is a something of a heroine while 'The Little Flower', as Thérèse is somewhat nauseatingly called, represents all that is least attractive in Victorian Catholic piety. But they were pursuing the same ends, and by very similar means. In the destruction of their individuality, the mortification of all desire, a brutal practice of silence and self-punishment, they were both waiting for a desert God without a name to come to them in the darkness of their own emptiness and the silence of their hearts.

Thérèse writes:

I had been offering myself to the Child Jesus as His little plaything, telling him not to treat me as the sort of expensive toy that children only look at without daring to touch. I wanted Him to treat me like a little ball, so valueless that it can be thrown on the ground, kicked about and left lying in a corner . . . I wished only to amuse the Child Jesus and let him do with me exactly as he liked.[20]

Weil writes:

> The extinction of all desire – or detachment – or *amor fati* – these all
> amount to the same thing: to empty desire, finality of all content, to
> desire in the void, to desire without any wishes. To detach our desire
> from all good things and to wait. To wait through and across the
> destruction of Troy and of Carthage – and with no consolation. To
> wait as a door slave waits, listening attentively for his master, and to
> go on waiting even when he knows the master will not come.
>
> I do not ask you to believe in God, I only ask you not to believe in
> every thing that is not God.[21]

Despite the almost bizarre difference of imagery and language, they
are offering remarkably similar insights – slaves and toys are both
possessions, have no rights, no independence, no instrumentality, no
true personhood. There was in both of these women an almost
inhuman rigour, a willed decreation, which determinedly eliminated
human love, not just sexual but even real friendship, spiritual con-
solation, in the sense of mystical experience, and in the end the will
to life itself. They both buried themselves in a dark silence and
stayed there waiting for God. They have some other interesting
things in common too: they are both women and both French; they
both wrote extensively and then refused to take responsibility for
their own writing – giving it away at the point of death with instructions to their editors to do what they wanted with it; they both
rejected normal forms of human relationship; they both gloried in
suffering and they both died too young, from causes undeniably
associated with their courageous assault on their own egos, using
silence as their murder weapon. In a sense they were both throw-
backs to a pre-modern sensibility.

I am very much aware that this sort of spirituality is repugnant to
many people. But it is not repugnant to me. It is challenging and
somehow thrilling. It is also terrifying. I do not know who I would be
if I gave myself away, silenced my own words and sat waiting on
God in the darkness.

Some of this repugnance is, again, the fault of hagiography; the genre loves penitence and suffering. Atonement for sins and renunciation of 'the world' sit awkwardly, in any narrative, with deep delight or joy – that ineffable *jouissance*, which I have suggested is part of the common experience of silence and which is likely (at the very least) to be enhanced if an individual interprets the joy as a sign of the presence of God. When Athanasius wrote about Anthony he had a point to make – everything he did was about contesting the Arians' heretical Christology and he wanted to haul Anthony and Anthony's immense prestige on to the side of anti-Arian orthodoxy. He needed to give Anthony *gravitas* and the best way to do that was to stress the painful rigour of the ascetic life. He was not very likely to say, 'Look, this great warrior of God, the founder of the eremitical life, the hero of Christ, was having a great deal of fun in the desert.' After Athanasius there was not much space for anyone to talk about happiness, joy, pleasure.* The genre requires hideous penitential practice and grim suffering. Even Bede, apparently in himself so gentle and sweet a personality, feels he has to present Cuthbert in gloomy sacrificial terms, giving up his bishopric and struggling deathwards in penitential solitude, despite the fact that all the evidence suggests that Cuthbert was deeply joyful to get back to his island.

But – this is the point – despite the whole literature being set up this way, the hermits' *joy* keeps breaking through. When I first read Athanasius's description of Anthony finding his final hermitage in the Inner Mountain, I wept. I wept because Anthony's delight was so patently revealed. I think perhaps I wept with longing for myself as well, but what it seemed to be (and I believe was) was a kind of moved sharing in the simple sweetness of his delight in his homecoming.

---

* There is a nice little example of the pressure towards suffering in hagiographical literature in *The Penguin Dictionary of Saints*, edited by Donald Attwater. Although this is not really a 'pious work' it falls into a number of genre-coded traps. Describing Bernadette of Lourdes, Attwater comments that she was a 'pious BUT cheerful' child. Even in his scholarly mind there is a contradiction between happiness and holiness.

Despite the privations, the discipline and the sheer hard work, hermits like their lifestyle. They find joy there.

Charles de Foucault wrote in a private letter:

> I find this desert life profoundly, deeply sweet. It is so pleasant and so healthy to set oneself down in solitude, face to face with the eternal things . . . I find it hard to leave this silence and this solitude and to travel.[22]

(Being Charles de Foucault, he does his 'hagiographic work' on himself by immediately turning to a self-denying piety and continuing, 'But the will of the Beloved, whatever it may be, must not only be preferred but adored, cherished and blessed.')

Thomas Merton's pure pleasure, after waiting so long, at being in his little hut in the woods, alone in silence, has something of the same quality about it:

> What a thing it is to sit absolutely alone in the forest at night, cherished by this wonderful, unintelligible, perfectly innocent speech . . . the talk that rain makes by itself all over the ridges . . . As long as it talks I am going to listen. But I am also going to sleep, because here in this wilderness I have learned to sleep again.[23]

> Everything the Fathers of the Church say about the solitary life is absolutely right. The temptations and the joys, above all the tears and the ineffable peace and *happiness.* The happiness that is so pure because it is simply not of one's own making but sheer mercy and gift.[24]

Dalrymple gives a lovely example of this in *From the Holy Mountain.* He was staying with an Egyptian hermit:

> I asked him about his motives for becoming a monk and why he had left the comforts of Alexandria for the harsh climate of the desert.
>
> 'Many people think we come to the desert to punish ourselves,

because it is hot and dry and difficult to live in,' said Father
Dioscuros. 'But it's not true. We come because we love it here.'

'What is there to love about the desert?'

'We love the peace, the silence. . . . You can pray anywhere. After
all, God is everywhere, so you can find him everywhere.' He gestured
to the darkening and dunes outside: 'But in the desert, in the pure
clean atmosphere, in the silence – there you can find *yourself*.'[25]

It is about joy – and love and happiness and beauty. The Chinese
poet Jia Dao wrote, 'On Looking in Vain for the Hermit' in which
the poet goes to massive efforts to track down a hermit but never
finds him.

> I questioned the boy under the pine trees.
> My master went to gather herbs.
> He is still somewhere on the mountain side,
> So deep in the clouds I do not know where.[26]

The last night I was in Sinai I kept an all-night vigil, just sitting
and watching and listening to the silence. I watched the moon cross
the sky casting sharp shadows, so clear that I could see the shadow
of wisps of my own hair that had escaped from my plait, and
changing the shapes of everything. It seemed to tow an indigo sky
with very bright stars in its wake. Later the moon turned yellow like
an egg, and slipped over the horizon; as the glow of it faded I
watched half an hour of dancing stars, with Venus hanging huge in
the east, and then the grey light moving towards sunrise and a spectacular performance of colour as the rising sun moved in a visible
sharp line down the rock faces and they changed colour from grey
to pink, to red and then to gold.

Through the whole night I listened – listened to *nothing*.

The silence was very pure. Down in the camp, all the sounds
were precise breaks in the silence, very distinct, separate from each
other. There was no ambient sound, no background. Just noises
laid on to the silence – like pebbles on a still pond. Or rather not

like that, because there were no outspreading ripples, just a single
sound 'chomp' (camel); 'rustle' (sleeping bag) or my cigarette being
inhaled. Round like a stone – and then the silence returned unbroken, each individual noise carrying very clearly, but without
any 'residue'. The sounds seemed to alight quite gently on the
silence – and the silence gobbled them up, or swallowed them
down.

It was absolutely still, absolutely silent. The desert night was not
very dark and the sky was *deep* – the stars did actually 'twinkle', and
I had a sense of their distance – some are nearer, seem nearer, as
well as larger or brighter. The sky was not a black ceiling, but an
infinite recession. In the night the starlit silence, the time, the distance – the infinite. Yet underneath my hand when I reached out
from the sleeping bag, the sand was made of *tiny* grains, very cool
and clean, fine-textured, soft against my fingers. It was probably the
most profound silence I had ever engaged with. It was this intensity
of silence that I had come to listen to; this was the silence that the
desert hermits sought here in this desert, while they engaged in their
enormous courageous battle against 'the world, the flesh and the
devil' and their own noisy selves.

Through that desert night I conceived a vast, lovely and
awestruck sense of God. God, in this desert context, does not say be
safe, be cosy, here's a woolly blanket, a tidy cocoon, a place of
refuge. God says, 'If your eye offends you pluck it out; if your hand
offends you cut it off.' Bend and break the will, discipline and
scourge the flesh, face blindly the unknown, the enormous, the terrifying. Love your life and you'll lose it. Risk it and maybe, just,
you'll totter into heaven – the place of both annihilation and total
knowledge; the place of beauty and joy. The risk is absolute, you'll
get nothing else out of it, not pleasure, not health, not affection, not
comfort and certainly not safety. Just the beauty of God.

Later in the night I began to hear John Cage's 'sound of silence'
in a new way. It was not my nervous system or my circulation; it was
not the last murmurs of almost silenced chatter, nor the shifty movements of the tectonic plates. I thought I heard the singing of the

spheres. The classical and early Christian world believed that the heavenly bodies sang as they spun through their orbits; each had its own unique and perfect note that reverberated in perfect harmony with the others. With a geocentric universe there were eight such spheres – the sun, the moon and the six visible planets (Uranus, Neptune and Pluto cannot be seen with the naked eye, so they were not known until there were telescopes); this created the perfect eight-note scale. The singing was silent and could only be sensed or imagined at moments of heightened and joyful awareness. The sound of silence, in that desert night, was the song of *jouissance*, of bliss.

In the desert I realised that there is something hideous, especially to a contemporary Western sensibility, about a systematic and determined attempt to break down, or thin out the boundaries of the self and become open to, participate in, the undefined, illimitable freedom of the divine. It is also very hard work. One of the Zen monks at Throstlehole remarked to me once, 'It is strange, everyone says they want to *meet* a saint, but no one actually wants to *be* one. It's too tiring even to think of it.' The experience of both East and West is that silence is the ground for this work.

Whether or not silence is also the goal of the task is a slightly different question.

In the desert I learned that silence is more for me than a context for prayer, or a way of creating more time (though those are important). It is, in itself, a form of freedom; it generates freedom, free choices, inner clarity, strength. A freedom from one's self and a freedom to be oneself.

I started to think that perhaps silence *is* God. Perhaps God *is* silence – the shining, spinning ring 'of pure and endless light'. Perhaps God speaking is a 'verb', an act, but God in perfect self-communication, in love within the Trinity, is silent and therefore is silence. God is silence, a silence that is positive, alive, actual and of its 'nature' *unbreakable*. Perhaps the verb 'God' – speaking, creating – is one more reflex of the infinite generosity, the self-giving abandonment, the kenotic love of God. Perhaps the incarnation of the

Word is but a secondary expression of that 'for our hardness of heart'. Far from 'all silence is waiting to be broken' perhaps all speech is crying out 'like a woman in travail' to be reabsorbed into silence, into death, into the liminal space that opens out into the presence of the everlasting silence.

Did I dare to find out; did I dare to give the absolute a whirl?

7

The Bliss of Solitude

Then, very soon, and wilfully, I turned my attention to what felt like the opposite sort of silence; Kafka's idea that 'there can never be enough silence around one when one writes'. My whole idea of what it is to be a writer was profoundly formed within a post-romantic model of the creative artist. I wanted to undertake an adventure in romantic silence that I could balance against my desert experience and try to learn more precisely how they were both the same and different and what I might do about that.

What I should probably have done was go to the Swiss Alps. The Alps were, for the leading romantics, the apotheosis of the sublime – beautiful not in the orderly, balanced and serene style of classicism, but in a new aesthetic – which meant that a kind of wildness, horror or terror should pervade a view and intensify the emotions. In the previous classical period the Alps had appeared so chaotic and uncivilised that the man of sensibility on his way to Italy for the Grand Tour was supposed to pull down the blinds of his carriage lest he be driven mad by such grotesque excess; some people apparently even had landscapes with tidy Greek temples and other classical scenes painted on the inside of the carriage blinds to protect them against the vast disorder outside. This doubtless made them all the more attractive to the would-be rebel poets of the early Romantic Movement. In Britain, at least, there was nothing comparable, so the high mountains of the Alps had an additional exotic ambience, which was attractive. Shelley in 'Mont Blanc' – his great poem of 1817 – captured and refined a cultural moment:

Far, far above, piercing the infinite sky,
Mont Blanc appears – still, snowy, and serene;
Its subject mountains their unearthly forms
Pile around it ice and rock . . .

Mont Blanc yet gleams on high: – the power is there,
The still and solemn power of many sights . . .
       Winds contend
Silently there, and heap the snow with breath
Rapid and strong, but silently! Its home
The voiceless lightning in these solitudes
Keeps innocently, and like vapour broods
Over the snow. The secret Strength of things
Which governs thought, and to the infinite dome
Of Heaven is as a law, inhabits thee!
And what were thou, and earth, and stars, and sea,
If to the human mind's imaginings
Silence and solitude were vacancy?

This elevated understanding of mountains, and particularly the Alps, led moreover to the original solitary adventurers. Walking and climbing alone, in marked contrast to team sports and their rules and regulations, became activities appropriate to a man of genius. Coleridge led the way by semi-addicting himself to vertigo, running preposterous risks in high places in order to enjoy the sensation of terror.

There were, however, some practical reasons why I did not go to the Alps. The most important one was about *solitude*. It was not physically possible (for me) to go to the desert alone, but I had found going in company difficult. I wanted to explore the romantic 'bliss of solitude'. I did not have the knowledge or the physical skills to climb high alone and I did not want to do it with anyone else. Moreover, I had learned that rock climbing scared me, and not in any 'sublime' way.

I also needed to distinguish this investigation from the long silence in Skye. This was to be a very different sort of journey. Then I had wanted to sit in silence and see what happened. Now I wanted to replicate the particular sort of silence that romanticism has made central to our culture and see how that related to my own ideas about my writing and my growing sense that this was a profoundly different silence from the silence of the desert. I decided that what I should do was go for a very long walk, the sort of walk that Dorothy Wordsworth describes so often in her *Journal*. Day-long hikes in wild, high hill country, followed by quiet evenings at home seems to have been the Wordsworths' circle's recipe for productive poetic work.

The obvious choice, for anyone who is seeking such silence on these terms, would be the Lake District, Wordsworth's own country, but unfortunately the Lakes are now so popular and crowded that they cannot represent silence or solitude for me. The success of the idea that wild nature is somehow 'good for us' is reflected in the recent proliferation of long-distance walks throughout Britain. There are several wonderful trails now – but for various reasons they did not feel right. The Pennine Way was too near home; the West Highland Way too closely associated with Skye. St Cuthbert's Way, particularly the bold clean hillsides over the northern shoulder of the Cheviots and coming down to Lindisfarne, held an enormous attraction for me, but planning this trip, it seemed too closely associated with the eremitical silence of the desert. I am fully aware that the Border Hills do not look in the least like the Sinai Desert, but I know I read all landscapes with a pre-formed imagination; try as I will, there is no pure unmediated seeing for me. Cuthbert had been trained at Melrose in the Irish tradition, with its complex association with Sinai itself and with the hermits. Moreover, it was not coasts I wanted this time but mountains, harsh rock faces, hideous slides of scree, waterfalls, rainbows and long views obscured by moving cloud and mist. The odd storm would be an additional benefit – but even in my most romantic moods I know that I cannot summon the lightning or call up the thunder.

In the end I followed Wordsworth biographically rather than geo-graphically. The Lake District was where Wordsworth had grown up. Like him I went 'home', to walk in the mountains and hills of my childhood in Galloway. Galloway – the old County of Wigtown and Stewartry of Kirkcudbright* – is strangely, though fortunately, unknown. The area has the second-lowest population density in Britain (only Caithness, now part of Highlands and Islands Region, is less inhabited) and that population is very predominantly located on the coastal plain. This leaves a large wilderness, without roads, houses or much else, between the coast and Ayrshire, includ-ing a number of significantly large hills, with the Merrick, the highest point on the Range of the Awful Hand, at 843 metres the highest mountain between Scafell Pike in the Lake District and the Highlands. (This in itself is a blessing – another mere 70 metres and the Merrick would become a Munro – one of the 284 mountains in Scotland over 914.4 metres, or 3,000 feet when the list was made in 1891. Munros lure walkers and break up silences.) The Southern Upland Way crosses the southern edge of both the Merrick and the Rhinns of Kells, between Newton Stewart and St John's Town of Dalry, then passes below the Black Shoulder of Cairnsmore of Carsphairn, but most of this part of the route is through forestry plantations, cunningly hiding the mountain wilderness beyond. This is as near as we can get, I believe, in the UK today, to the romantic wilderness scenery that the Lake District offered Wordsworth 200 years ago. It has everything I needed for the expedition I was plan-ning – high hills with enormous views, rough walking, waterfalls and tiny lochs, roofless castles and abandoned farmsteads. Unlike the Lake District, northern Galloway is *more* desolate than it was in 1800 because the population has declined. As a bonus it is scattered with prehistoric sites – standing stones and barrows – often miles from

---

* It is not clear why Kirkcudbright was a Stewartry (the only one in the UK) rather than a county, except for the obvious fact that it had a steward instead of a sheriff – but so it is. 'Kirkcudbrightshire' was a term invented by the Post Office at the end of the nine-teenth century – and the area is still called 'The Stewartry' for the purposes of the local Regional Council.

any road, which stand as gaunt reminders of a culture entirely silenced and, to fuel a sense of freedom and fervour, it is also the setting for Robert the Bruce's early guerrilla campaigns against English imperialism.

There were other, less high-minded reasons for choosing south-west Scotland. One of the problems with walking alone in areas without much public transport is that you have to walk in circles, or carry too much heavy baggage. In Galloway this was not a problem – someone, usually my mother – would come and pick me up at a pre-appointed rendezvous; and this meant that I could walk further and cover more territory. A final factor was cost: at this time my mother had furnished a redundant farmhouse, about a mile from her house, specifically for her daughters and their families and friends. It felt worth sacrificing some silence in exchange for free board and lodging, and a chauffeur.

So I went to Galloway and walked for ten days, on the high, windswept hills, seeking that release of expressive imagination that Wordsworth calls the 'bliss of solitude'. It was rough and wild and silent and beautiful – and there are few physical sensations as profoundly pleasing as the tiredness at the end of a long day's walk.

The silence on a high hillside is aurally very different from the silence of the desert. In the first place it is nothing like as silent – there is always the wind moving through, across or over things. The wind is like a cellist's bow – it itself is silent but it draws sound out of things in a surprising and rich range of tones, wind in grass, wind in reeds, wind in heather, wind on water, wind squeezed between rocks. The wind driving rain against a waxed jacket makes a different sound from the wind driving rain against a cagoule. There is also the 'sound of many waters'. Linguists, rather sadly, now teach that the claim that Inuit languages have all those words for snow is a myth; but it is a credible myth to me because of how many words English has for the sounds of running water: babble, bubble, burble, ripple, splash, gush, cascade, run, rush, spout, spurt, dribble, drip, drizzle, trickle, flow, ooze, roar . . . and a day spent walking in these sorts of hills will reveal most of them, usually overlaying each other and creating a kind of orchestral effect.

Presumably, high up above the snow line these sounds would vanish as the water no longer runs.

I am not enough of a physicist to know whether hot air carries sound waves differently from cold air, or dry air from wet air, but it certainly feels as though this were true. Hillwalking is bracing – you do not sit mute and still in a cleft in the rocks while the sun dries you out and empties your head. The reverse happens. It is not necessarily cold in the hills (though it often is) but what makes you warm is the expenditure of your own energy – you make your own heat actively, rather than absorbing the sun's passively. There is more external stimulus – you have to look where you are going and there is a lot else to look at too. The view changes quickly, the weather changes quickly – the clouds shift and there is the summit of the Merrick like a hooked beak above you; or Loch Enoch shining like a coin framed by its unexpected white beaches, a hundred metres below you. You can't help looking: was that a deer, or even a wild goat? There are golden eagles in these hills, though I have never seen one; it is hard not to look speculatively, hopefully, at every large bird in the distance. Views like this make you look outwards rather than inwards as you do in the desert.

One lunchtime I found myself eating a hard-boiled egg sitting on a stone on the ridge beyond Benyallery. This ridge, called the Nieve of the Spit locally, affords enormous views both east and west. It was stunning countryside, with the Merrick big and grey in front of me and a 'vast vacuity' below; huge empty distances and golden grass blowing, and here and there patches of bright green sward – very closely sheep cropped. And *nothing*: miles and miles of nothing and no one. The clouds in procession bore down towards me from the north with the sun dodging them almost playfully. More hills for ever away into a blue mist and the wind, coming and going with moments of real calm. I felt strong and free, and the world seemed holy and whole. I thought, 'Earth hath not anything to show more fair.' It was one of those memorably happy moments. I thought, too, that perhaps the effort, the sheer hard work of getting up there from Loch Trool, somehow added to the pleasure – a bonus sense of achievement.

I walked high and hard, and was exhausted every evening. I tried to contrast this experience with sitting in a nook of the desert rocks and trying to empty my mind and my heart of *everything*; and I also tried to think about authenticity and 'coming to voice' out of the silence around me. I learned some things.

I had loved and felt deeply drawn to the silence of the desert hermits – who chose, so strenuously, to empty their minds and hearts. But I was also aware that this concept is profoundly alien in our culture. I started to think about why this should be so and what had changed.

In Europe until well into the seventeenth century most serious-minded people would have accepted the hermits' underlying motivation as a normal and healthy one, even though some of the more extreme forms in which this was expressed raised a few eyebrows. The sensible person practised disciplines, like an athlete in training, in pursuit of the radical freedom to choose the good, unhampered by the pressures of the ego and the weakness of the flesh. Above all, pride, any sense of self-sufficiency or autonomy, and particularly self-love, needed to be wrestled with and overcome: *low* self-esteem was considered a moral good. Now there is something outrageous and wrong in the very idea. This is made more complicated because of the accompanying emulsion of self-abnegation and joy, almost like salad dressing – the emollient of sweet oil and the sharp acidity of vinegar shaken together. This is now hard to understand. The post-Enlightenment, post-Freudian mind cannot find bliss in self-abnegation and if or when someone does, this is swiftly pathologised as self-hatred, repressed guilt or masochism.

Gradually I came to see the movement as historical and that at the Enlightenment a very profound change in how we understand identity itself occurred. Every definition of the Enlightenment ends up proving unsatisfactory, but here I am using it fairly loosely: by the Enlightenment, I mean that shift which surfaced in the seventeenth and eighteenth centuries by which individualism, freedom and change replaced community, authority and tradition as core

European values. The Enlightenment was optimistic, secular and rationalist, and developed an ethical language of natural law, inherent freedoms and self-determination.

Inevitably Enlightenment thinking moved towards a greater respect for the autonomy of the individual and for the positive nature of desire. Romanticism, critical of the excessive civility of the eighteenth century,* focused on the emotional and subjective experience of the individual. Under the pressure of this shift certain relevant words began to change their meaning. Etymologically it is much less common for words to 'improve' their standing than for them to decline in status – villain, gossip and spinster show a typical progression from something positive or neutral to something pejorative. So when I noticed a whole group of words becoming *less* negative in their connotations I got curious. What is going on when words like imagination, self-esteem and above all pride simultaneously move from being negative moral terms to being virtues or positive attributes?

For instance, the word 'genius' changed meaning at this time. Today, as the OED recognises, it almost exclusively refers to a person endowed with:

> native intellectual power of an exalted type, such as is attributed to those who are esteemed greatest in any department of art, speculation or practice; the instinctive and extraordinary capacity for imaginative creation, invention or discovery. Often contrasted with *talent*.

This sense of the word does not seem to have existed before the mid eighteenth century. Prior to that the word, derived from Latin, had only its classical meaning of the 'tutelary god or attendant spirit

---

* Civility – like 'civilisation' – is derived from the Latin word *civis*, 'city' (just as 'polite' is derived from *polis*, the Greek word for 'city'). In the classical period the countryside was seen as uncivilised and 'rude'. Much of eighteenth-century neoclassical culture was built on this notion that nature was the enemy of humanity and needed to be brought under control.

allotted to people at their births – to govern their fortunes, deter-
mine their characters and finally to conduct them out of this world'.
Places and institutions had similar spirits. A Christianised version of
this story allowed people two 'geniuses' – a good and a bad one,
who were often identified as angels; and the phrase someone's 'evil
genius' is a throwback to this original usage. From here the word
developed to mean characteristic disposition or turn of mind, and
thence a 'natural ability or capacity'.

In the early eighteenth century this sense came to be applied with
increasing frequency to the kind of intellectual power particular to
poets and painters – and given the way artists were making increasingly grandiose claims for themselves, it is not altogether surprising
that the word began to denote:

> That particular kind of intellectual power which has the appearance
> of proceeding from a supernatural inspiration or possession and
> which seems to arrive at its results in an inexplicable and miraculous
> manner.

Although this use of the word 'genius' originated in English, it
was taken up enthusiastically by the German Romantic Movement,
to such an extent that their literary and artistic revival is often
known as the *Genieperiode*. The major influence of German writers
on early English romantics meant the term was reimported with
particular overtones.

(I strongly suspect that the word 'genius' was given added amelio-
rative impetus by the enthusiasm at the time for Arabian and Persian
culture – for example, in the growing popularity of *The Thousand and
One Nights*. The word 'djinn' was translated as 'genie', with the plural
'genii', which is the same word as the plural of the Latin genius. This
placed the powerful magic spirits very close to the 'genius' of the
classical world, but with an added frisson of exoticism.)

But for me the most important of these upwardly mobile words
was 'individual' itself. It has acquired a totally new meaning over the
last two centuries.

It is fairly obvious that 'individual' has its roots in 'that which cannot be divided'. And in fact until the late seventeenth century, it meant very much the same as 'indivisible': different parts that cannot be broken down into smaller units. Before about 1650 the most common English usage was theological, specifically as a way of describing the Holy Trinity: 'To the glorie . . . of the hie and indyvyduall Trinitie' (1425) is the first example in the OED: the Trinity is made up of three 'bits', which cannot be divided, which cannot be made sense of except in an indivisible unity. It also referred to married, or conspicuously loving, couples. Shakespeare, in *Timon of Athens*, can talk of 'individual' mates, or Adam can address Eve, in *Paradise Lost*,

> . . . to have thee by my side
> Henceforth an individual solace dear,
> Part of my soul I seek thee, and thee claim
> My other half.[1]

In the eighteenth century the word began to shift. First it became a zoological term meaning a single example of a whole species. Its move from adjective to noun is, I think, as indicative as its change in meaning. Interestingly, it was one of the earliest words to make this grammatical shift – to be swiftly followed by terms like homosexual, feminist, lunatic and so on, words that may well have required the present understanding of 'individual' to achieve their contemporary noun status. William Godwin, Mary Wollstonecraft's partner and a leading radical philosopher, seems to be the first person to use 'individual' in our contemporary sense. It was not until the early nineteenth century that human beings' individuality was deemed not to extend beyond the boundaries of their own skin. That which was not breakable down, divisible into further constituent parts, was the *self* – the individual in whom innate human rights and self-authenticating emotions could reside.

Through the twentieth century the word 'individual' increasingly developed positive moral connotations – it is now a good thing to be individual, unique and separate. Its ascent is still in process: my 1933 edition of the OED has not yet quite caught up with contemporary 'individualism' and still describes it in negative moral language as 'self-centred conduct or feeling; egoism'. In current usage, though, I think it has transcended this obloquy and now means something nearer to 'original', 'independent', or 'well-integrated'.

For many of the intellectuals of the early classicist phase of the Enlightenment the very notion of a hermit was repellent to a civilised person:

> There is perhaps no phase in the moral history of mankind of a deeper or more painful interest than this ascetic epidemic. A hideous, distorted and emaciated maniac, without knowledge, without patriotism, without natural affection, spending his life in a long routine of useless and atrocious self-torture and quailing before the ghastly phantoms of his delirious brain, had become the ideal of nations which had known the writings of Plato and Cicero and the lives of Socrates and Cato.[2]

And, most famously, Edward Gibbon, with what Helen Waddell was to call his 'slow-dropping malice', wrote:

> The ascetics who obeyed and abused the rigid precepts of the Gospel were inspired by the savage enthusiasm which represents man as a criminal and God as a tyrant. They seriously renounced the business and the pleasures of the age; abjured the use of wine, of flesh and of marriage; chastised their body, mortified their affections and embraced a life of misery.[3]

In the *Decline and Fall of the Roman Empire*, Gibbon also wrote the much-quoted line: 'Conversation enriches the understanding, but solitude is the school for genius.'[4] He clearly felt then that there were two different sorts of solitude – the 'genius' post-Enlightenment kind and the 'savage' solitude of asceticism.

This view remained in currency into the nineteenth century, when James Wilson, on tour in the Scottish Highlands, wrote:

> On Eilan-na-Killy are the remains of some ancient habitation, the supposed dwelling of an ascetic monk, or 'self-secluded' man, possibly a sulky egotistical fellow, who could not accommodate himself to the customs of his fellow creatures. Such beings do very well to write sonnets about now that they are (as we sincerely trust) all dead and buried, but the reader may depend upon it they were a vile pack.[5]

I suspect it is a view that many people would fundamentally agree with now.

But by the end of the eighteenth century the idea that the individual was of supreme importance launched a movement that saw itself as being in total opposition to the values of the civilised ('city based') rationalism of the early Enlightenment, although ideologically it drew on the same concept of the autonomous individual. To the idea that an 'individual' was a single unique person, indivisibly contained within a single body, the Romantic Movement attached quite a specific package of philosophical attitudes. Among the most relevant of these are:

- An elevation of emotion over reason and of the senses over the intellect.
- Introspection and a fascination with the self; a sort of heightened awareness of one's own moods and thoughts.
- A fascination with the genius, the hero, and the exceptional personality, and particularly his inner struggles.
- A construction of the artist as a free creative spirit – whose expression of authentic personal emotion was more important than form.
- An emphasis upon imagination and spontaneity as a way to spiritual truth.
- The idea that children were born naturally free and even perfect – and that social life and its demands corrupted them. They came

into the world 'trailing clouds of glory', but 'shades of the prison house' ensnared them all too fast.
- A heightened appreciation of the beauties of nature, particularly the sublime.

The romantic genius or artist had somehow to escape the coils of social convention and slip back into primal innocence so that he would be able to access his deepest emotions. Obviously solitude and silence in nature proved useful here; as I have discovered, these do indeed intensify feelings and sensations. Untrammelled by the demands of social life, the genius will find his inner true authentic self, buried under the layers of false consciousness, and be free to express it.

The 'he' and 'his' throughout this passage is not accidental; the original romantic hero-artist was definitely male. Although a woman, ideally in a doomed love relationship, could and ought to be his muse, she was more often his nemesis, demanding his return to the chains of conventional society.

And so the romantics sought out solitude and silence in order to 'find themselves', just as the desert hermits sought out silence and solitude to 'lose themselves'. It is not coincidental that while the hermits generally preferred the word 'silence', the romantics tended to use 'solitude'; they certainly did not want to be silenced; they wanted to use silence as a way to finding their own individual voices. Periods of silence and solitude modelled on the idea of the religious 'retreat' were considered valuable for developing independence and authenticity, and for allowing an individual to stand outside the conforming pressures of 'civilised' life. They also talked about it a great deal.

> We must reserve a little back-shop all our own, entirely free, wherein to establish our true liberty and principal retreat and solitude.[6]

> No man will ever unfold the capacities of his own intellect who does not at least checker his life with solitude.[7]

Under all speech . . . lies a silence that is better. Silence is deep as
Eternity; speech is shallow as time.[8]

When from our better selves we have too long
Been parted by the hurrying world, and droop,
Sick of its business, of its pleasures tired,
How gracious, how benign is solitude.[9]

Heard melodies are sweet, but those unheard
Are sweeter; therefore, ye soft pipes, play on:
Not to the sensual ear, but more endear'd
Pipe to the spirit ditties of no tone.[10]

To be honest, I find it hard to suppress a certain sense of relief
when I find George Eliot bringing her caustic scepticism to bear on
all this:

Speech is often barren; but silence also does not necessarily brood
over a full nest. Your still fowl, blinking at you without remark,
may all the while be sitting on one addled egg; and when it
takes to cackling will have nothing to announce but that addled
delusion.[11]

On my Galloway walks I took not *The Sayings of the Desert Fathers*
but Wordsworth's *Prelude*.

Wordsworth wrote *The Prelude* in 1805, although he continued
revising it and it was not published until after his death in 1850.
Its title makes clear that it was intended to be an introduction to
The Recluse – the great philosophical epic containing his views on
'Man, Nature and Society' that he never completed. He published the second of its three intended parts as *The Excursion* in
1814; and in the preface to that, he described his overall intention. The editor of the 1850 posthumous publication of *The
Prelude* used that preface to *The Excursion* in his own introductory
remarks.

Several years ago, when the Author *retired to his native mountains with the hope of being enabled to construct a literary work that might live*, it was a reasonable thing that he should take a review of his own mind, and examine how far Nature and Education had qualified him for such an employment. As subsidiary to this preparation, he undertook to record, in verse, the origin and progress of his own powers, as far as he was acquainted with them.

That work . . . has been long finished; and the result of the investigation which gave rise to it, was a determination to compose a philosophical Poem . . . to be entitled the 'Recluse'; as having for its principal subject *the sensations and opinions of a poet living in retirement* [my italics].[12]

What Wordsworth does in the first and second books of *The Prelude* is describe and celebrate his rural childhood. This is no innocent autobiography, it is a treatise on the making of a genius, and in particular it lays out the relationship between the poet and the landscape – that is to say, the natural world imbued with long associations.

In the opening passages of *The Prelude* the poet has first to gain his freedom, 'dear Liberty', by escaping from the city into the country:

> Whate'er its mission, the soft breeze can come
> To none more grateful than to me; escaped
> From the vast city, where I long had pined
> A discontented sojourner: now free . . .

Once away from the pressures of society he can start to think again and have access to his own true feelings and ideas, which will manifest themselves as *poetry*:

> I breathe again!
> Trances of thought and mountings of the mind
> Come fast upon me: it is shaken off,
> That burthen of my own *unnatural self*,

This moment of peace and quiet *naturally* turns his attention back to his childhood and the sublime beauties of the Lakes, which had given him:

> Amid the *fretful dwellings of mankind*
> A foretaste, a dim earnest, of *the calm*
> *That Nature breathes* among the hills and groves.
> . . . thus from my first dawn
> Of childhood didst thou intertwine for me
> The passions that build up our human soul;
> Not with the *mean and vulgar works of man,*
> But with high objects, with enduring things –
> With life and nature

> And I was taught to feel, perhaps too much,
> *The self-sufficing power of Solitude.* [my italics throughout]

I chose *The Prelude* because it was written explicitly to explore how solitude in nature influences creativity by strengthening the individual against the '*mean and vulgar works of man*'. Wordsworth is of course particularly concerned here about how childhood experiences of silence can develop these creative capacities, and also how language, specifically poetry, can represent them.

Wordsworth, and the Romantic Movement more widely, put a new emphasis on the experiences of childhood and its effect in later life. It was Wordsworth who coined the phrase, 'the child is father to the man', in his 1802 poem, 'The Rainbow'.* Since he believed that children were uncontaminated by society, and therefore spontaneously both wise and creative, returning to the scenes of his childhood, alone and in silence, allowed him to access this primal innocence and with it his own poetic voice.

One afternoon, sitting in thin sunshine under the shelter of a dry-stone wall and looking down on the forestry plantations around the

---

* In *Jane Eyre* (1847) Charlotte Brontë, the great romantic novelist, was the first author to give a first-person voice to a child, a stylistic and structural strategy which is now commonplace.

Clatteringshaws reservoir, I suddenly and vividly remembered something that I had forgotten for years. For her fourth-birthday treat my youngest sister had decided she wanted to climb the Merrick – it is a big walk for such a small child, but she did it. She was jollied but not carried. What I experienced was a whole, rounded memory – the kind that is entirely visualised but has nothing outside its own frame. I don't remember why we decided to do this, but remembered vividly the doing of it, the breaking out of the pine trees into the huge upper air, her determined sturdy walking in little red wellington boots, the enormous sense of victory that we all had at the top – and the huge view from the ridge.

This made me notice something interesting: this silent walking seemed to improve my memory. Increasingly, throughout the week, I had a very sharp recall of episodes, events, even emotions. Not just of 'significant moments' but of small things like walking up the Merrick for Maggie's birthday. Things from far back in childhood. They felt at least like 'true' memories and were quite detailed, and usually came as whole, nicely shaped stories. At first I thought this was about coming back to the terrain of my childhood. But soon I realised that it was not just memories of childhood but of later events, which had nothing at all to do with south-west Scotland. One of the things I gained during this week, in this specific silence, was a much stronger narrative of my own life. It was not until after I went home that I became aware of how much – how many anecdotes – I had added to my conscious memory bank. The effort to eliminate ego and silence the mind, heart and imagination destroys a clear sense of time and therefore of narrative, but the attempt to use silence deliberately to stimulate internal states of imagination has exactly the opposite effect. I'm guessing, of course, that this is related to silence – it could just be chance, or menopause or something, but I really do not think so.

One reason that I do not think so is because it seems to have been the experience of more individuals than just me. You go out into the wild and you 'discover who you are', you 'establish your individual voice', or 'your authentic identity'. One of the definitions

of identity or selfhood being explored at present in both philosophy and psychiatry is the idea that the ability to construct a
coherent narrative of one's own life circumscribes identity – to
be an individual is to own a narrative self. Choosing to be alone,
solitary, particularly in a place that is 'sublime', is one way of
establishing contact with such a narrative, unmediated by other
people's interpretation. I came to feel that it really is about going
down (or in/up/through/over) a level internally – and there are
memory gobbets just lying about down there. Silence firstly puts
one in that 'other' place and secondly gives one an opportunity,
without interruptions or comments, to retrieve and shape those
memories. This gives a poignant sensitivity to Storr's observation, 'I regret that the average mental hospital can make little
provision for those patients who want to be alone and would
benefit from it.'[13]

This confirmed for me a validity in the romantic claims for
silence as a deep well of creativity, provided, of course, that you
accept the underlying premises – that our 'inner' self is more 'true'
and more 'real' than the socially constructed *persona* (mask) that we
put on in social circumstances, and that great art is the exploration
and exposure of that hidden self.

This time in the hills made me happy. My body liked being fit
and tired. The walks themselves created a shape and narrative for
each day. It was all extremely simple and pure. And one night I had
an adventure that encapsulated and expanded the whole experience. I had decided there were two walks I wanted to take in the
most northerly part of the region; to save time I decided I would
sleep in my car up in the hills rather than go back down to the coast.

The first of the two days was lovely, bright and clear, but the
walking was strenuous and I got back to the car weary. I snuggled
down into my sleeping bag and was asleep before it was fully dark.
At about 3 a.m. the stars woke me. I did not immediately know that.
I woke up quite gently and lay there, half awake. Then I blinked my
eyes open – and STARS. I have never seen stars like that night, not
even in Sinai. There were so many that they lit up the sky; 'starlight'

took on a specific meaning like sunlight and moonlight. I was hurtled from my bed by them – driven or called, or both, to pull on my jacket and shoes and be outside. It was completely calm and silent. The sky was perfectly clear across the zenith, although there were low, darker bands of clouds north and east. The hills bulked up, clear blacker outlines below the black sky, but high above me was a fabulously dense Milky Way – 'The White Lady's pathway' and 'the Goddess's milk' as it has also been called. There were so many stars it was impossible for me to pick out the constellations that I did know. It was not 'flat'. I had a real sense of the three-dimensionality of the sky. Did the ancients really see it as a flat 'dome' or single layer? I was breathless with awe and excitement. Eventually I found the Pleiades and with the help of binoculars I could distinctly see each of the Seven Sisters, including the fainter Merope, and a dusting of tinier stars within the cluster, like icing sugar on a cake. I had never before really managed to see their different colours – blue, yellow and a brilliantly pure white. As I grew used to the panoply I identified Orion, and picked out the stars of Ursa Major from among the hundreds that seemed to obscure the pattern. There was no moon but there were shooting stars, random, sporadic, but frequent, and some with long flaming tails like the great dragon of the apocalypse.

I didn't know it at the time that it was the peak night for the Orionids – one of the regular meteor showers. So the dragon metaphor was better than I meant; meteor showers are caused by the discarded dust fragments of comets' tails burning up as they encounter our atmosphere. And the whole sky was twinkling, dancing, singing silently. It was gratuitous, that extraordinary sense that it was somehow alive, not flat and dead and distant, but immensely present and vital. Eventually some clouds drifted up or I got tired and the intensity faded. Half exalted, half exhausted, I climbed back into my sleeping bag and drew breath.

Two breaths.

The first breath was for the enormity of the silence.

The silence of the stars is unthinkable. They burn and burn at unimaginably high temperatures for unaccountably long aeons. They blaze and blast and spark, and they do it all in silence. The explosions of their births and deaths go unheard throughout the whole cosmos. Sound waves, unlike light waves and radio waves, cannot carry through a vacuum; space itself is silent. Out there, beyond the atmospheric blanket, is an immeasurable vast and everlasting silence, 'the vast vacuity' through which Milton's Satan fell. No wonder the devil likes noise.

The scale of it all is outrageous. There are about the same number of stars in the Milky Way, our own galaxy, as there are cells in my body and there are at least 125 million other galaxies. The numbers themselves lose meaning; there have not been a million earth days since the birth of Christ, but when I try to talk about astronomy I start treating 'millions' casually because there is no other way to speak. Between each of the stars is an enormous distance – our nearest star, *alpha proxima*, is about five light years away from the sun.* Between each star is silence. According to the Yale Bright Star Catalog there are 9,110 stars with a magnitude of 6.5 or brighter, that is to say visible to the naked eye (assuming ideal conditions and good eyesight). Because space stretches out in every direction you will never be able to see this many at once – only half of them could possibly be visible in each of the hemispheres; nor will you see that many at any one time because the earth spins them into view throughout the night. Nonetheless 4,500 stars is generous enough.

But wait. Pick up a reasonably good pair of binoculars, the same ones you use for birdwatching, and you multiply the number of cosmic bonfires you can see by about ten. So now, if you have a very clear night and a high place to view from, you can see 45,000 stars.

Get a telescope and . . . the present 'best estimate' of observable stars using available telescopes is seventy sextillion (seventy thousand million million million). That is more than all the grains of sand on

---

* In a vacuum, and space is a vacuum, light travels at 1,079,252,849 kilometres per hour. A light year is the distance that light would travel in a whole year: 1,079,252,849 x 24 x 365.

all the beaches and in all the deserts on this planet, but it is not all the stars; it is only the number within the range of our technology.

Standing there in the cold night, I made an effort not to think about antimatter. Cosmologists are currently saying there is not enough matter, enough material objects, molecules or atoms, out there to allow the cosmos to function. There has to be some dark material, invisible, immeasurable, but somehow *there*. They do not know what it is or how to find it. I can be overwhelmed by the idea that antimatter is all the concentrated silence of space. Silence so dense and heavy that it takes on materiality.

The second breath was a sharper intake, more of a gasp. I realised that almost the first thing I had done, confronted with that enormous brightness, was look for patterns, for *stories*. I had instinctively and very swiftly groped about for something I knew a story for. The Pleiades, for example, are named after the immortal sisters, daughters of Atlas, who were placed in the heavens because of their beauty. One of the seven stars is fainter than the others and called Merope because she alone married a mortal while the other six took gods as lovers. The visible astronomical objects are not named randomly: Mercury was the messenger of the gods with winged heels, and the planet Mercury moves faster than any other, whizzing round the sun at high speed. Venus, named after the goddess of love, appears in the evening and the morning, serene and beautiful. Mars looks red in the night sky, red was the colour of war and Mars was the god of war, hence the term 'martial arts'. Jupiter was the king of the gods and is the largest planet; it is surrounded by an exceptionally large number of moons, each named after one of his exceptionally large number of lovers.

Each constellation is a story too: Orion, the hunter, with his sword belt, is visible in the sky of the northern hemisphere only during the hunting season. As Orion disappears to the west in March, Scorpius is rising in the east: Orion was killed by a scorpion, a punishment for boasting there was no living creature who could conquer him, and the scorpion still chases him across the night sky. I find it hard to remember that these patterns are arbitrary and that

the stars in each constellation have no necessary scientific relationship to each other. Chinese astronomy imposed completely different
patterns on the same stars: it was not that they had different names
for the same constellations but that they saw different patterns, different stories. For example, Chinese constellations were smaller than
Western ones and did not depict myths but facets of Chinese court
and social life, such as *Dizuo*, the seat of the emperor; and *Tianshi*,
the celestial market.

(I have subsequently used a Creative Writing exercise with
people who have no knowledge of the stars. I hand out star maps
with no names or constellations marked on them, and ask people to
find and name their own patterns, then write a story to explain why
that figure is in the skies. Almost everyone can do this with an ease
that often surprises them; and, unless they have some elementary
knowledge of astronomy, no two people ever see the same patterns.)

Like everyone else I love stories; I hear, use and tell stories. My
right, earned for me by the Romantic Movement, to tell my own
stories about myself and hear other people's has been precious to
me and has also been how I have earned my living. But that night,
in the frail but magical starlight, it seemed an intolerable arrogance
and even weakness. It came between me and the true silence of the
moment – that rush to narrative seemed little more than chitter-
chatter.

It would appear, too, that there was something accurate in the
idea that silence inspires creative, particularly literary, activity. If I
had had someone else with me, we would have dissipated the energy
of that search for stories verbally – rather than piling it up inside
and generating written words. We would probably have competed
to identify or at least have discussed the location of further constellations. We would probably have had slightly different versions of
the names, 'The Great Bear', 'Ursa Major', 'The Frying Pan', and
of the stories that went with them. Someone would have known
more and had more authority. The author is the person with the
authority to tell the stories.

Romantic silence, as I experienced it in Galloway, sharpened my memory and generated stories. Whether this demonstrates that there is an inner hidden self that is somehow truer, more real, than the 'socially constructed self' and that exposure to that self, through isolation and silence, will strengthen an individual is more dubious. But it is deeply embedded in the Western cultural psyche. Wordsworth felt he needed to encounter and fortify his true self in solitude, *so that he could speak that self truly* in his poetry. This is the basis of the idea that solitude nourishes creativity and all artists need it.

It's not very difficult to see a rather close connection between the idea of an 'authentic' inner self obscured and weakened by excessive social demands and classical Christian dualism, with the 'true' soul trapped within a 'corrupt' body, and a corrupt material world. One would expect a philosophy like romanticism, opposed to classical dualism, also to reject the idea of a pure inner nugget of true being, but this is not what has actually happened. The belief in the true inner self has been promulgated as a new and radical posture by all sorts of movements throughout the nineteenth and twentieth centuries. This idea was fundamental to Radical Feminism: there was a 'pure'* woman-self, which had been obscured and repressed by layers of social conditioning. The emergent feminist had only to strip away these layers of 'false consciousness' (it was always and necessarily false) and find her 'real' or true inner self and become liberated. By seeing 'woman' as a category that has been excluded from culture and therefore not responsible for society, feminists did not need to withdraw from it into solitude or silence. This liberating work could best be done *in the company of other women*. Our medium of liberation became the group, the naming and sharing of experience through language, even though the need to do so was fundamentally based on the idea that men owned language and women did not.

---

* This analysis rather deftly dodged the idea that 'pure' means 'purged' rather than 'essentially innocent'.

There is something wrong here. It seems nonsensical to suggest that talking in groups can do exactly the same thing as silence and solitude are held to do: shore up the individual's boundaries against social construction. If the romantics realised that they needed silence and solitude to find their authentic voice, then how can the same authentic voice be found through speaking in groups?

I think what may have happened is that two different 'liberation' movements bumped into each other in the second half of the nineteenth century. Romantic individualism, with its ideas about personal freedom, encountered and was engaged by political freedom movements: nationalism and anti-imperialism were important to some of the romantics, who had many of their philosophical and political roots in the aspirations of the French Revolution: organised labour, anti-slavery, early women's rights and other emancipation movements all claimed the attention of romantic artists. Byron died defending the freedom of Greece.

By the end of the nineteenth century the conviction that the artist was entitled – indeed, was morally obliged – to abandon social obligation, to strengthen his ego through solitude, had become almost a cliché. But, more important, this idea began to extend itself (like the franchise) further and further into the general population. Everyone had the right to individual expression, everyone was entitled to shake off the shackles of social obligation and aspire to self-actualisation. Everyone had a true inner self and was entitled to assert it over any social conventions or obligations. This applied especially and particularly to groups who had been oppressed or marginalised by society. However, the overall experience of the oppressed was that they had been *silenced*, rather than freely choosing silence. It was not that their truths were being corrupted by too much social chatter, but that they were not free to speak at all – or at least not audibly. Many radical thinkers found themselves engaged on two fronts: they were active in political reform movements and at the same time advocates of individualism and therefore set against any social order. The political freedom movements saw the right to speak, and to be heard, as absolutely crucial.

For many of them this overrode the belief that the solution to the problem of the self lay in escape from the conventional restraints of society and in a retreat into solitude or 'nature'.

Squeezed between the belief that social intercourse corroded freedom and the belief that naming oneself and one's oppression in solidarity with others was a fundamental pre-necessity of freedom, something had to give. This pressure produced an extremely interesting development: a brand-new kind of silence. The individual would speak out and be heard. The silence, which would allow and shape that free speech, would be located not in the oppressed individual, but in a separate person: a listener or hearer. After a long and complex journey through the nineteenth century these needs and desires found a form: the psychoanalyst.

This idea of a silent listener, one who can hold the silence so that others can speak their true selves into it, is an extraordinary development. The analyst's capacity to hold the silence is quite different from anything in religious life; the function of confessors, spiritual directors, gurus, sheiks, teachers is explicitly directive, instructive, even judgemental. Of course these roles require good listening, but in the context of hearing enough to know what to say back, how to advise, direct and assist the speaker in the task of escaping from the ego and finding their own silence, so as to hear and incorporate the divine. Even those who teach through their own silence, like Meher Baba, the influential and popular twentieth-century guru who claimed to be the Avatar, the human form of God, are *teaching*.

From 1925 until his death in 1969, Meher Baba was silent. He communicated first by using an alphabet board, and later by hand gestures, which were interpreted and spoken by one of his disciples. He insisted that his silence was not undertaken as a spiritual exercise, nor as a vow, but solely in connection with his universal work.

Man's inability to live God's words makes the Avatar's teaching a mockery. Instead of practising the compassion He taught, man has waged wars in his name. Instead of living the humility, purity, and truth of his words, man has given way to hatred, greed, and violence. Because man has been deaf to the principles and precepts laid down by God in the past, in this present Avataric form, I observe silence.[14]

Psychoanalysts (and other therapists) in theory do not teach, direct, judge or instruct. They create and hold the free silence in which the subjects of the process may struggle to name themselves. They have become like God is to the contemplative.

During my brief brush with psychoanalysis in the 1980s I myself never encountered this liberating silence, and through it some place of truth and self-knowledge; I always felt every bit as much constructed by Freudian theory as I was by any other social circumstance. The psychoanalytical silence does depend on an article of faith: that naming, speaking oneself, is essential to freedom and integrity, and I was never sure enough that I believed this. Now I would question whether psychoanalysis is appropriate or even possible for anyone who is seriously given to contemplative prayer, partly because of Freud's determination that all faith in God was necessarily neurotic, and partly because so much of the encounter with God in prayer is not merely silent but is ineffable. It cannot be spoken or described and yet it is experienced as completely real. Despite this caveat, the capacity to create such a listening silence is a strange and beautiful thing. So many people, when I have asked them about positive experiences of silence, have mentioned this psychoanalytic silence that I do not want to ignore it here.

Certainly the sort of speech, of self-knowing, drawn out by a good listener has a creative quality to it that often surprises the speaker, even in situations less consciously constructed to do so. In 2001 I wrote *Other Voices*, a drama for BBC radio. It was an attempt to present to a wider audience some of the contemporary and more radical ideas about hearing voices – a phenomenon that has been too simply treated as a psychotic symptom, usually associated with schizophrenia.[15] One strand of the play was documentary – and, with extraordinary generosity and courage, several members of the

Exeter Voice Hearing Group agreed to talk about their experiences. Sara Davies, a BBC producer, recorded over six hours of interviews with them. The tapes are beautiful, surprising, open-hearted and intensely personal. When I talked to some of the group they all said they were taken aback by how freely they had spoken – some of them saying they had heard themselves say things that they had never said or even known about themselves before. They all insisted that this was because Sara Davies was 'such a good interviewer'. The fascinating thing about the tapes is that she says practically *nothing*. There are frequent pauses and silences, and even on the tapes this listening silence collaborates with the speakers. It generates the confidence that allows the spoken word proper space. For me these tapes have a redemptive quality. One of the biggest problems (after social stigmatisation) that many voice hearers experience is the difficulty of creating any silence internally. Too often there simply is no silence ever. Davies's capacity to create that silence was a revelation.[16]

These were the issues I was trying to think about as I strode across the hills of my childhood. After Sinai I had begun to feel that all my own inclination and endeavours were towards the eremitical silence – the harsh wrestling with the strength and tenacity of the ego – rather than the romantic notion that the ego needs shoring up, but during those long, lovely, strenuous walks I learned that I underestimated how much my perception of nature and of religious experience, and indeed of my own self, is grounded in a romantic model.

The romantic poets were so influential and important to me as an adolescent, especially in giving me a point of reference, a way of seeing myself as a writer, or potential writer. How much I got from them – even my name. I had an 'h' on the end of my name when it was given to me by my parents. When I was seventeen I was in love with Samuel Taylor Coleridge. Both Coleridge's wife and his mistress were called 'Sarah' and he had made them each drop their final 'h', describing it as a 'singularly ugly aspirant'. I cancelled my 'h' immediately.

The romantics' quasi-mystical approach to nature had given me a way of interpreting experiences which I could not, as a sceptical adolescent, have happily called holy and which, without some kind of romantic interpretation, might well have driven me mad. Instead, I think that heightened intuitive response to the world did nurture some sort of creativity. The lens of romantic ideology legitimated my feelings. Moreover, a romantic idea about madness – that it marked one as a 'special' person – is useful to all adolescents. The sense of being fragmented, worthless, 'out-of-control' can be balanced and made bearable by the idea that there is a *meaning* and truth that can only be discovered through experiencing extreme emotion – and valuing it. I am increasingly persuaded that both the worrying increase in mental health problems and the demonstrations of antisocial, even violent, behaviour in younger people in the West at present must be related to a lack of silence and a lack of training in how to use silence.

Towards the end of my walking, I did indeed encounter the storm I would not have dared to summon. A dark-green evening of increasing oppression and rumblings in the distance burst into one of those spectacular night thunderstorms where the lightning really does flash like strobe lights – illuminating everything in a weird, violent monochrome like an overexposed photograph. The wind got up and the rain pounded on the roof of the car. I was a little scared, but more exultant, excited and emotionally somewhat hyperactive. I realised that there are two distinct strands to this engagement with solitude and silence in nature. There is the moralistic strand that argues that a person will grow in freedom, integrity, authenticity and courage if nurtured by nature – the good mother – that her stern, even austere, though profoundly rich regime will make one a nobler, better person than the soft, smothering, but restrictive and conventional love of society. This is the tradition of Rousseau, Wordsworth, Thoreau and Annie Dillard, at least in *Pilgrim at Tinker's Creek*. Then there is the other tradition – the tradition of the wild, of Shelley, Emily Brontë, Poe and Kerouac – which is amoral at bottom. It claims that 'nature' and solitude will open up an individual to the wild and mad, which is lurking there, barely contained by civilisation.

What I ultimately learned from those walks is that I had been right: there is something profoundly different about this romantic understanding and the older religious view of silence. Religious or eremitic silence, not just in the Christian tradition but in Buddhism as well, is about inner emptiness – emptying the mind and the body of desires, being purged and therefore pure: a kind of blank, a *tabula rasa*, on which the divine can inscribe itself. It is a discipline of self-emptying, or, to use a theological term, of kenosis, self-outpouring. Whereas romanticism uses silence to exactly the opposite ends: to shore up and strengthen the boundaries of the self; to make a person less permeable to the Other; to assert the ego against the construction and expectations of society; to enable an individual to establish autonomous freedom and an authentic voice. Rather than self-emptying, it seeks full-fill-ment.

As the imagery and the practices of both these interpretations of silence are very closely related (as the use of 'retreat' in the Montaigne quotation at the beginning of the chapter suggests), in any specific modern life there is bound to be a good deal of confusion about precisely which sort of silence someone is enjoying at any particular moment. There seem always to be multiple layers or fragments of identity, rattling around within an individual. Nonetheless, there are some real differences in the self-understanding and indeed 'well-being' produced by each kind of silence; and for me they seemed to be in direct conflict. Some of the points of conflict could be simplified into binary oppositions: a person pursuing desert silence seems more likely to have a sense of time as space, compared to the romantic notion of time as narrative; to delight in ineffability rather than struggle for self-expression; to value openness and humility over autonomy and self-esteem; and perhaps above all to desire *jouissance*, the infinite opening out into eternity rather than resolution or closure, represented by a finished work of art.

I have come, for my own convenience, to use the terms 'permeable' and 'boundaried' selves, or identities, to sum up the two positions; with desert silence seeking to make the self as open as possible and romantics trying to wall off the self from outside influences.

To put the matter somewhat simplistically, at this present cultural moment, certainly in the West, we tend to see 'normal', healthy people as firmly, though not excessively, boundaried. A person is, or should be, autonomous, integrated, whole, rational and independent. These socially approved boundaries are expressed, more or less, by the skin; the 'self' starts, and stops, at the margins of the body. Such a self is fulfilled: filled full of self. It is neither a sucking vacuum of need nor an overflowing intrusion into other people's space. This clear-edged person does not exist without a social framework, but there should not be very much confusion between inside and outside. The self is seen as a tiny nation state, with the rights and obligations of that sovereign entity. A nation state has the right to police its borders, repel invasion and form self-interested alliances with others. In the individual, as in the nation state (and of course these two concepts developed together), authenticity and authority depend on a smooth continuity and a firm narrative of the self. Most psychoanalysis is directed towards bolstering this sense of identity.

Permeable selves, on the other hand, tend to be less rationalist and less atomised. Religious identity, for instance, tends to be affiliative rather than nationalist. I suspect that this is why in the West, still dogged by nationalism, we have great difficulty in coping with the international dimension of Islamic politics, for good or ill. The number of newspapers that rushed to tell us, in slightly shocked tones, that the Beslan terrorists 'weren't Chechnyan' as though somehow they should have been, is interesting. In many of Bush's statements about 'the evil ones' there is the subtextual suggestion that part of their evil is that they aren't 'patriotic' in the old nationalist sense and cannot, therefore, be addressed with the old rules of play: diplomacy, bribery, threat and ultimately war.

In the context of the modern boundaried self, Freud is right: religious belief is neurotic, and spirituality delusional and an inappropriate form of self-expression. If a person believes in a God (any

God) as an external Other who has a value equal to or higher than the individual's, then ego boundaries are necessarily going to become shaky: the thrust of most traditional spiritual practice is to make them ever more shaky. If there is a God – if there is truth and meaning other than the purely material – outside the self, then the self that is permeable has greater access to such truth than the more strictly boundaried self. In this narrative the appropriate identity may well be one that allows in the most from outside, which allows the Other to break down or through the boundaries. When a community collectively accepts the existence of powers outside the individual, then anyone who has access to those powers has a value to the community.

So a modern narrative will say that anyone who lets the (divine or delusional) Other too far in, who weakens their own boundaries, or has them weakened, is 'mad', as we see extensively in modern psychiatric discourse. While a religious or spiritual narrative will tend to sense that those who will not consent to be used by the forces of the Other are the mad ones.

I certainly do not want to be seen to be saying that a religious structuring of identity is somehow 'better' than a romantic one, or vice versa. There are downsides to both models. For example, within a religiously framed understanding, weaker boundaries are a good thing. But what often actually seems to happen is that the boundaries are re-erected elsewhere – often around the community of believers. Although behaviour that the boundaried self would need to describe as delusional can be contained, 'heresy' cannot. Societies that are tolerant of excess at an intra-personal level, are frequently very intolerant of ideas that threaten the wider framework – and punitive of originality, intellectual challenge, or unbelief. Constructing identity around a religious understanding may also be guilt-inducing. If you believe there is a God out there who is both good and powerful (and very few societies go for a deity who is mean-minded and impotent), then if something goes wrong it has to be someone's fault. Blame and guilt become commonplace, and potentially destabilising. Finally, if one allows for the intrusion into the daily of 'spiritual forces', one is also likely to allow the incursion of other powers of the irrational. These are often very dark forces. Weakened ego boundaries do not protect a person the way a sense of autonomy does; they let things in, because they are designed to. Undefended, these can be devastating to the self.

But equally there are negative effects of constructing identity around romantic ideas of authenticity, including the concept of the true inner self. Individualism requires a belief that all rights are equal and that they cannot be in competition – but actually what we have seen in the past few years is that this is simply not the case. The right to have freedom of speech and the right not to have one's religion held up to mockery are demonstrably incompatible. Democratic voting systems do not deliver freedom and equality. Assertions of independence weaken communities. Another negative effect of tight boundaries is the inability to accept any authority, so that a personal response to something can become more important than the facts or reasons that triggered the response: 'I feel' becomes synonymous with 'I think' and 'I believe'.

And perhaps the most interesting things about all this is that neither model seems to be very efficient at delivering its promised goods. Under an ascetic, disciplined spiritual model of identity in which the ego is to be stamped out and the self made available to the Other, the ego fights back with astonishing energy and success. Religious societies are not havens of peace and serene joy, never mind of kenotic self-giving. At the personal level, achieving enlightenment or canonisation or sheik status or holiness or right standing or serenity or wisdom or bliss (or any of the other ways in which the permeable self has been described) has been extremely rare – and the virulent insurrection of the indomitable ego is usually held to blame. However, 250 years of being nice to the ego, paying attention to it, focusing on it, indulging it and valuing it, does not seem to have strengthened or secured it at all: this authentic or true self turns out to be distinctly feeble. Identity is more at risk now than it has been for centuries. Replacing the core values of community, authority and tradition with the new ones of individualism, freedom and change does not actually seem to have enhanced a sense of identity – indeed, rather the reverse. Alienation, a sense of loss, self-harming activities and mental health difficulties are more frequent rather than less frequent. A sense of the 'common good' has apparently evaporated. The right to the 'pursuit of happiness' does not deliver happiness.

For my final walk, I did not go up into the hills, but westward along a section of the Southern Upland Way to the Laggangairn standing stones. These are two tall stones, the remaining evidence of a lost stone circle, probably from the third millennium BCE. They are a long way from anywhere, in a clearing in the ubiquitous forestry plantations, and they are strange and rather wonderful, partly because their isolation means that they are less guarded about with fences and interpretation boards than most ancient stones remains. You just come upon them standing there, over four miles from any public road or human habitation, as they have stood for 5,000 years. They are scored with carved crosses, Christian symbols, but very ancient ones cut in the eighth century. Laggangairn was on the old pilgrim route to Whithorn, where St Ninian first established Christianity in Scotland, in the fifth century. What I had not known until I walked there, though, was that there is also a ruined steading at Laggangairn; once, probably in the last 200 years, this almost unbelievably remote site was someone's home. It was probably not as isolated, of course – there are ruined steadings all over the hills, as there are on the outer isles; they are the shadows of a whole way of life that has been silenced by modernity itself. Suddenly, I was confronted with a whole complex history of silences. We know virtually nothing about the people who with such labour created the stone circle; we know remarkably little about Ninian and his *Candida Casa* (white house), the original church at Whithorn, which remained a place of pilgrimage and a cathedral until the Reformation. Even his role as Scotland's 'evangelist' has been silenced in popular culture in preference for the later Columba, and the more romantic glamour of Iona. And until I saw the abandoned farm I had not really thought about the 'Lowland Clearances'.

Almost everyone knows about the Highland Clearances. During the century between the 1780s and the 1880s approximately half a million Gaelic-speaking Highlanders were 'cleared' from their traditional homelands and way of life. A large number of them emigrated to Canada, USA, Australia and New Zealand. In many cases this relocation was forcible and violent, or, as John Prebble puts it, the history of the Clearances is 'the story of people, and of how sheep were preferred to them, and how bayonet, truncheon and fire were used to drive them from their homes'.[17]

These clearances were processed with considerable violence: one contemporary account describes a clearance in vividly painful terms:

> The consternation and confusion were extreme. Little or no time was given for the removal of persons or property; the people striving to remove the sick and the helpless before the fire should reach them; next, struggling to save the most valuable of their effects. The cries of the women and children, the roaring of the affrighted cattle, hunted at the same time by the yelling dogs of the shepherds amid the smoke and fire, altogether presented a scene that completely baffles description – it required to be seen to be believed.[18]

The empty isolated silence of the Highlands was created by the wanton destruction of a whole culture; there was not even any intention of creating something beautiful, just a desire to make more money out of land. One of the reasons why the Highlanders were so vulnerable is that Gaelic culture did not see land as something *ownable*: there were no tenancy agreements or tenancy law in the Highlands. Clan culture was one of reciprocated needs, not landownership.

But at least there is a history and a folk memory of the Highland Clearances. The clearances in Galloway are almost entirely unknown, although they were probably extensive and raised rather more resistance. The landowners had to call the army out to deal with groups calling themselves 'levellers' because they levelled the

stone walls that were being built to enforce enclosure of fields that
had once been common land. Galloway had its own Gaelic language, as one might guess from the name itself; unlike Highland
Gaelic it has completely disappeared.[19]

Standing in the clearing at Laggangairn, looking at three different silenced societies, I was filled with sadness, and the sadness was
part of the beauty. This beautiful wild silence exists under the
shadow of the people silenced in order to create it. The silence of
oppression, the silence that does 'wait to be broken' and needs to be
broken in the name of freedom, exists inextricably entangled with
the *jouissance*, the bliss of solitude. At least the Desert Fathers did not
have to worry about that – no one wanted their desert. The price of
this silence is silence. And it suddenly felt very expensive.

8

Coming Home

After this expedition, when I returned to my own house in Weardale I did not feel the easy welcome, the sense of slipping into my own steady silence that I had become used to. I felt unsettled, restless and frustrated. I had clarified to my own satisfaction that there were indeed two different sorts of silence. But I did not see how I could have both. Too much attention to kenotic, self-emptying prayer, to decreation, breaks down the boundaries of the self; weakened boundaries prevent the creation of strong narrative. And vice versa. But I still wanted both.

The frustration was made more annoying because I had a powerful inner sense that somewhere beyond the divisions I was experiencing there was a way of living and writing that could integrate these two silences. I started to look for people who had indeed done both – had sought their own inner silent emptiness in communion with their God *and* created literature. At first sight there appeared to be a long and encouraging tradition. Hildegard of Bingen, the wonderfully eccentric twelfth-century German mystic and polymath, produced a string of remarkably original works, both about her own interior life and about the world more widely – including perhaps the first description of female orgasm[1], and a feminist precursor to oratorio, a mystery play with an all-women cast, except for the devil who is male and, because of his fall from grace, cannot sing. There is a strong strand of poetry whose authors seem to find their voice from profoundly contemplative experience, like the Spanish Carmelite monk, John of the Cross. Above all there is a great deal of very fine non-fiction, from personal accounts of spiritual experiences, like the *Shewings* of Julian of Norwich, through spiritual teaching, to memoir and autobiography. There is also a long tradition of nature or travel writing, like Annie Dillard's *Pilgrim at Tinker's Creek*. Above all, perhaps, there is Thomas Merton. The deeper he plunged into silence the more he seems to have written – autobiography, spirituality, politics, poetry, theology – increasingly responsive to the world outside his hermitage and increasingly conscious of and attuned to the act of writing itself.[2]

What is missing from this list is fiction and especially novels. It seems very curious to me that the usual prose form of individuals deliberately engaged in trying to empty themselves of self is autobiography. Before he went to Gethsemane, the Trappist monastery in Kentucky in 1941, Merton wanted to be a writer, but his two novels had failed to find a publisher. In his journal he comments on this:

> I have tremendous preoccupations of my own, personal preoccupations with whatever is going on inside my own head and I simply can't write about anything else. Anything I create is only a symbol of some completely interior preoccupation of my own. I only know I am writing well when [I am writing] about the things I love.[3]

This does not sound like a self emptied of self – it sounds like raging egotism – and yet, in the last count, even people who build in a rhetoric of self-abnegation – 'I write only in obedience' (Thérèse of Lisieux is an example of this strategy), 'I write at God's direct instruction, contrary to my own desires' (Hildegard of Bingen), 'The writing is worthless, do whatever you want with it' (Simone Weil) – end up writing autobiographically. Why should this be so? Perhaps it is because fiction involves creating whole new worlds and this requires a greater assertion of the ego than recording what comes, as gift, into your own silent life. Perhaps true silence is such a absolute engagement that there is finally nothing else to write about except the struggle to lose that very last *thing* (the ego) that binds you.

All silence is a search for a particular kind of truth; perhaps metaphor, and particularly the sustained metaphor of fictional characters, comes to feel, even to be, a lie, an untruth. Novels require narrative, plot and resolution or closure, all of which are linear and time-bound and therefore deeply alien to silence.

I did not have any answers, but I experienced a deep restlessness and, with it, a writerly curiosity. I wanted to be both a silence dweller and a writer. I wanted to write silently, somehow to *write silence*. I did not know how it could be done; I did not even know if it could be done. But I very much wanted to try to find out.

Over the following months this imperative but uneasy quest led me to some practical decisions. The first was I would move house again. If I was not feeling comfortable about what I might write, it seemed important to 'downsize' financially. If I wanted more silence, I did not need or even want such immediate neighbours nor so much space – Weatherhill's three bedrooms, two living rooms and big kitchen were considerably more than any solitary requires. What I wanted and needed was a hermitage.

Finding one turned out not to be at all easy. In the first place there are not that many houses that are both truly isolated and very small: isolated houses, especially those in the sort of wild austere scenery that I had identified as my terrain of silence, are usually old farmhouses, which tend to be substantial, and the more isolated the more substantial, because before cars they needed to be fairly self-sufficient. In wild places even the farm workers' cottages are very often within or adjacent to the steading. I knew that the kind of house I wanted did exist, but they aren't exactly hanging around waiting, especially in this era of second homes.

It is also surprisingly complicated to try to buy a house based on its topography. Despite the anxieties about Britain being overcrowded, there are in fact a substantial number of places in which it is possible to find the long views and austere lonely spaces that I craved. Indeed, in theory there was no reason why I had to stay in Britain at all. I could go anywhere in the world. In *Silent Dwellers*, her book about being a contemporary solitary, Barbara Erakko

Taylor tells a very funny story about her search for the perfect hermitage:

> I dreamed of leaving the area, of finding an acre or two and build-
> ing a small four-room house. I searched the newspapers for ads,
> drove to distant places looking for this wilderness Shangri-La. I felt
> I could not become a real hermit without it . . . I ended up buying an
> RV. It was my 'hermitage on wheels'. I abandoned the monetarily
> simple life and complicated it by adding a second home. Then I
> drove it all over the country – from Maryland to Colorado, from
> Maryland to Florida, from Maryland to Minnesota. Then I sold it
> for an older cheaper one I found in Washington state and drove that
> one home across the entire United States. Altogether I spent nearly
> three months on the road in my quest for absolute solitude in a
> wilderness setting . . . When I came home from the last trip
> exhausted and lonely, my home became a hermitage.[4]

I did not want that level of complexity – I wanted to get a move
on. Although I indulged in fantasies about Greece, about Morocco
and even about New Zealand, I knew that was what they were. I
decided to limit my choices and soon afterwards to limit them to
Scotland. It was partly sensible, because property prices are lower,
because I knew how things worked there and I would not be a 'for-
eigner'. It was partly aesthetic – there is more of the sort of
countryside I wanted there than anywhere else – and it was partly
sentimental – I wanted to go home.

Of course it all got complicated. The problems co-ordinating selling a house in England and buying one in Scotland, where the
system is different, are convoluted and anxiety-inducing. By the time
I did finally sell Weatherhill it was midwinter; not the best time to
find and buy an isolated rural property at the colder end of the
country. As a temporary expedient I rented the lodge at the bottom
of my mother's drive. The idea originally was that I would just stay
for a few months while I found myself the home I wanted, but in the
end I stayed for over two years. It was a strange sort of regression,

really, back in the cosy, noisy embrace of my childhood family, and made more complicated by the fact that my mother was clearly beginning to fail. She had had major surgery the year before and was simply not getting better; she was increasingly dependent and demanding in ways that I had not anticipated. She had no intention whatsoever of going 'gentle into that good night'. And why, indeed, should she? She had little interest in or respect for silence and she seriously disrupted mine.

There were two unqualified good things about living in the North Lodge. One was that it was genuinely small, and this gave me an opportunity to explore how much space and how much stuff I really did need to live happily.

I had now been through over a decade of getting rid of things. There is nothing like moving house frequently to make you address this. 'Is this worth putting in yet another packing case?' sharpens the moment of decision. In ten years I have shed over thirty yards of books and can honestly say I have seldom missed any of them.

I tend to be rather sceptical about an aesthetic of 'simplicity'. Often those pure white loft spaces and their tasteful minimalism are not merely uncomfortable, they are expensive and time-consuming to maintain. They need more heating, more tidying, more cleaning. They are also noisier as there are fewer soft surfaces to absorb the natural echoes of normal living. Nonetheless, I began to recognise that silence and simplicity do have a connection. I found myself immensely encouraged and influenced by Henry Thoreau. As well as his best-known work, *Walden, or Life in the Woods* (1854), he also wrote with a sort of eccentric independence on various subjects, including abolitionism and civil disobedience. But one thing I found particularly helpful, and have increasingly adopted, is his economic theory. Thoreau argued that we should not calculate our wealth by how much we had or owned, but by how much free time we have. How much time there is left over when our needs have been met is the best measure of wealth. This means, of course, that the less you need the richer you are. Thoreau became a master of his own philosophy, and ended up needing only to do a couple of weeks of physical labour a year in order to sustain his chosen lifestyle – he was in the millionaire category. I was beginning to learn that a life of silence and prayer is immensely time-demanding – and no one was going to pay me for that time. So, in Thoreau's terms, the fewer things I felt I needed the richer I would be. I started asking myself about everything I thought about buying not, 'Can I afford this?' but, 'Am I prepared to spend X hours working at something less interesting than silence in order to have it?' It was amazing how often the answer was 'no'.

At first this paring down of possessions was about silence in the simplest sense – I got rid of things that made noises. As I've explained, I never had a mobile phone to get rid of, but the television went very early on, before I even left Northamptonshire. Next I shed the radio and the speakers, and all the sound-generating programmes on the computer. I kept the car radio longer, but eventually it broke and I have not replaced it.

Soon I discovered that a person living alone in the country does not need a doorbell or a microwave oven and certainly has no real use for a tumble dryer. One of the things about this list is that, with the exception of a radio, these are all inventions of the last half-century. So I do understand why people started to accuse me of being a Luddite, but in fact I don't think this is true – some modern inventions make silence a great deal simpler. Email is a wonderfully non-intrusive communication tool, a telephone answering machine means that I can unplug the phone without inconveniencing anyone, even myself, and online shopping resolves a great many dilemmas. A deep freeze and a breadmaker actually make more silence possible. Above all, in my case a computer goes a very long way to solving the financial difficulties of living in extreme rural solitude: I live now mainly by teaching creative writing online in various ways. It is silent; it is flexible; it keeps me in touch with writing at the technical level and it allows me not to have to churn out new writing while I brood on the complexities of narrative and silence.

I have made some failed experiments too. I tried to live without clocks, without imposing that sort of artificial time and its demands on the rhythm of my days: I felt that even the implicit 'tick-tock' of time measured and meted out the silence of eternity. This turned out, at least then, to be a silence too far. It was too countercultural, and to avoid mismanaging things seriously and inconveniencing others I found myself adding anxiety and also cheating – it is cheating to turn on your computer *just* to find out what time it is; it is cheating to shatter your silence with a wake-up call from BT. One of the great advantages of silence in community – and this seems to be one of the things that crosses the boundaries between different religions – are the bells. Time is marked out in beginnings and ends but there is no anxiety for individuals in silence because they do not have to 'keep an eye on the clock' for themselves. I stopped wearing a watch and gave up having an alarm clock, but have come to accept that I need a clock in the house.

I discovered, helpfully, how little I really did need in a material sense and that was encouraging. And as I pared down my possessions I began to develop a more conscious clarity about what I was trying to do. I am not a 'back to nature' survivalist. I do not think it is possible, or at least not in this country, to live wholly outside the cash economy. I do not know if it would be possible to be food self-sufficient; I do know it would be extremely hard work. It would become an end itself; it would not increase my sense of freedom, space or silence. I do not want to grow all my own vegetables, live without cigarettes or coffee, knit or weave my own clothes or write with a quill pen and home-brewed ink. I do not want to struggle each day to milk my goat, or forage for wood for my fire. And even if I did, there would still be council tax. What I want to do is live in *as much silence as is possible at this point in our history.*

The other unqualified good thing about living in the North Lodge was that it was situated overlooking an estuary, the kind with a good deal of tide and a great expanse of reed beds. This daily silent rhythm of the tide affects everything; it causes the colour of the reeds to change constantly, reflecting the water through the reeds or flattening out the light when the tide is low; even the birds are affected by it – you see different species on the mud flats at low tide than in and around the reeds when the water is high. This sense of the daily ebb and flow of the oceans affected the rhythm of my days. I started to keep an estuary journal, in which I tried day after day to capture the silent moments of change. It was tricky because the tidal timetable is not synchronised with the twenty-four-hour day, so the change happens at a different hour each day. The rise and fall of the water changes with each tide too and the quality of the light is affected by the level of the water. Tides are deeply mysterious, caused by the gravitational pull of the irregular moon in relation to the regular sun.* I took out my nephews' little rowing boat and paddled about in the reed beds waiting for the kingfishers, herons and goosanders to appear or disappear. I watched for reflections too; when the water was as still and clear as a mirror, and when it ruffled and swayed in the wind. One night when the tide was full there was an evening so still that I could see reflections of the stars. Reflection is a magical silent thing – and the double meaning of the word doubles the magic; I reflected, silently, on the silent reflection of the stars in the water, and the reflections of dragonflies coming up from the depths to meet the real dragonflies as they skim down on to the surface, which is a skin between the two worlds of air and water. I would stand on the little stone bridge for hours trying to learn to see fish, which can look like the reflection of trees but are not.

There was morning and evening; there was high tide and low tide – they were like silent counterpoint. They created a lovely rhythm and on good days I could sense in them a model, or image, for the double silence of prayer and writing that I wanted to explore.

* High tide occurs approximately every twelve and a half hours (with some variations); so on most days there are two high tides. In the Solway where I was living the height of the tide varied through the year from 5.7 metres to 9.4 metres – and was further affected by the amount of water coming down the river into the estuary.

Then my mother died.

She did not die as abruptly as that sentence. She was in hospital for a long stretch of the spring and early summer and in pain, but no one thought she was going to die. She wanted to come home and we set about making that possible with complicated but optimistic plans for her care. I don't think we were deluded or closing our eyes to reality, her doctor was predicting 'months' and worrying about how on earth we were going to keep that house warm enough for her through the winter. My poor sisters, who unlike my brothers and me were not in Galloway, were constantly coming and going. Perhaps more touchingly, so were her nineteen grandchildren, who adored her, and proved it, not just visiting but participating in her care in very hard practical ways.

Towards the end of June she was indeed brought home, but within days it was clear that all that planning for a future had been pointless. Not that anyone felt it was a waste – we are the sort of family who believes that people ought to die in their own place with their family around them. She died in the first week in July, on her wedding anniversary, 'peacefully at home' as they say. My youngest brother was with her, and the rest of us were around and prepared.

There is a silence in death that is absolute; especially, perhaps, in deaths like this where people are ready and have slipped outside medical intervention and fuss. The noisy churning body is silent, and that silence somehow spreads outwards and fills the room, and then the whole house. That huge, inconvenient, welcoming, sociable house was silent. There was a long hush. I have been 'in the vicinity' of several deaths now, different people in different circumstances, but even where the external events are noisy or dramatic there is still, at the centre, a final silence. My mother lay in her big bed in her sunny bedroom and there was silence.

Death itself is silence; which may be why we think that silence is death. In one sense death is the only silence. Most of us are not conceived in silence; in the womb there is no silence, there is the steady maternal heartbeat, and we are led to understand a constant bubbling, churning, rhythmical 'tune' of pulse and energy. As soon as we are born we are encouraged to yell, to make a noise, to announce our arrival. But in death the silence sneaks in and sets up home. Death is a very concrete physical event, so its silence is also concrete and physical, but it is also made more intense by the emotional silence that is necessarily present. All the things that were not spoken will never be spoken, for good or ill. The living have to shut up; there is nothing more to be said.

The silence of death is unbearable to a noisy society like ours. There can be no other reason why all our customs around death are designed to make the whole thing as noisy and fraught as possible. I thought with great longing and envy of those societies where the dead must be buried before sunset; of those societies where the bereaved are 'supposed' to pull down the blinds, dress in darkest black and not communicate with anyone for a while; even of those societies where everything is ritualised and ordered, and with such clarity that you do not have to discuss what to do next; you are free of all those decisions that have to be made – cremations, dates, places, whom to contact, whom to visit, whom to telephone. We do not allow ourselves enough time to be in the silence of death and honour it. I was shocked and, I admit, saddened by the general family sense that we did not want a 'coffin funeral' – but instead some sort of 'thanksgiving service'. It seems to me still that to have the dead person there, there in the church or wherever, there physically but also somewhere else, silent, boxed up but nonetheless *there*, ought to be a natural and proper acknowledgement of the great silence that we want so much to block out and drown in waves of sound – with cheerful hymns and cucumber sandwiches.

There are advantages to large families in times of death – the burden and the loss are shared, and if the members of that family are halfway decent people (and it turned out that we were) a kind of disciplined care for each other imposes order and contains self-seeking indulgence. However, there is also necessarily a great deal of chatter and negotiation and compromise and planning that has to go on; no decisions can be taken without hours of consultation.

My daughter, flying back from the USA for the funeral, said perceptively, 'The trouble with you [me, her aunts and uncles] is that there
are always too many chiefs and no Indians, but it is worse than usual
at the moment because all the chiefs are trying to pretend to be
Indians.'

We did well, I think. But death shattered a lot of the silence that
I had been trying to develop and live within. The following few
months were without question the most difficult time I have had
since I started looking for my silence. I learned a bit about the
strengths of self-discipline: how to hold back, how not to speak my
mind. I learned the comfort of a practice of silence, a habit of meditation. But that was not enough. I felt thrown from my path and
without the right to blame anyone, even myself. I did often think
that if I had stayed in Weardale I would not have had to endure all
this, but I also knew that it was good and useful that I was there. It
is the only time in my life (except when I have to change a double
duvet single-handed) that I have felt the lack of a partner, felt lonely
and different. I have no inclination to be the 'oldest daughter' or 'big
sister' and yet, quite simply, I was. That was the reality and without
choice I had to accept that death pulls us back into patterns laid
down, usually unspoken, unexamined, un-negotiated – silently –
throughout childhood.

That autumn, as I moved away from the immediacy of death
and the closeness and warmth of my family, I found myself
increasingly impatient – to find a house, to get settled down, to
get back on track. I spent hours on the web and hours in my car
looking for my house. I had decided that in the Highlands the
winters were just too long, there was too much darkness for too
much of the year, and in most cases the mountains were too
demanding, so I was searching mainly in the southern uplands, in
what is now the Border Region, and in the Galloway, Ayrshire
and Lanarkshire hill country. But I could not find a house that
called to me, that did for me what his first sight of the Inner
Mountain did for Anthony, a place that said, 'Here. Here you can
be happy and silent.'

I knew what I wanted. I wanted a small house with a big room: I wanted to integrate living, working and praying into a single whole and I did not want any rooms that I did not use. I also wanted this house to be in a very particular landscape.

Landscape seems to be particularly important to solitaries. The word landscape did not originally mean the shape and look of a view itself – but a picture of that view. Until the eighteenth century a landscape was – like a portrait, conversation piece, still life, narrative painting and so on – a painter's technical term. Quite deliberately, stressing their emphasis on design rather than nature, the new 'landscape gardeners' of the eighteenth century claimed the word to describe their *art*. They made nature into pictures (at that point pictures as like a neoclassical landscape painting as they could contrive – Claude Lorrain was a popular model). All views are seen in the mind as landscapes. The landscape of my silence had become very clear to me. It is high moorland: a long view across rough grass and an unbroken line where the hill meets the sky. It is not being tucked in under a steep mountain, or in a wood, but open to the wind. Equally, it is not about dramatic and challenging peaks. It is a huge and silent nothing of peat bog, rough grass, bracken, broken walls enclosing no fields and the harsh cry of curlew on the wing.

One day, driving fretfully home from inspecting yet another impossible house, I had a sharp consoling memory. Once, years before, on holiday in Italy with my family, we had had lunch near Arezzo and in the afternoon had walked up a steep path in the Apennines, through pine trees dappled in sunshine, and had come out of the woods to the monastery at Camadoli. The Camadolese Fathers, founded by St Romauld at the very end of the first millennium, was the order that Merton thought he might join when he found that the Trappists could not offer him the solitude that he craved. The Camadolese monks live as hermits – each monk has his own hermitage separate from the others. Their Rule instructs them to:

sit in your cell as in paradise . . . watch your thoughts as a skilled fisherman watches for fish . . . remember always that you are in the
presence of God . . . Abandon everything and wait, dependent on
the grace of God, like the fledgling who eats only what its mother
brings it.[5]

Each hermit-monk has two rooms – a room for living in, for
praying, studying, eating and everything else, and a bedroom – and,
opening directly off the cell, he has his own little walled garden,
sheltered and completely hidden. (The monks do not need a kitchen
because the meals are prepared separately – by the non-hermits in
the order, often novices who are awaiting their opportunity to
become hermits – and brought to the cell ready cooked, where they
are 'posted' through a hatch in their front door.) I recalled it with
vivid precision, the sunshine, the scent of pine trees, the walk from
cell to church, the children's fascination and the great quiet. That,
that was what I wanted – except I would need a kitchen and a bathroom. My would-be asceticism does not run to cold-water strip
downs in the washing-up bowl, even in my most self-inflated fantasies. Nor, I suspect, would Planning or Health and Safety
regulations permit it.

Somewhere in all this I began to think about self-building. It is a
dream that a lot of people seem to share – to make our own house.
The popularity of television programmes about doing just this suggests that it catches at a very specific desire. My friends Will
Anderson and Ford Hickson were doing it in south London – building their lovely house, based on their passionate eco-aesthetic.[6] This
was encouraging. Discouraging, on the other hand, was the non-
silence that would be involved; the very proper difficulty of getting
planning permission to build on a green site; and the cost, which
rumour warned would be astronomical.

I was mulling this over when something that retrospectively feels
magical, even graced, happened. I had been to look at a (totally
unsuitable) house in the Machars, the more easterly of the two
Galloway peninsulas that stick down into the Irish Sea towards the

Isle of Man, and later in the day had an appointment to view another (also, it turned out, totally unsuitable) house near Girvan in southern Ayrshire. It is hard to imagine any other pair of locations that would have caused me to notice that on the map there was a tiny little road that ran north from the A75 to Barrhill. I thought it would be a short cut through pleasant rural countryside, pretty and convenient. So I headed up the Luce valley. North of the village of New Luce I entered a new world, one that I had not known existed, a swath of moorland and, moreover, one that had not been taken over by modern forestry plantings. Here the high hills only a few miles further east, which I had walked in two years before, were ground down by the glaciers of the last Ice Age, leaving the undulating peat and granite moors of my dreams stretching empty for miles. The land here is so infertile that it was left alone in the nineteenth century and is still liberally scattered with Bronze Age remains, which elsewhere were obliterated by enclosures and agricultural improvements. The road, single track with passing places, wound its way up over singularly decrepit cattle grids and little bridges; the upper reaches of the Cross Water of Luce, somewhere between river and stream, bubbling over stones or lying in still long pools, wound serpentine down the shallow valley. And there was the huge nothing.

Here, here was where I wanted to live. Like Anthony, here was the place that fed my 'appetite for the absolute',[7] that would place me, as his wood and pond had placed Thoreau, in a 'naked condition in front of the universe' and in front of God as well. But when I got home and started asking around it became clear that the chances of my finding a place to live up on that moor were effectively non-existent. There were very few houses in any case, and almost all of them were tenanted farmhouses and the Stair Estate, which owned it all, had a policy of not selling land – they preferred levelling unused homesteads and expanding the few remaining hill farms. I tried to shrug my shoulders and I went on looking.

Just over a month later, for reasons that the local population still do not understand, the Estate put two sites on the market. One was a substantial old farmhouse and the other was its derelict little shepherd's house nearly a mile away. In the days when hill farming was profitable, most of the old farms had a farmer and probably a couple of workers, but also a shepherd, who lived further up, where the sheep roamed freely. It gives me a special joy that the last person to shepherd here was Jock Welsh, the international sheepdog trial champion and judge. The house was collapsing even when he was an apprentice, and when he got married he and his wife Christine moved first into a caravan behind the house and later off site, but it seems a noble heritage and gives me encouragement in my rather different 'trials'.

Of course I bought it. The house had been empty for nearly half a century. It had no roof, no working water supply; it had two feet of cow and sheep manure on all the floors and a tree growing out of the front wall. This was not a conversion job; the works were done as 'new build' but it was enough of a house not to run into trouble with green-site building restrictions. It was sufficiently derelict for me to do whatever I wanted; its situation and the long view down the valley were the landscape I craved, and it even had an attached barn, roofless but with its old stone walls intact that would be my Camadolesian walled garden.

Building a house is not a silent activity – the pause in my silence seeking extended itself for another eighteen months, during which I experienced some of the highest levels of anxiety that I have ever had to endure; more meetings and conversations and negotiating with strangers than I could have imagined; and a very great deal of fretful activity. But always, running like a thread through the difficulties and complications and delays and expense, and the unnerving awareness that a great many people – from my brothers to the surveyor – clearly thought I was slightly deranged, was a strand of absolute certainty. This was my house, my hermitage, my home.

I built my house as I wanted my house to be. I wanted it to sit in its landscape as it has always sat, four-square, solid, like a child's drawing of a house, two windows with a front door between them and a chimney pot at either end. Driving up the road from New Luce you can see the house from over two miles away; I wanted nothing in that seeing to change and it makes me happy when people tell me how lovely it is 'to see lights in Dirniemow again' as they had stopped hoping they ever would. Neither the inhabitants nor the landscape itself would have welcomed a contemporary design. But inside there is one big room that is kitchen and study and eating place and sitting room, open plan, and behind it there is one bedroom. The bedroom has french windows, which open directly on to my walled garden – which at the moment I confess is still two feet deep in cow shit awaiting 'development'. Visitors can sleep in the attic – this is illegal and none too comfortable, but it suits me – and, yes, there is a bathroom. There is a proper cold larder too and an open fire and underfloor central heating.

I was impatient to get settled. I finally moved in on 16 February 2007, although at that point there was no kitchen sink and no bath; I still had to balance up a plank to get through the front door; the Internet connection did not connect; and I was broke. It took the rest of the spring and summer to get the work finished. It was not a peaceful or a silent time.

But I had learned a lot in the previous decade.

After her twelve years in the Tibetan mountains Tenzin Palmo, the British Buddhist nun, commented:

There are many approaches, many ways. What is unrealistic, however, is to become a mother or a businesswoman and at the same time expect to be able to do the same kind of practices designed for hermits . . . Whether one is a monk, a nun, a hermit or a businesswoman, at one level it's irrelevant. The practice of being in the moment, of opening the heart, can be done wherever we are . . . It's just that it's easier to do in a conducive environment away from external and internal distractions . . . The advantage of going to a cave is that it gives you time and space to be able to concentrate totally. The practices are complicated [and] require much time and isolation. Going into retreat gives the opportunity for the food to cook. You have to put all the ingredients into a pot and stew it up. And you have to have a constant heat. If you keep turning the heat on and off it is never going to be done. Retreat is like living in a pressure cooker. Everything gets cooked much quicker.[8]

I want that 'pressure cooker' and that means that I need to look at the practicalities with a certain caustic realism.

I am learning not to be too sentimental about silence. The glorious intensity of those six weeks in Skye is not, in the long term, sustainable. You can, of course, get more silence than I have, but only at the price of less solitude. In any case you can do a surprising number of things without speaking; one of the seldom mentioned advantages of supermarkets is that you can shop without exchanging a word, smiling at the staff's mechanical greetings and fixing your eyes on your list in order to avoid eye contact with anyone. But for me, in the end there is something bogus about that, and rude. I am walking, say, alone and high on a narrow track, the day has been silent except for the sound of streams and a distant caw from a crow – and lo and behold, coming towards me is a group of cheerful walkers. I know they will say 'hello' and what do I do? Duck behind a rock, although I know they will have seen me? Pass by on the other side, with a haughty expression? Increase my pace and smile swiftly as I pass? It is less 'noisy' and more rational to say 'hello' back.

The reality is that it is impossible to live in complete silence for very long in the developed world in the twenty-first century without various and extensive negotiations, in part with oneself.* And particularly if you need to earn a living.

---

* In one sense this is not true. People with aphasia do not speak. People using sign languages do not speak. Karin Paish, the conceptual artist, went for six months without speaking at all, even to her partner, while carrying on her normal daily life. However, instead of speaking she wrote. It is interesting to me that she saw this as an 'exercise in communication' rather than an exercise in silence.

I used to worry about this, or even feel that when people asked me how I manage that I was being accused somehow of cheating. I kept telling myself that if only I were better organised, more disciplined, stronger willed, I would have to speak less but, reading and thinking about silence, I came to realise just how much talk there was inside even the great famous silences. Everything we know about the early Christian hermits, many of whom could not read or write and most of whom chose not to, we know from the conversations they had: the contemporary records of their lives and spiritual adventures are called *The* Sayings *of the Desert Fathers*. Almost all the solitaries – even the anchorites like Julian of Norwich – had servants or disciples who negotiated the outside world for them. Thomas Merton tells us about the deep silence of Gethsemane and then – in a casual aside – mentions that he was 'helping the abbot with translating for foreign visitors'. And where there is pure silence, it is always serviced by someone else who is not silent. Even Tenzin Palmo, in her three years of complete silence high in Himalayas, had someone who, although he did not speak or break her retreat, nonetheless brought her, by pre-arrangement, necessary survival supplies. I have come to the decision, for both economic and ideological reasons, that I will be my own servant, service my own silence and accept the technical breaches of silence that this entails.

So the questions have really become about how much silence I can create, and how much of the intensity and beauty of Skye I can bring into dailiness, into a continuing life that is both rich and sustainable.

I have inevitably given a good deal of attention to the practical problems of living in silence. The whole business of how I actually manage my life is something that interests people very much. In my experience silent housekeeping requires a high level of commitment and a hefty dose of good administration; the latter is not something that comes very easily to me.

At a very basic level, for example, it is important to eat properly and this requires shopping. However, I live nearly fifteen miles from any proper food shops. I do go to church every Sunday, but on Sundays the only shop that is open is the supermarket. How should I balance the ecological and neighbourly imperatives to use local shops and local produce against the carbon damage of taking the car out during the week and the loss of silence and stillness that this entails? Now I try to do a big shop once every four weeks – and do without whatever I fail to remember to buy. On Sundays after Mass I buy milk and sometimes fruit and vegetables and I collect free-range eggs from a farm on the way home. I try to think about it – to pay precisely enough attention to eating and house-cleaning and the rest of the administration of my home and life so that it takes up the least possible time. Mostly I do not succeed.

At the moment I am aiming for 80 per cent silence on the grounds that it is good to have a target. Two days a week I unplug the phone and with it the Internet and email; I would really like a third day and am working on that, but it takes a good deal of efficient time management and forethought. I try to limit all social activities to a maximum of six days a month, but it can be tricky, because unexpected things happen and people other than I have needs and desires too. I comfort myself with one of my favourite stories from the desert hermits:

> A brother came to a certain solitary, who gave him a meal and ate and talked with him. When he was leaving, he said, 'Forgive me, father, for I have made thee break thy rule.' He answered and said, 'My rule is to receive thee with hospitality and send thee away in peace.'[9]

I pray for about three hours a day; for much of this time, when I can, I try to hold that apophatic imageless silence, that complete emptiness, but often I need to ground myself in biblical meditation, in other sorts of imagery and in the discipline of the psalms or other texts. I do it for myself, in truth, but I also pray for others and pray that my silence may be useful somehow in the noisy world.

I earn my keep, I walk, I read, I do my sewing. I think about silence. I am extremely happy in my little house. But although I am happy and hopeful, or perhaps *because* I am happy and hopeful, I still find silence deeply mysterious.

Over and over again, for nearly ten years now, I go back to Janet Batsleer's letter and wrestle with it: 'Silence is the place of death, of nothingness . . . All silence is waiting to be broken.'

Silence is a lack, an absence, a void – silence is the negation of speech, and therefore of meaning and freedom. In the beginning was the word. I go on being certain that this is wrong, but I cannot pin down quite why it is wrong. I have been collecting and experiencing so many strongly positive instances of silence, moments in human experience where there is no speech, no noise, but clearly no sense of loss or deficiency. I don't mean just my own 'happy moments' of silence, but more widely acknowledged cultural moments.

There is the exquisite intimacy between mother and infant at the end of the night feed, when the baby is contented, on the edge of sleep, and you are there with it and with yourself.

There are those awed responses to certain demonstrations of the 'natural' world, in which words, and even normal emotional reactions, fail or rather step back from the experience. Some natural phenomena, even though silent in themselves, tend to bring on sensations of peace or contentment, rather than awe and ineffability. For the full effect of the sublime to work there has to be an element of *power* and of something essentially inhumane. Different phenomena do it for different individuals: mountain ranges, meteor showers, large waterfalls and long views from high cliffs are examples of the kind of silencing events I am thinking of here.

There is the positive psychoanalytic silence that seems to allow a new kind of self-knowing and recreation of the wholeness and integrity of an individual.

There is the aftermath of seriously good sex, when you are with the other person without demand or need. In fact, there is a silence around sex, which is quite other than the silence of shame. There is something about sexual passion that language cannot comprehend or represent and at its best there is no reason to try.

There is the silence of mystical experience, in which the silence becomes the content as well as the context and which is felt to be ineffable, somehow impossible to pull into language.

There is the silent, even ecstatic, euphoria which so frequently precedes psychotic, and indeed epileptic, episodes. I feel that perhaps this is the same silence as mystical silence, but contemporary culture has rigorously separated them.

There is the particular silence in some sorts of reading where a balanced communication is created and the generous-hearted writer opens the silent space for the attentive reader and the two of them work (or perhaps play) at meaning-making together.

There is the silence in listening to music – especially instrumental music (as opposed to the human voice). Music is complicated in this context. If music is an aural language 'intelligible but not translatable' as Anthony Storr has called it, or even more crudely a set of *sounds*, in what sense can it be called 'silent'? This is why I have emphasised *listening* to music, rather than the music itself. A silencing of the heart and mind, and an inability to speak about its meaning, emotional or intellectual, while being very clear that it has an important meaning, is a common response to certain kinds of music, and it is one of the cultural experiences that people come up with frequently if you ask them about positive experiences of silence. Sometimes I think that music mediates between silence and language; sometimes I see it as a particular language of its own – like BSL (the most common hand/eye, as opposed to mouth/ear, language of the British deaf community) or mathematics.

There are the great cosmic forces, on which we depend, although they are silent and indeed invisible: light, organic growth, gravity, electricity, tides, rotation, the movement of the tectonic plates. Air, earth, fire and water.

There is the silence of death.

All these silences have some quite specific things in common: for example, a sense of 'givenness' – that this experience comes from 'outside' the normal self and cannot be commanded or controlled, though it can be evaded or avoided. At the same time they are experienced as integrative; the whole self is engaged and *known* to itself, in a new way. Even more common and profound is the lack of boundary – people feel they are outside watching themselves, 'from a great height', but without any sense of separation or split. A grasp of the difference between Self and Other, between I and Thou becomes unclear – except that there is no loss of integrity. It is usually the reassertion of the ego, of self-consciousness, that brings this state to an end.

Perhaps more relevantly here, there is a very strong sense of ineffability – the experience is not only very hard to speak about, it is actually very hard to recall, remember, to reconstruct emotionally. It can even be somehow 'content-free' or meaningless – 'outwith language'.

I am labouring the point. Put simply, it does seem to me that to describe all these experiences of silence in terms of 'lack' or 'absence' is inadequate, if not stupid. Concepts of 'excess' seem rather more appropriate, if undeveloped in Western psychology. Whether we see silence as the way to access these states – that is, whether we see it as a liminal state or a doorway – or whether we see silence as the autonomous space within which these experiences are happening, we cannot just say this is void or negative; that all silence is waiting – or wanting, needing, yearning – to be broken. Or that it ought to be broken.

Silence does not seem to be a loss or lack of language; it does not even seem to be the opposite of language. I have found it to be a whole world in and of itself, alongside of, woven within language and culture, but independent of it. It comes from a different place altogether.

Silence apparently happens in a different part of the human brain from speaking or hearing or even *thinking* in a rational and orderly manner; a part of the brain separate from where language happens. Neurologically this has in fact been demonstrated, through a fascinating series of experiments scanning individuals while they are practising meditation, or other forms of self-consciously chosen silence. It isn't that the brain blanks out or closes down if a person is silent, but that the electrical activity takes place elsewhere – somewhere different.

The experiences of silence are somewhat resistant to the usual brain-activity-measuring devices of modern medical science. I am very aware of the dangers of bad science and I do not want to get trapped within the mind/brain debate, but it does seem to me that neurological research is providing a remarkably good metaphor to look at what might be happening. Within current brain descriptions there is a broad agreement that language is controlled from a part of the brain within the cerebral cortex – predominantly the left per-sylvian region. This is a language zone, *not* a speaking/hearing zone (language for signers is also located here, not within the visual zone, nor within the right cortex's spatial organisation areas. Signers, for instance, lose their language capacity after left-brain lesions or strokes exactly as speakers do). However, all non-linguistic vocalisa-tions – laughing, sobbing, moaning, shouting in pain (and bizarrely enough a range of swear words, as is famously recognised in people with Tourette's syndrome) – are controlled not by the cerebral cortex but by a phylogenetically older set of neural structures in the brain stem and limbic systems, usually described as the 'subcortical areas'. Suppose one imagines (at least) that it is by silencing the cere-bral cortex that we can access this subcortical zone and its powerful emotional content. It is quite literally a different level of conscious-ness – a silent level.

I wonder if all 'the inarticulate sighs and groans' of Protestant seventeenth- and eighteenth-century prayer; the ecstatic swoons and howls of pentecostalist deliverance ministries; glossolalia (speaking in tongues); the superficially psychotic disturbances of mysticism and its related spiritual phenomena; and the euphoric ecstasy of certain meditation practices are all instances of subcortical expres-sion, emerging – as they so frequently do – from silence, by freeing up space in the brain more commonly suppressed by language and linear thought.

Perhaps this is why silence is so often presented as though it were a subcortical brain function: animal, semiotic and emotionally chaotic. This does mirror (perhaps in a rather distorted way) the actual experiences of silence, inasmuch as we can access them. Almost universally, silence practitioners comment on the difficulty of recalling, remembering, focusing on, reporting with any satisfactory accuracy, let alone articulating what it is or was that they felt or experienced. The effort of transferring the content from one part of the brain to another seems to burn away the content – rather like a space ship re-entering the atmosphere. The ineffability of the event is an essential part of the event; as though silence itself were the 'whereof we cannot speak, thereof we must keep silent'.[10]

Julia Kristeva, the French psycholinguist, suggests that although language – complex grammared language, which can articulate the self into being and which she calls the *symbolic* – is only accessible through cutting a deal whereby individuals give up certain sorts of freedoms in exchange for what she calls the 'phallic' law, there is nonetheless a 'pre-phallic' pool of articulation which, while not fully linguistic, is nonetheless capable of emotional expression, which she names the *semiotic*.

Psychoanalysis offers to help people find material that, because of assorted traumas, got 'stuck' in the semiotic, and bring it into the conscious and articulate sphere of the symbolic. But for me personally what I experience is not a struggle to emerge from the semiotic into the fully symbolic, but the reverse: I find it difficult to move down and access that range of expression, to be more permeable, available to whatever there is 'down' or 'out' there. It seems to me that silence offers those people who want it a return journey into the semiotic, the seedbed of the self. And some of what we find there is both rich and exciting.

In my search for silence I have become increasingly interested in destabilising my own autonomous independent self, losing ego rather than establishing it in logical linear language. This is not a very 'modern' project; modernity has made enormous sacrifices for rational order and for individual logical self-expression. But I am certain that our cultural repudiation of silence and our determination to define it as nothing more than a lack or absence is a sacrifice too far.

But . . . but here I am, sitting on my doorstep in the sunshine, looking out at my huge nothing, delighted by a passing hen harrier, smug about my Completion Certificate and full of hope. Thoreau wrote (in *Walden*) about how I am feeling:

> If a man walks in the woods for love of them half of each day, he is in danger of being regarded as a loafer. But if he spends his days as a speculator, shearing off those woods and making the earth bald before her time, he is deemed an industrious and enterprising citizen.[11]

People talk about 'sinking' into the 'depths' of silence. It is a good metaphor in lots of ways; there is profundity in silence. Silence absorbs me and the further in I go the more I am pressurised by it. In silence, as in deep waters, you are free from gravity. In his book *The Silent World* Jacques Cousteau describes the almost ecstatic freedom of the very first aqualung dive:

> I swam across the rocks and compared myself favourably with the sars [bream]. To swim fishlike, horizontally, was the logical method . . . To halt and hang attached to nothing, no lines or air pipe to the surface, was a dream. At night I had often had visions of flying by extending my arms as wings. Now I flew without wings. Since that first aqualung flight, I have never had another dream of flying. From this day forward we would swim across miles of country no man had known, free and level with our flesh feeling what the fish scales know. I experimented with all possible manoeuvres – loops, somersaults and barrel rolls. I stood upside down on one finger and burst out laughing . . . Delivered from gravity and buoyancy I flew around in space.[12]

And, like the deep water, you can drown in silence. The peril is always there.

It is a good image, but at present I favour a different one altogether. Cousteau also describes later in his book one way of coming up from the depths of the seabed: you strip off all your equipment, leaving your heavy weights and breathing equipment at the bottom and the ascent is:

> an enjoyable rite. As you soar with [your] original lungful, the air expands progressively in the journey through the lessening pressures, issuing a continuous stream of bubbles from puckered lips.[13]

Silence is soaring into a new lighter atmosphere, weightless and free, and when it works a stream of bubbles, bubbles of joy, float up around you and rise ahead of you towards some bright surface you cannot yet see clearly.

I am beginning to flourish in this new atmosphere. This summer I saw something new – something I did not even know happened so I was not looking for it; in fact, it took me a little while to work out what I was seeing. The house martins came back all the way from Africa to their old nests. For generations they have nested in their elegant closed mud nests stuck on the old cracked stone walls under the broken eaves. But while they were away last winter I had restored the roof, straightened the walls and destroyed their homes. I am not sure where, or even if, they did nest instead. But all summer they came, swooping on the wind, graceful, skilful, skimming up and under the new wide eves, one by one. Each in turn, they were placing tiny specks of mud and spittle on to the new roughcast wall. By the end of the summer they had cemented a small shelf into place for next year's nests. Sometimes there were thirty of them busy at this work. I watched them for hours, yet I never saw them so much as graze wings with each other. I feel very close to them. I deeply hope they will be back next summer and raising their broods here.

I think, at this present, it is the silence I want most. I want silence to be actual and real and structured into my daily life: I do not want to lose a crudely real, embodied definition of 'silence'. I don't want to turn it into a philosophical or spiritual abstract or 'state of mind' – and that tends to happen very easily. Indeed, it tends to happen as soon as you start writing about it! Max Picard, for example, writes with a lyrical beauty about silence.

> Still like some old forgotten animal from the beginning of time, silence towers above all the puny world of noise; but as a living animal not an extinct species, it lies in wait and we can still see its broad back sinking ever deeper among the briers and bushes of the world of noise. It is as though this prehistoric creature were gradually sinking into the depths of its own silence. And yet sometimes all the noise of the world today seems like the mere buzzing of insects on the broad back of silence.[14]

But although it is lovely, it does not actually mean very much. It is more or less impossible to imagine getting up in the morning and *doing* Picard's silence: it lacks the tough reality of either Kafka at his desk, or de Foucault in his desert.

I know now that when I started this adventure I underestimated the power of silence itself. If, and I think it is true, silence really does produce the effects I was investigating in Skye and have been working with ever since, especially the collapse of time and space – those boundary confusions – that is not going to be too good for prose fiction, which utterly depends on specific times and place. Plot (the idea that things happen in an orderly pulse of cause and effect) just doesn't work any more. Narrative doesn't drive anything forward in the silent vacuum. Perhaps, although silence has no narrative, it does have a rhythm. That would be an interesting idea because it would align silence with *music*.

> Since music is the only language with the contradictory attributes of being at once intelligible and untranslatable, the musical creator is a being comparable with the gods and music itself the supreme mystery of the science of man.[15]

How nearly could I say the same thing about silence? In all my researches into silence I have never encountered a silent heaven, even from those mystics who used silence most directly as a way of achieving heaven. Apart from the horrified 'little hour' of silence and the occasional casting down of golden crowns, what the heavenly hosts do in a Christian heaven is sing. They sing; they make music. Perhaps a writer's job is finally co-operative, creating the words for that eternal choir, so that the endless song of 'Holy, holy, holy' never becomes boring.

So yes, I want to work on that. I want to work on seeing if it might be possible to give 'ineffability' a good shaking up and invite it to reveal its secrets. I want to encode silence, so that out there in all that noise, people can access and love it. I am not sure that this is possible, but it seems worth a try.

But actually I just want to do it. I want to sit in the sunshine on my doorstep and listen to the silence. In the morning I want to stare at the sheep – I am getting fonder and fonder of the sheep around here. They seem rather more professional than the fat complacent lowland sheep. I watch them and note various things about them. They like to walk neatly along the paths. The ewes around the cottage seem busy and gossipy, and go about in little gangs. Today a small group of five or six came almost trotting past the house while I was sitting there. They all had ridiculous punk hairstyles: a splendid tuft of neon turquoise above their foreheads. (This is in fact a very simple way of marking the sheep you have treated in some way and distinguishing them from the ones you haven't yet dosed or wormed or whatever you have done to them.) They had surprisingly neat white coats and charming black faces with neat curled horns. But what really struck me were their elegant legs – some were all black and some had black and white stripes like Pippy Longstocking's leggings. Hard businesslike legs and sharp elegant little feet, like old ladies who have gone plump in their bodies but still have smart legs and ankles for which high-heeled court shoes seem designed. I want time to notice sheep's feet.

I want to say my prayers and write some new sorts of stories and make a garden and read some books and walk up the hill behind the house so that I can see the sea when the weather is clear. And just sit. Yesterday evening I saw my owl, though who can say 'mine' to a barn owl who happens to live in a ruin you happen to own? This spring when the local 'owl man' came to ring the fledgling owlets, four of them, so white and fluffy and sweet, he said they were the 'most forward brood in the county' this year, and I surprised myself with a surge of maternal pride.

In fact, there are a pair of barn owls, who live in an owl box in the old bier just up the hill from the house, but I tend to think of them in the singular because I have never seen more than one at a time, either suddenly, a white, fast-moving shape in the car head-lights, or as a darker shadow across the dark night sky. So I do not really see my owl very often and then usually fleetingly: the ideal silent neighbour. Barn owls are genuinely more silent than tawny owls, who make the traditional 'twit-twoo' sound. However, my bird book says that barn owls are not only nocturnal but also 'crepuscu-lar' – a fabulous new word for me, another gift from my owl; it means, 'of, or associated with, the twilight' – and sometimes they hunt at dusk, and so it was yesterday.

The wind tends to drop at sundown and the colour fades out of the rough grass, and there is often a moment of almost perfect still-ness. Yesterday, just then I came round the corner of the walled garden and there she was, perched on the dyke. She has feathered legs, like snug plus-fours; her heart-shaped face and wide black eyes really did look wise. She took off at once, of course, immensely strong and smooth, with her deep owl wing beats, stiffer than the flop of other owls, and her talons hanging down beneath her with the claws bunched neatly; powerful, silent, smooth across the hill-side, then she floated behind the broken gable of the bier and was gone. I want to get to know her comings and goings.

I want to watch for young foxes, for the occasional deer, for the first swallow, for the moment when the grass turns from green to gold. I want to sit out at night and count all the 4,500 visible stars.

I want to have a long long time to do all this, so that the silence has a chance to work on me and in me. And then I do not really know what will happen next.

Sometimes I think that silence is like a Black Hole: in a Black Hole the gravitational force is so great that nothing, not even light, can escape outwards. Anything that comes within the range of that force is irreversibly attracted, sucked in, compressed, squeezed, compacted until it collapses under the concentration of its own mass. Time itself slows down. As if in slow motion, once the process has begun, any object – even a human ego – will be stretched, warped, twisted and contracted as it is drawn towards the centre, the singularity, and thence – the physicists are not quite sure what happens next either – perhaps into an alternative universe beyond the laws of physics and psyche, into a new universe, into God.

This is death, of course; but it can also be birth, depending on the position of the observer. Whatever there is the other side of the singularity may be watching with excitement the slow transformation, understanding the breakdown of all the rules, waiting with a fierce joy to welcome the hermit into the infinite. I want to find out, and I know that for me silence is the only way to do it.

I am finding it hard to finish this book, because I don't feel that I am at the end of anything. Back in Warkton, at the very beginning, I tried to design a garden that would open out into infinity; that would forgo the satisfaction of closure, in the hope of finding the *jouissance* of the unresolved, the open-ended. Now I am trying to design a whole life that will do that. For me silence is both the instrument and content of that life. I don't feel worried about falling over the edge of a bottomless chasm, but rather I have a sense of moving up a level, into some finer cleaner air.

It is risky, I have always known it would be risky, and I was raised in a risk-averse culture. I hope I do not underestimate the risk. But I am willing to face it.

Terror and risk walk hand in hand with beauty. There is terror, there is beauty and there is nothing else.

And the rest, I hope, is silence.

ACKNOWLEDGEMENTS

This book has been a long time in the writing, which means there are a lot of people to thank.

Apart from Janet Batsleer and John Russell I have discussed the ideas in the book with a wide range of individuals and I thank them all.

I especially want to thank Joe Cassidy, my spiritual director.

Very early in the process Elaine Graham and Frankie Ward invited me to give a paper at the Manchester Contextual Theology Seminar, which was inspirational and immensely helpful to me; Emma Loveridge and everyone at Wind, Sand and Stars made my trip to Sinai possible; Deirdre Peppe owns Allt Dearg, the cottage on Skye, and did everything imaginable to support my long stay there; Christopher Rowland is an inspired and inspiring biblical guide. *Sine qua non.*

As a writer I owe an enormous debt to my wonderful agent Jenny Brown; and to Sara Holloway and Lindsay Paterson at Granta, Claire Malcolm at New Writing North, Graham Mort at Lancaster University and to the Society of Authors and the Scottish Arts Council who both gave me grants.

Ronnie and Sheila Lambton, in Weardale, taught me in practical terms how to live in wild places – and did so with constant kindness and good humour. John Freeburn, master builder, and his gang, built my house for me.

My neighbours in Glenwhilly – all the Donnans, Jasmine and John Thorpe, Marie and Billy Furguson, Alex McColm – have made me welcome here.

Alan Wilkinson, Tessa West, Adam, Fred, Jock and Thomas Maitland all worked on Dirniemow with me; Will Anderson was both an inspiration and an unfailing support.

Mildred and Adam Lee, Ros Hunt, Stella and Phillip Thomas,

Alan Green, Sabine Butzlaff, Ford Hickson and Will Anderson, Sebastian Sandys, Jane Havell, Peter Daly, Sue Dowell, Peter Magee, Harriett Gilbert and Trevor Richardson RIP are all owed thanks of various kinds.

And finally I thank Frippy Fyfe, Jamie Maitland, Robert Maitland and Maggie Lawrence (my brothers and sisters) for an act of generosity far beyond the requirements of justice.

NOTES

1 Growing up in a Noisy World

1 Angela Carter in *Gender and Writing*, ed. Michelene Wandor (Pandora, 1985).

2 Psalm 131:2 (interestingly, most modern translation omit the word 'weaned', returning us to the more sentimental/pious suckling image, but my experts assure me that *weaned* is the intended meaning – a child who is intimately with the mother, but without *needing* her for anything).

3 Helene Deutsch, *The Psychology of Women* (Grune & Stratton, 1944), p. 477.

4 Sara Maitland, *On Becoming a Fairy Godmother* (Maia Press, 2003). I had the greatest difficulty getting this collection published – and even wonderful Maia Press drew the line at the original subtitle, 'Role models for the menopausal woman'!

5 One of the stories in *On Becoming a Fairy Godmother*, 'Bird Woman Learns to Fly', explores this lovely natural phenomenon in more detail.

6 Dylan Thomas, 'The force that through the green fuse drives the flower', *18 Poems* (Fortune Press, 1934).

7 Sara Maitland and Peter Matthews, *Gardens of Illusion* (Cassells, 2000). (We wanted to call the book 'A Cunning Plot' but the marketing people wouldn't let us!)

8 John Cage, *Silence: Lectures and Writings by John Cage* (Wesleyan University Press, 1961), p. 8.

9 Janet Batsleer, personal communication.

10 George Mallory became obsessed with climbing Mount Everest and in the end he died there, last seen 'going strongly for the summit'. Legend claims that when asked why he wanted to climb it he replied, 'Because it's there.' In fact, he never said this – the phrase, as an explanation of apparently senseless ambitions, appeared in a

1923 article about Mallory and other climbers, and was not even ascribed to him. However, it has become inextricably attached to Mallory.

11 Henry Thoreau, *Walden, or Life in the Woods* (1854).

12 Richard Byrd, *Alone* (Putnam 1938), pp. 3–7.

13 *The Sayings of the Desert Fathers*, trans. Helen Waddell (Constable, 1936), p. 157.

14 Edward Gibbon, *Decline and Fall of the Roman Empire*, ed. Bury (London, 1898), vol V, p. 337.

15 John Keats, 'Ode on a Grecian Urn' (1820).

2 Forty Days and Forty Nights

1 I am rashly assuming that readers can remember Enid Blyton's 'Famous Five' stories. I owe this accurate and evocative description to Ford Hickson.

2 Byrd, *Alone*, chapter 1.

3 There is a fine selection of photos of the cottage and the locality at www.drynoch.demon.co.uk.

4 Revelation 14:2.

5 There is a biography of Tenzin Palmo: Vicky Mackenzie, *A Cave in the Snow* (Bloomsbury, 1998).

6 John Hunt, *Ascent of Everest* (Hodder & Stoughton, 1953).

7 Quoted in Fergus Fleming, *Killing Dragons: The Conquest of the Alps* (Granta, 2001).

8 He later explained this nausea by saying that he 'had made a pact with the gods' in reparation for what he saw as a bad and dishonest previous book, and felt strongly that circumnavigating for a possible cash prize would sully the whole enterprise.

9 Robin Knox-Johnston, *A World of My Own* (reissued Adlard Coles Nautical, 2004).

10 Byrd, *Alone*, foreword to UK edition, p. 6.

11 Many of the Desert Fathers paid for their few necessities by weaving baskets from rushes and selling them in the local villages. Given how many hermits there were at some points, and how few villages, I have this pleasing image of infuriated but affectionate villagers reluctantly buying yet more redundant baskets because of their concern for the well-being of the monks, their small houses or tents crammed

with useless baskets, much the way twenty-first-century parents go on sticking their children's nursery artwork on to the fridge.

12 Byrd, *Alone*, p. 83.
13 Christiane Ritter, *Woman in the Polar Night*, trans. Jane Degras (Allen & Unwin, 1956).
14 Quoted in Fleming, *Killing Dragons*.
15 Jon Krakauer, *Into the Wild* (Villard, 1996), p. 138.
16 Nicholas Wollaston: *The Man on the Ice Cap: The Life of Augustine Courtauld* (Constable, 1980).
17 Journal, Day 15.
18 *Observer*, 10.2.2002, p. 9.
19 Peter Nichols, *A Voyage for Madmen* (Profile Books, 2001), p. 214.
20 Bernard Moitessier, *The Long Way*, (Doubleday, 1971), p. 164.
21 Journal, Day 9.
22 Journal, Day 27.
23 Charles Lindbergh, *Spirit of St Louis* (Scribner's, 1953), p. 109.
24 Nichols, *Voyage for Madmen*.
25 William Howell, *White Cliffs to Coral Reef*, (Odhams, 1957).
26 Ann Davison, *Last Voyage*, Heinemann, 1951.
27 William Wordsworth, 'A slumber did my spirit seal', *Lyrical Ballads* (1800), line 7–8.
28 Byrd, *Alone*, p. 85.
29 *Song of the Siren – The World About Us*, BBC television, 1971.
30 Moitessier, *The Long Way*, pp. 101–4.
31 Ritter, *Woman in the Polar Night*.
32 Geoffrey Williams, *Sir Thomas Lipton Wins* (P. Davis, 1969), p. 115.
33 Jean-Jacques Rousseau, *La Nouvelle Héloïse* (1761), quoted in Fleming, *Killing Dragons*, (2002), p. 90.
34 Jacques Yves Cousteau, *The Silent World* (Hamish Hamilton, 1953).
35 Goutran de Procius, *Kablina*, quoted in Max Picard, *The World of Silence*, trans. Stanley Godman (London, 1948).
36 The hideous consequences of this effect are detailed in Jon Krakauer's *Into Thin Air* (Random House, 1997), his account of a disastrous twenty-four hours on Everest in which nine people were killed, almost entirely through 'disinhibited behaviour' of one sort or another.
37 John Dennis, letter, 1688, quoted in Robert Macfarlane, *Mountains of the Mind: A History of a Fascination* (Granta, 2003), p. 73.
38 Macfarlane, *Mountains of the Mind*.

39 Exodus 3:1–6.

40 Frank Mulville, 'The Loneliness of the Long Distance Sailor', *Yachting Monthly*, no. 132, May 1972, pp. 686–8.

3 The Dark Side

1 Liddel and Scott, *Greek–English Lexicon* (1843).

2 Moitessier, *The Long Way*.

3 Byrd, *Alone*.

4 Web advertisement.

5 www.wikipedia.org.

6 www.salon.com/news/feature/2007/06/07.

7 Stuart Grassian, *Journal of Law & Policy*, vol. 22:325, 1986.

8 There is a certain confusion in this story. While all the old narrators (including Ovid) agree that there were two sisters – Procne and Philomel – there is no agreement about which was the wife and which the rape victim. Because Philomel is a name for a nightingale that can sing and Procne for a swallow that was classically held to be silent (although actually it is not) I prefer to give the name Procne to the tongueless victim, and Philomel to the sad but vocal wife.

9 Genesis 16–21.

10 Captain John Phillips, clause 4, ship's articles, *Revenge* (1724).

11 Marguerite of Navarre, *Heptameron*, Tale LXVII (posthumous pub., 1588). Marguerite of Navarre bowdlerised the story she had learned from Alfonce, to minimise de la Rocque's 'immorality' and possibly to exonerate Roberval.

12 Sara Maitland, 'The Tale of the Valiant Demoiselle' in *Far North and Other Dark Tales* (Maia Press, 2008). Other fictions based on this adventure include a narrative poem of 1916 by Isabel Ecclestone Mckay, and novels by Elizabeth Boyer (1977), Charles Goulet (2000) and Joan Elizabeth Goodman (2006).

13 Richard Steele in *The Englishman* (periodical), issue of 1.12.1713.

14 Ibid.

15 Joe Simpson, *Touching the Void* (Cape, 1988).

16 Ibid., p. 206.

17 Ibid., pp. 141 and 147.

18 Ibid., p. 195.

19 Krakauer, *Into the Wild*.

20 Nichols, *A Voyage for Madmen*, p. 273.

21 Waddell, *Desert Fathers*, p. 228. The Gray referred to here is Thomas Gray, the poet who wrote the famous 'Elegy Written in a Country Churchyard' and who lived most of his life at Pembroke College Cambridge, where he was first a student and subsequently a fellow. He seems to have suffered most of his life with some sort of depression or accidie.

22 Cassian of Marseilles, *De Coenobirum Institutis*, in ibid., pp. 229–31.

23 Anthony Grey, *Hostage in Peking* (M. Joseph 1970). This is from the new and expanded edition (Tagman Press, 2003), p. 110.

24 Ritter, *Woman in the Polar Night*.

25 Psalm 91: 5–6. Modern translations give us 'scourge' or 'destruction' rather than 'demon' – but the eremitical tradition used 'demon' consistently.

26 Richard Burton, *The Anatomy of Melancholy, What it is: With all the Kinds, Causes, Symptomes, Prognostickes, and Several Cures of it. In Three Maine Partitions with their several Sections, Members, and Subsections. Philosophically, Historically, Opened and Cut up* (complete modern edition by New York Review Books, 2001).

27 Cassian, in Waddell, *Desert Fathers*, p. 232.

28 Ibid.

29 Adam Nicolson, *Sea Room* (HarperCollins, 2001), p. 156.

4 Silence and the Gods

1 Janet Batsleer, personal communication.

2 Genesis 1:1–3.

3 John 1:1.

4 Genesis 1:1–5.

5 John 1:1–3.

6 P. B. Shelley, *Prometheus Unbound* (1820).

7 In Greek there are two words that are translated by a single English word – time. *Kronos* means time in its literal and measured-out sense – as in chronology or chronometer. *Kairos* means time in the sense of 'the right or opportune moment', an undetermined period of time in which something takes place. Naming their ur-god Kronos (rather than Kairos) therefore has a metaphorical depth that is quite hard to express in English.

8 Keats, 'Ode on a Grecian Urn'.

9 Almost the only personification of silence I have seen is a picture of *her* in a nineteenth-century mural in the old British Foreign and Commonwealth Office.

10 George Steiner, *Real Presence* (Faber & Faber, 1989).

11 *OED*. Both these possibilities are mentioned, although they are rejected.

12 Figures comparing the 1991 with the 2001 census. The present population of the Scottish islands is now just under 100,000.

13 C. S. Lewis, *The Screwtape Letters* (Geoffrey Bles, 1942) reissued Fontana, 1973, p.114.

14 Ernest Gellner, *The Psychoanalytic Movement* (Paladin, 1985), p. 154.

15 Anthony Storr, *The School for Genius* (André Deutsch, 1988), p. xiii. This excellent book has been reissued in a revised edition with the simpler title *Solitude* (HarperCollins, 1994).

16 Revelation 8:1.

17 Philip Howard in *The Times*.

18 John 19:9

19 Attributed to Bodhidharma (fifth century CE) and first recorded in *Ts'u-t'ing shih-yuan* (1108).

20 Douglas Hofstadter, *Gödel, Escher, Bach,* (Harvester Press, 1979) p. 248.

21 Ibid., p. 251.

22 Ibid., p. 255.

23 Pierre Lacout, 1969 www.quaker.org.uk.

24 John Russell, personal letter.

25 Evelyn Underhill, *Mysticism: A Study of the Nature and Development of Man's Spiritual Consciousness* (1911).

26 Jenny Uglow, *Nature's Engraver* (Faber & Faber, 2006), p. 99.

27 Saint Augustine, *Confessions*, vi:3, trans. R. S. Pine-Coffin (Penguin, 1961).

28 The principal scholarly positions are laid out by Balogh in 1927 and Knox in 1968. In *A History of Reading* (Viking, 1996), Alberto Manguel lays out the case for the lay reader. In 2007 in the *Guardian* James Fenton challenged this, but I remain persuaded by Manguel.

29 1 Timothy 2:11–14.

30 Adam Phillips, *Promises, Promises* (Faber & Faber, 2000), pp. 373–5.

31 William Dalrymple, *From the Holy Mountain* (HarperCollins, 1997), p. 290.

5 Silent Places

1 Henry Thoreau, *Journal*, 7.1.1857.
2 Thomas Merton, *Journal*, 27.2.1963.
3 These concerns are reflected in my fiction, especially in *Three Times Table* (1990) and *Home Truths* (1993), and in many of my short stories, but most particularly in 'A Big Enough God' (1995), an attempt at a theology of creation post-Einstein.
4 Annie Dillard, *Pilgrim at Tinker's Creek* (Cape, 1975), p. 165.
5 Anthony Gormley, interview, *Guardian* 14.6.2005.
6 Psalm 124:7
7 Nicolson, *Sea Room*, p. 29.
8 'St Columba's Island Hermitage', Irish, twelfth century, anon. From *Celtic Miscellany*, ed. Kenneth Hurlstone Jackson (Penguin Classics, 1971).
9 William Cowper, 'The Solitude of Alexander Selkirk', *Palgrave's Golden Treasury*, (Oxford, 1907) p. 114. Oddly enough, far from being a paeon to solitude and ownership, this is a very depressing poem about the pains of isolation and the pointlessness of ownership – the opening four lines are entirely ironic and quite bitter, but they have been removed from their original context and are frequently quoted as positive pleasure.
10 The Forestry Commission has recently taken on a great number of these concerns – both planting with more diversity and opening out the forests for recreational use. Far more than private landlords, they have taken on board not just the legal obligations of the new access laws but their spirit also.
11 Kenneth Grahame, *The Wind in the Willows* (1908).
12 Bruno Bettelheim, *Uses of Enchantment* (Thames & Hudson, 1976). One of the places from which silence is conspicuously absent is the index to this fascinating book. Bettelheim, a psychologist, sees no value in silence and overrides it in his work.
13 *Maitland Miscellany*, vol. 2, part 1 (Edinburgh, 1840), pp. 187–91.
14 In some tellings there are seven or twelve brothers; and in some versions they are not swans but crows or ravens. I am not sure why they are always either pure white or pure black.

6 Desert Hermits

1 Franz Kafka, letter to Felice Bower, 14–15 February 1913, *Letters to Felice*, trans. James Stern (Schocken Books, 1973).

2 Charles de Foucault, letter to Father Jerome, OCSO, 1901, quoted in Ann Fremantle, *Desert Calling* (1950), pp. 162–3.

3 Gertrude Bell, quoted in Janet Wallach, *Desert Queen* (Weidenfeld & Nicolson, 1996), pp. 54 and 108.

4 Wind, Sand and Stars publicity brochure. (The company's name is derived from a book of the same title by Antoine Saint-Exupéry, an extraordinarily lyrical memoir of the desert.)

5 Cage, *Silence: Lectures*, p. 8.

6 Martin Buckley, *Grains of Sand* (Vintage, 2001), p. 49.

7 My own free reworking of 1 Samuel 1:1–20.

8 Personal communication.

9 Amos 8:11–12.

10 Indeed, someone has done so. Rudolf Bell's *Holy Anorexia* (1985) is a tediously reductionist attempt to present a wide range of medieval women saints as case studies in anorexia. To achieve his purpose he has to strip them of all cultural context and all self-awareness. If he is right, the only reasonable conclusion is that the medieval Church was better at treating anorexia than modern medical science is.

11 Even in the early nineteenth century Jane Austen, in *Northanger Abbey* (1818), has Eleanor Tilby (a model of rational good sense and refined taste) support the view that it is perfectly proper for historians to invent speeches for historical characters.

12 Waddell, *Desert Fathers*, pp. 289ff.

13 Nicolson, *Sea Room*, p. 156.

14 Athanasius, *Life of Antony*, in *Early Christian Lives*, trans. Carolinne White (Penguin, 1998), p. 39.

15 See, for example: Derwas James Chitty, *The Desert a City* (Blackwell, 1966); Peter France, *Hermits* (St Martin's Press, 1996); Andrew Louth, *The Wilderness of God* (Darton, Longman & Todd, 1991).

16 John Cassian, 'On Mortification', in Waddell, *Desert Fathers*, pp. 232–4.

17 Waddell, *Desert Fathers*.

18 France, *Hermits*, p. 139.

19 There is some disagreement about this. Some argue that she sought

and received baptism in the hospital shortly before her death; some that she was baptised without her explicit consent after she lost consciousness. Here I am following Simone de Petrement, her friend and biographer, who writes persuasively against any regular form of baptism; *La vie de Simone Weil* in (Fayard, 1973).

20 Thérèse of Lisieux, *The Story of a Soul*, trans. M. Deig (Source Books, 1973).

21 Simon Weil, *Waiting for God* (Routledge & Kegan Paul, 1951), p. 116.

22 De Foucault, letter to Marie de Bondy, 15.7.1906, quoted in Philip Hillyer, *Charles de Foucault* (Minnesota, 1990), p. 129.

23 Thomas Merton, *Raids on the Unspeakable* (New York, 1964), quoted in M. Furlong, *Merton, a Biography* (London, 1980), p. 283.

24 Merton, *Journal*, 16.12.1965.

25 Dalrymple, *Holy Mountain*, p. 410.

26 Jia Dao (779–843), James J. Y. Liu, *The Chinese Knight Errant* (Routledge & Kegan Paul, 1967).

7 The Bliss of Solitude

1 John Milton, *Paradise Lost*, Book iv, 481–8.

2 William Lecky, quoted in France, *Hermits*, p. 22.

3 Quoted in Waddell, *Desert Fathers*.

4 Gibbon, *Decline and Fall*, chapter 37.

5 James Wilson, *A Voyage around the Coasts of Scotland and the Isles* (1841).

6 Michel de Montaigne, *The Complete Essays*, trans. M. A. Screech (Penguin, 1987). I find it fascinating that Montaigne should have picked this particular image. He himself was from a noble family and probably never entered a 'back-shop' in his life – 'trade' being even more despised by the French landed classes than by their English equivalents. While Catherine of Siena, who grew up over her family's dyeing shop, had spoken of a 'hermitage of the heart' where she could retreat to be with her beloved, Montaigne chose the commercial metaphor.

7 Thomas de Quincey, *Collected Writings*, ed. Masson (Edinburgh, 1890), p. 235.

8 Thomas Carlyle, *Critical and Miscellaneous Essays* (1838).

9 William Wordsworth, *The Prelude* (1850).

10 Keats, 'Ode on a Grecian Urn'.

11 George Eliot, *Felix Holt* (1866).

12 Wordsworth, 'The Advertisement' to *The Prelude*.

13 Storr, *School for Genius*, p. 33.

14 Meher Baba, 'Meher Baba's Universal Message', World's Fair pamphlet, 1964.

15 See chapter 2 for more on this topic.

16 Sara Maitland, *Other Voices*, produced by Sara Davies for BBC Radio 4, *Afternoon Theatre*, 2001. The play later won a Media Mental Health Award. My deep gratitude goes to Sara Davies and the Exeter Group of the Voice Hearing Network.

17 John Prebble, *The Highland Clearances* (Secker & Warburg, 1963), p. 10.

18 Donald Ross, *Scenes at Knoydart* (1853), quoted in Prebble, *Highland Clearances*, p. 278.

19 The 1901 census lists ninety-one individuals in Galloway as Gaelic-speaking.

8 Coming Home

1 Quoted in Sabina Flanagan, *Hildegard of Bingen, 1098–1179: A Visionary Life* (Routledge, 1998), p. 97.

2 Thomas Merton's autobiography, *The Seven Storey Mountain* (Harcourt, 1948), made him famous, but it was followed by a long string of publications, covering a wide range of subjects and genres.

3 Thomas Merton, *Journals, Vol. 1, 1939–41* (HarperCollins, 1995), p. 118.

4 Barbara Erakko Taylor, *Silent Dwellers* (Continuum, 1999), p. 32.

5 Camadolesian short rule, *Catholic Encyclopaedia*, 1913.

6 See Will Anderson, *The Diary of an Ecobuilder* (Green Books, 2007).

7 Adam Nicolson's description of his islands in *Sea Room*.

8 Mackenzie, *Cave in the Snow*, pp. 197–8.

9 Waddell, *Desert Fathers*, p. 160.

10 Ludwig Wittgenstein, *Tractatus Logico-Philosophicus* (Kegan Paul, 1922).

11 Thoreau, *Journal*, 17.6 1853.

12 Cousteau, *Silent World*, p. 16.

13 Ibid.

14 Picard, *World of Silence*, p. 22.

15 Claude Levi-Strauss, *The Raw and the Cooked* (Cape, 1970), p. 18.

INDEX

'A slumber did my spirit seal'
(Wordsworth), 63
Abraham and Sarah, 93, 194
accidie, 108–14, 293
Achilles, 31
Adam, 120, 201–2, 232
adventure writing, 44–5
Aeneid, 150
Aeolian harps, 85
affect, lack of, 108
Africa, 56, 193, 283
aggression, 132
agoraphobia, 131
Alaska, 103–4
alcohol, 92, 131
Alexander, Mrs C. F., 27
Alexandria, 205, 218
Alfonce, Jean, 97
Ali, Tariq, 9
alienation, 255
Allt Dearg, 38–9, 76
Alps, 43, 196, 223–4
Ambrose, Bishop of Milan, 148–9
Anatomy of Melancholy, The (Burton), 113
Ancren Riwle, 111
Anderson, Will, 270
Andes, 100
Anglo-Catholicism, 10–11, 14
anorexia, 296
Antarctica, 30, 42
anti-imperialism, 246
antimatter, 243
Apennines, 269
aphasia, 274
applause, 135
archaeopteryx, 19
Arctic, 43, 51–2, 97, 174
Arezzo, 269
Arfderydd, battle of, 176

Arianism, 205, 209
Aristotle, 148
Armistice Day, 136
Arthur, King, 176
asceticism, 103, 108, 110, 112, 171,
184, 191
and desert tradition, 203–4, 208,
213–14, 217
and romanticism, 233
astronomy, Chinese, 244
athletes, 110, 229
Atlantic Ocean, 56, 78, 105, 193
Attwater, Donald, 217
Atum, 123–4
auditory hallucinations (hearing voices),
14, 57–62, 78, 91, 101, 205
and *Other Voices* radio drama, 248–9
aural overstimulation, 131
Austen, Jane, 296
Australia, 43, 64, 256
aboriginal mythology, 124–5
Authumla, 122–3
autism, 179
Ayrshire, 226, 268, 271
Aztecs, 129

Bacon, Francis, 21–2
Baghdad, 193
Baldur the Beautiful, 129
Balmat, Jacques, 51–2
banishment and exile, 92–4
Barrhill, 271
Barthes, Roland, 74–5, 186
bathing, 53–4
Batsleer, Janet, 28–30, 117, 277
Batt, Mike, 197
Bell, Gertrude, 43, 194
Bell, Rudolf, 296
bells, 264

Beltane, 129
Benedictines, 144–5, 174
Benyallery, 228
Bernini, Gian Lorenzo, 72, 146
Beslan school siege, 252
Bettelheim, Bruno, 179
Bewick, Thomas, 155
Bible, 19, 93–4, 97
  Apocalypse, 135–6
  creation story, 119–21, 201
  and silent prayer, 199–201
Big Bang, 118–19, 121, 125, 128
birds, bones of, 19–20
Black Holes, 157, 287
blue-tits, 16
Blyton, Enid, 290
boarding schools, 6
Bodhidharma, 138
body temperature, 49
Boethius, 41
bones, 19–20
boundary confusions, 68–72, 74, 78, 91,
    199, 205, 279, 284
brain
  and language, 59–62, 279–80
  and silence, 279–81
  and sound, 187
  subcortical functions, 280–1
Brazil, 136
British Sign Language, 147, 278
Brontë, Charlotte, 238
Brontë, Emily, 250
Bronze Age, 34, 80, 271
Brown, Peter, 203
Buber, Martin, 73
Buckley, Martin, 197
Buddhism, 152, 213–14, 251
  and hagiography, 206
  see also Zen Buddhism
Buddhists, 17, 159
  hermits, 50
  and vows of silence, 41, 208
Bunyan, John, 41
Burton, Richard, 112
Bush, George W., 252
buzzards, 2, 155
Byrd, Richard, 30–1, 36–7, 42, 47, 51,
    53, 64, 83, 114

Byron, Lord, 246

Cage, John, 26, 197–8, 220
Caithness, 226
Camadolese Fathers, 269–70
Cambridge, 5, 7
camels, 195
Canaanites, 194
Canada, 96, 173, 256
Candida Casa, 255
cannibalism, 93
Cantor, Georg, 188
Cape Horn, 43, 56, 65
Cape of Good Hope, 56, 105
Caribbean, 78
Carmelites, 19, 144
Carthusians, 144–5
Cartier, Jacques, 96–7
Cato, 233
chastity, 50, 203
Cherokee, 124
Cheviots, 23, 225
Chichester, Francis, 43
childhood, 237–9, 249
children, feral, 94
Children of the Book, 119, 125, 194
Chile, 98
China, 102, 138
Chinese, 102, 114, 147
Christianity, 8, 23–4, 194, 208, 214
  and creation story, 117, 119–20
  early, 149, 202–3
  and imagination, 37
  and reading, 151–2
  in Scotland, 255
churches, 137, 145
Cicero, 233
Cinderella, 178, 182
claustrophobia, 131
Clinton, Bill, 9–10
clochans (beehive huts), 169
clocks, 264
'cloud of unknowing', 213
clouds, 158–9
Coleridge, Samuel Taylor, 224, 249
Common Law, 137
computers, 3, 133, 263–4
constellations, 243–4

convalescence, 112
Counter-Reformation, 203
County Durham, 33–4, 84, 166
County of Wigtown, 226
Courtauld, Augustine, 43, 52–4, 57, 81
Cousteau, Jacques, 46, 70, 282–3
Cowper, William, 295
creation stories, 117–28
creativity, 32, 127, 190, 192–3, 223, 240, 244–5
Crete, 175
Crosby, 164
Crow's flight, 124
Crowhurst, Donald, 41, 44, 67, 83, 89, 104–7
Cuban missile crisis, 5
cuckoos, 160
Cuillin, the, 38, 76
curlews, 160
Cyril of Jerusalem, 148–9
Cyrillic, 147

Daedalus, 163
Dalrymple, William, 152, 218
Daughter of Jerusalem (Maitland), 13
Davies, Sara, 249
Davis, Paul, 121
Davison, Ann, 62
de Foucault, Charles, 191–2, 214, 218, 284
de la Rocque, Marguerite, 95–9, 103
Dead Sea, 87
death, 266–8, 278, 287
Decline and Fall of the Roman Empire (Gibbon), 233
Defoe, Daniel, 41, 98
deipnosophy, 13, 24
democracy, 254
depression, 111–13
Desert Island Discs, 165
desert lassitude, 70, 198–9
deserts, 22, 46, 109, 128, 193–200, 219–20, 257
    desert hermits, 31, 83, 169, 191, 193–4, 199, 203–14, 220, 229, 235, 275–6
    Jesus Christ and, 46, 202
Deutsch, Helene, 18
devils, 204–5, 258

Dillard, Annie, 160, 250, 259
Dirniemow, 273
disciplines, 229
disinhibition, 52–5, 57, 72, 78, 91–2, 199, 291
divorce, 15
Drake, Robert, 86
drugs, 92
dualism, 245
Durham, 35, 141
Durham Cathedral, 170

earth, 20–1, 128
Eastern Orthodox Churches, 152
Eastgate, 35
Egypt, 50, 109, 113, 169, 194, 203, 207, 209
Egyptian mythology, 123–4
eider ducks, 170
Eilean ArdNeimh, 168
Einstein, Albert, 106
Elgol, 76
Eliot, George, 236
Eliot, T. S., 186
email, 263, 276
embroidery, 47
emotions, 49–50
Englishman, The, 99
Enlightenment, 205, 229–30, 233–4
epilepsy, 278
Equal Opportunities Act, 6
Errako Taylor, Barbara, 260–1
Euphrates, river, 193–4
European Union, 136
evolution, 126–7
Excursion, The (Wordsworth), 236
Exeter Voice Hearing Group, 248–9

Fairbairns, Zoe, 12
Famous Five, 35
Farne Isles, 165, 167, 169–70
fasting, 204, 212
feldspar, 34–5
Female Eunuch, The (Greer), 10
female orgasm, 258
feminism, 8, 10–11, 245
feminist writing, 13, 175
First World War, 136

flotation tanks, 86–8, 90, 186
flowers, 159, 161
flying, 20, 72, 161–3, 195
Foot and Mouth Disease, 83–4, 86
forests, 173–80, 184, 295
France, Peter, 214
France, 96, 136, 209, 211
freedom of expression, 137–8, 254
Freire, Paolo, 28
French Resistance, 215
French Revolution, 246
Freud, Sigmund, 173, 248, 252
Friends, 149
fungi, 21

Gaelic, 38, 256–7, 298
Galloway, 23, 226–7, 236, 245, 256–7, 266, 268, 270, 298
gannets, 165–6
Gap Years, 7
gardens and gardening, 20–3, 157, 287
Gateshead, 131
Gaul, 109
Gautama Buddha, 46, 160
Gellner, Ernest, 134
'genius', 230–1
George V, King, 136
Germany, 174–5
Gethsemane monastery, 259, 275
Gibbon, Edward, 233
Gilbert and Sullivan, 45
Girvan, 271
'givennness', sense of, 62–6, 78, 91, 111, 278–9
Glen Affric, 176–7
Glenbrittle, 62–3
glossolalia, 280
Gnostics, 126
God
  name of, 201–2
  nature of, 74
Godwin, William, 232
Golden Globe race, 41, 43–4, 46, 55, 104
golden plover, 166
Goldilocks, 48
Goldsworthy, Andy, 146
Goldsworthy, Joanna, 17
'Goose Girl, The', 179–80

Gormley, Anthony, 164
Göttingen, 175
Goutran de Procius, 71
Gowdie, Isobel, 181
Grand Canyon, 7–8
Grand Tours, 223
Grassian, Stuart, 89–92, 94
Gray, Thomas, 109, 293
Great Caledonian Forest, 176
Great Chthonic Terror, 128–30
Greece, 136, 152, 209, 246, 261
Greek, 108, 128, 139, 293
Greek deities, 178
Greek temples, 223
Greer, Germaine, 10
Grey, Anthony, 102–3, 110, 114
Grimm, Jacob and Wilhelm, 175, 178–9
Guinevere, 180

Hadrian's Wall, 34
Hagar, 93
hagiography, 205–7, 217–18
Hamilton, Ian, 22
happiness, pursuit of, 255
Haran, 194
Harris, 168
Hawking, Richard, 101
hearing, 49, 51–2, 59
hearing loss, 132
Heathery Burn, 34
heaven, 285
Hebrides, 167
Heliopolis, 124
hen harriers, 2, 282
heresy, 253
Hermaness bird sanctuary, 166
hermits, 22, 42, 144–5, 184, 190, 290–1
  and accidie, 108, 110, 112
  Buddhist, 50
  desert, 31, 83, 169, 191, 193–4, 199, 203–14, 220, 229, 235, 275–6
  English, 35
  island, 167, 169–71
  and joy, 217–20
  modern, 103
  and romanticism, 233–4
  and sexual torment, 50
Hermopolis, 124

Hexham, 35
Hickson, Ford, 270
Highland Clearances, 36, 81, 256
Hildegard of Bingen, 258–9
Hillary, Edmund, 42
Himalayas, 22, 42, 275
Hofstadter, Douglas, 138, 140
Holy Trinity, 232
honeymoons, 37
hortus conclusus, 22
house martins, 283
House of Commons, 6
housekeeping, 275–6
Howard, Philip, 136
Howell, Bill, 62
human rights, 127
Hume, Cardinal Basil, 15
Hunt, John, 42, 47
hypertension, 132

Ibn Tufail, 94, 98
Ice Age, 271
Iceland, 167
identity, 240, 251–4
'If' (Kipling), 105
ikebana, 139
India, 138
Indian Ocean, 56
individualism, 229, 231–4, 246–7, 254
Industrial Revolution, 35, 133
ineffability, 41–2, 74, 78, 91, 248, 251,
      277, 279, 281
   negative, 101
infanticide, 93
infinity, 188
insects, 159, 163, 173
insomnia, 132
integrity, 184
'Intimations of Immortality' (Wordsworth),
      75
Inuit languages, 227
Inverness, 184
Iona, 167–8, 255
Iraq, 193
Ireland, 55, 165, 167–9, 171, 209
Irish poetry, 171–2
Irish Sea, 164, 167
Ishmael, 93–4

Islam, 117, 119–20, 151, 190, 194, 209
   political, 252
islands, 165–72
Islay, 167–8
Isle of Man, 165, 271
Isle of Wight, 59, 165
Israel, 194
Italy, 209, 223, 269

Jane Eyre (Brontë), 238
Japan, 138
Jenks, Charles, 22
Jerusalem, 203, 206
   destruction of the Temple, 201
   fall of, 200
Jesus Christ, 24, 210, 213–15
   birth of, 242
   fasting in desert, 46, 202
   and martyrdom, 203
   trial of, 137
Jia Dao, 219
Jones, Rhys, 135
Jordan, 193
joy (*jouissance*), 62, 74–8, 91, 115, 217–21,
      229, 251, 257
Juan Fernandez, 98
Judaism, 117, 120, 151, 190, 193, 200–1
Julian of Norwich, 111, 259, 275
Jung, Carl Gustav, 53–4
Jungle Book, The (Kipling), 94
jungles, 46

Kafka, Franz, 191–2, 223, 284
Kennacraig, 168
Kennedy, Robert, 7
kenosis, 213–14, 221, 251, 254
Kentucky, 156, 259
Kerouac, Jack, 250
Khemnu, 124
Kierkegaard, Søren, 191
King, Martin Luther, 7
Kipling, Rudyard, 94, 105
kites, 164–5
Knox-Johnston, Robin, 43–5, 53, 56, 61,
      105
Knoydart, 76
Korea, 138
Krakauer, Jon, 52, 103–4

Kristeva, Julia, 281
Kronos, 125
Kyle of Lochalsh, 38
Kylerhea, 81

La Nouvelle Héloïse (Rousseau), 66
Lacout, Pierre, 141
Laggangairn standing stones, 255, 257
Lake District, 23, 225–6, 238
Lanarkshire, 268
landscape, 269
language, 54, 59–60, 94, 281
    and creation, 118, 120, 125–6
    and pauses, 185
    and reading, 147, 151
    and silence, 27–8, 146, 151–2, 279–80
    and the sun, 130
    women and, 245
    and Zen, 139
Latin, 58–9, 61, 92, 98, 108, 132, 230
le Guin, Ursula, 77, 182
lead mining, 34–5
Leonardo da Vinci, 163
Leppard, Tom, 55
Lewis, C. S., 134
libraries, 137
lichens, 177–8
Liddell and Scott's Greek lexicon, 82
lighthouse keepers, 166–7
Lilith, 201–2
Lindbergh, Charles, 60
Lindisfarne, 35, 169, 225
literacy, 28, 149–50
literature
    and endings, 186
    genres of, 147
Liverpool, 163
Liverpool Cathedral, 135
Loch Enoch, 228
Loch Slapin, 80
Loch Trool, 228
Loki, 120
London, 4, 9, 15, 131, 215, 270
    East End, 13, 20
    London time, 67
London Labour and the London Poor
    (Mayhew), 132
Lord of the Rings, The (Tolkien), 129

Lord's Prayer, 202
Lorrain, Claude, 269
Los Angeles, 7
Lowland Clearances, 255–7
Luib, 80
Luther, Martin, 151

McArthur, Ellen, 45
McCandless, Chris, 103–4, 107
Macfarlane, Robert, 73
Machars, the, 270
madness, 250, 253
Maid Marian, 180
Mallory, George, 30, 289–90
Mao Zedong, 102
Maori creation story, 121–2
Mar Saba monastery, 152
Märchen (fairy tales), 175, 178–84
Marguerite of Navarre, 96–7,
    292
marooning, 92, 95–100
martyrdom, 169, 203
Mary, mother of Jesus, 73
masculinity, 44, 104
Matthews, Peter, 23
Mayhew, Henry, 132
meditation, 24, 56, 116, 154, 190, 199,
    276, 280
    zazen, 139–41
Mediterranean, 174, 202
Meher Baba, 247
melancholy, 112–13
Melrose, 225
memory, 68, 164, 240
    textual, 150
menopause, 17–20, 186
Merck, Mandy, 10
Merlin, 176–7
Merrick, the, 226, 228, 239
Merton, Thomas, 24, 71, 144, 156, 158,
    218, 259, 269, 275
Milan, 148
Milton, John, 242
Minch, the, 168
mind, and silence, 187, 280
Miner, Valerie, 12
miniskirts, 7
mobile phones, 3, 133–4, 263

Moitessier, Bernard, 43–4, 55–7, 64–5,
    83, 89, 102
monasticism, 22, 37, 50, 109, 152, 184,
    199, 207, 209
Mont Blanc, 51
'Mont Blanc' (Shelley), 223–4
Montaigne, Michel de, 251, 297
Morocco, 261
Moses, 73, 194
Mount Athos, 209
Mount Everest, 42, 289, 291
Mount Hira, 46
Mount Sinai, 194
mountain madness, 70
mountaineering, 43, 51–2, 71, 73, 100–2
Muckle Flugga, 166–7
Muhammad ibn Abdullah, 46, 194
Mull, 167
Mull of Kintyre, 168
Mulville, Frank, 78
Munch, Edvard, 136
music, 278, 284–5
'music of the spheres', 220–1
musical notation, 185
myths and traditional stories, 18, 92–4
    creation stories, 117–28
    Märchen (fairy tales), 175, 178–84
    and the sun, 129–30

nationalism, 246, 252
nature writing, 155
navigation, 67
Negev Desert, 194
Nemo, Captain, 56
New Luce, 271, 273
New York state, 10
New Zealand, 256, 261
Newcastle, 162
Newfoundland, 96–7
Newton, Isaac, 160
Nichols, Peter, 56, 61
Nicolson, Adam, 114, 168–9, 207
Nieve of the Spit, 228
Nile, river, 123–4, 193, 207, 211
noise
    ambient, 132–6
    sensitivity to, 90
Norman Conquest, 35

Norse mythology, 120, 122–3, 129
North Africa, 148
North America, 167
North Lodge, 262, 264
North Pole, 121
North Sea, 171, 270
Northamptonshire, 15, 20, 23, 157, 263
Northanger Abbey (Austen), 296
Norway, 32
novices, 184–5

Orion, 243
ornithology, 159–61, 165–6
oronyms, 60
osteoporosis, 20
Other Voices, 248–9
otters, 171
Outer Hebrides, 114, 168, 172
owls, 161, 286
Oxford, 8–10, 200
    Oxford time, 67
Oxford English Dictionary, Compact
    Edition, 140
oxygen deprivation, 70–1

Pacific Ocean, 56
Paish, Karin, 274
Palestine, 194, 209
Pangu and the Yellow Emperor, 124
panic, 82
Paradise Lost (Milton), 232
Paris, 215
patriarchy, 14
pauses, 185–6
Peking, 102
Pembroke College, 109
Pennine Way, 225
Pennines, 23, 174
Persephone, 184
Petronius, 149
Phillips, Adam, 150
Phillips, John, 95
Picard, Max, 71, 284
Picardy, 97
Pinker, Steven, 59
pirates, 95
plainsong, 58–9, 92, 98
planets, 243

Plato, 233
Pleiades, 241, 243
Poe, Edgar Allan, 250
Poland, 174
population density, 132–3, 226
porpoises, 64–5, 76, 166
porridge, 48, 90, 92
Port Ellen, 168
Portugal, 136
prayer, 23–4, 36–7, 116, 189, 192–3, 258
    'apophatic', 213, 276
    communal and silent, 199–200, 202,
        204, 209, 213–14
    Protestant, 280
    and psychoanalysis, 248
Prebble, John, 256
Prelude, The (Wordsworth), 236–8
privacy, 6, 150–1
Procne and Philomel, 92–3, 292
Profumo affair, 5
Prometheus, 120
protest, silent, 137
Protestantism, 152
psalms, 11, 276, 289, 293
psychoanalysis, 247–8, 252, 277, 281
punctuation, 151

Quakerism, 141–5
Quebec, 96
Quorr Abbey, 59

rabbits, 157
radio programmes, 137
radios, 26, 133, 263
rage, 50, 55
Ragnarok, battle of, 120, 129
railways, 35, 67
'Rainbow, The' (Wordsworth), 238
Raphael, 146
'rapture of the deep' (depth narcosis), 70–1
reading, 146–53, 278
Reformation, 203, 255
Reinhardswald, 175
relationships, 134–5, 216
religious communities, 17, 37, 54, 175
    see also monasticism
Remembrance Sunday, 136
Reoch, Elspeth, 181

retreats, 37, 144, 235, 251
rhetoric, 204
Rhine, river, 174
Rio Branco, Barão de, 136
risk, 72–3, 78, 91, 205, 287
Ritter, Christiane, 51, 65, 110, 114
    rituals, 102
    and prayer, 199
    and remembrance, 136
    and the sun, 129
Robert the Bruce, 227
Roberts, Michèle, 12–13
Robinson Crusoe (Defoe), 41, 98, 114, 165
Roman Catholicism, 15, 152, 215
Roman Catholics, on Islay, 168
Romans, 34, 136, 201, 203–4
romanticism, 42, 63, 193, 223–5, 230–1,
        234–8, 244–6, 249–50
    and identity, 251–4
Rome, 94, 148
Romulus and Remus, 94
Room of One's Own, A (Woolf), 192
Rothko, Mark, 145
Rousseau, Jean-Jacques, 66–7, 250
Rowland, Christopher, 200
Royal Navy, 43
'Rumpelstiltskin', 182, 184
Ruskin College, 10
Russia, 174

Sababurg Castle, 175
Sabine women, rape of, 94
sacraments, 206
Sahara Desert, 191, 193
sailors and sailing, 43–6, 55–6, 61–2,
        64–5, 67, 78, 104–7
St Andrew's, 38
St Anthony, 50, 204–5, 207–9, 217, 268,
        271
St Athanasius, 204–5, 207, 209, 217
St Augustine, 148–9, 151, 205
St Basil the Great, 202
St Bede, 170–1, 217
St Benedict, 114, 145, 152, 209
St Bernadette of Lourdes, 217
St Boniface, 174
St Bridget of Sweden, 19
St Catherine of Siena, 187, 192, 297

St Columba, 167–8, 255
St Cuthbert, 35, 169–71, 217, 225
St Helena, 57
St Hilda of Whitby, 19
St Jerome, 54
St John Cassian, 109–10, 112–13, 209,
    211
St John of the Cross, 258
St John the Baptist, 55
St Kenneth, 168
St Kilda, 165, 167
St Lawrence seaway, 95–7
St Mary of Egypt, 206–7
St Ninian, 255
St Paul, 148, 202, 204, 213
St Romuald, 269
St Teresa of Avila, 19, 72
St Thérèse of Lisieux, 215, 259
saints, women, 19, 296
San Francisco, 7
Satan, 133, 204, 242
Satyrica (Petronius), 149
Saudi Arabia, 193
Sayers, Dorothy, 33
Sayings of the Desert Fathers, The 204,
    210–12, 236, 275
Scandinavia, 175
Scafell Pike, 226
Schama, Simon, 145
scholasticism, 133
science, 156–7
Scilly Isles, 165
Scotland, 4, 38, 146, 167, 261
    and Christianity, 255
    forests, 174, 176
    south-west, 226–7, 239
    witch trials, 181
Scottish Highlands, 2, 23, 36, 158, 226,
    234, 256, 268
Scottish islands, 132, 167
Screwtape Letters, The (Lewis), 134
scripta continua, 147
seals, 166
Selborne, 155
Selkirk, Alexander, 41, 98–100, 102–3
sensory deprivation, 88–91, 187
sex, 50, 206, 277–8
sexual abuse, 180

Shakespeare, William, 232
Sharm el Sheikh, 195
sheep, 81, 256, 285
Shelley, Percy Bysshe, 120, 223, 250
Shetland Isles, 166
Shiant Isles, 167–9, 207
shopping malls, 131
sign language, 147, 274, 278, 280
silence
    and boundary confusions, 68–72, 74, 78
    communal, 199–200
    and danger, 80
    definition of, 25–8, 146
    and disinhibition, 52–5, 57, 72, 78
    and the divine, 73–4, 251
    early accounts of, 40–2
    eremitical silence, 249, 251
    fear of, 128, 130–1, 184
    and free choice, 92, 187
    and 'givenness', 62–6, 78
    and God, 221–2
    interior dimension of, 26
    and joy, 74–8
    and lack, 277–9
    and mental illness, 91
    and natural phenomena, 25–6
    and oppression, 28
    and organic growth, 21, 278
    personification of, 294
    and physical forces, 20
    and physical sensations, 47–51, 70–2, 78
    and risk, 72–3, 78
    and screaming, 81–2
    and secrets, 179–80
    and selfishness, 57
    and solitude, 16–17, 19
    'sound of silence', 197–8, 220
    and spiritual development, 32, 207
    and time, 66–7
    and transmitter/receptor problem,
        26–7
    trial by, 182–4
    types of, 186–8, 190, 192–3
    and visual austerity, 46
    and voices, 57–62, 78
    volumes of, 187–8
    vows of, 41, 208
    and weaning, 11–12, 277

silence, right to, 137–8
silkies, 76
Simpson, Joe, 58, 61, 100–3
Sinai Desert, 46, 50, 193–9, 209–10,
    219–20, 225, 240, 249
Sitka spruce, 173
Siula Grande, 100
'Six Swan Brothers, The', 183–4
Skjolden, 32
Skye cattle, 81
Sleat, 76
sleep deprivation, 204
Sleeping Beauty, 175, 180–1
Sligachan, 62
snow, 84–5, 108, 115, 187, 227–8
snow poles, 85
Snow White, 178
Snowdonia, 23
socialism, 8, 10–11
Socrates, 233
solitary confinement, 89–92, 94, 102
'Solitude of Alexander Selkirk, The'
    (Cowper), 295
Solomon, Andrew, 112
Solway Firth, 265
songlines, 125
South Africa, 44
Southern Upland Way, 226, 255
Southern Uplands, 23, 268
Soviet Union, 27, 89
Spain, 209, 215
spatial confusion, 71–2
spiders, 159
Stair Estate, 271–2
Stanhope, 34, 40
stars, 240–4, 286
Steele, Richard, 99, 102
Steiner, George, 127, 193
Stephen, Leslie, 43
Stewart Island, 65
Stewartry of Kirkcudbright, 226
Storr, Anthony, 134, 278
Strathaird peninsula, 76
stress, 58, 132
sublime, the, 23, 32, 72–3, 83, 240, 277
Suffolk, 162
sun, 129–30
    midnight, 166

Sunday Times, 43–4, 57
sunrise, 154–5
Syria, 193–4, 209

Tahiti, 56–7
taste, 48–9
Tate Modern, 145
tattoos, 55
Tecsa, 168
teenagers, 4–5
Teesdale, 34
televisions, 3, 133, 263
Tenzin Palmo, 42, 114, 273, 275
Tenzing Norgay, 42
terns, 170
Tetley, Nigel, 44, 105–6
Thatcherism, 13
Thevet, André, 97
Thoreau, Henry, 30, 42, 103, 155, 210,
    250, 271, 282
    economic theory, 262–3
Thousand and One Nights, The, 231
Throstlehole monastery, 138–9, 141, 144,
    187, 221
tides, 265
time, 293
    sense of, 66–7, 71
Times, The, 6, 136
Timon of Athens (Shakespeare), 232
tinnitus, 132
Titanic, 136
Tolstoy, Leo, 103
Torridons, 76
Tourette's syndrome, 280
Tower of Babel, 120
Trappists, 144–5, 191, 259, 269
trial by silence, 182–4
Ts'u-t'ing shih-yuan, 138
Tuareg nomads, 191, 214
Turner, J. M. W., 146
Twickenham, 22
Twin Towers, 136

Underhill, Evelyn, 143
United States of America, 7, 89, 136,
    155, 256, 261, 268
universe, origin of, 118–19, 126
Unst, 166

Ur of the Chaldees, 194
Uranus, 124
'urgencies', 37

Valentinus, 126
Valhalla, 129
via negativa, 213
Vietnam War, 9
vigils, 180, 184, 212
Vikings, 129
village life, 29
Virgil, 150
virginity, 203–4
Vishnu, 124
visual arts, 145–6
voices, hearing, *see* auditory
    hallucinations

Waddell, Helen, 109, 204, 210–12, 233
Walden (Thoreau), 262, 282
Wandor, Michelene, 12
Wareham, Anne, 22
Warkton, 15, 17, 20–1, 24, 29, 287
Washington, 7
Weatherhill, 138, 157, 208, 260–1
Weil, Simone, 215–16, 259, 297
Welsh, Jock, 272
West Highland Way, 225
Westminster Abbey, 145
White, Gilbert, 155

Whithorn, 255
William the Conqueror, 35
Williams, Geoffrey, 65
Williams, Rowan, 203
Wilson, James, 234
Winnicott, Donald, 11
witches, 181
Wittgenstein, Ludwig, 32, 188
Wollstonecraft, Mary, 232
wolves, 174, 177–8
women
    and language, 245
    and silent reading, 148–9
    saints, 19, 296
    women's rights, 141–2, 246
    see also feminism
Woolf, Virginia, 1, 43, 192
Wordsworth, Dorothy, 225
Wordsworth, William, 42, 63, 75, 225–7,
    236–8, 245, 250
writing, 189–90, 192–3, 223, 225,
    258–60
    feminist, 13, 175

Yates, Simon, 100–1
York, 34
Yorkshire dales, 23

Zen Buddhism, 138–42, 144–5
Zozimos, 206